Good Taste, Fashion, Luxury: A Genteel Melbourne Family and Their Rubbish

Sarah Hayes

Studies in Australasian Historical Archaeology
Volume 5

Australasian Society for Historical Archaeology

SYDNEY UNIVERSITY PRESS

Published 2014 by SYDNEY UNIVERSITY PRESS
University of Sydney Library
sydney.edu.au/sup
In association with the Australasian Society for Historical Archaeology
asha.org.au

© Sarah Hayes 2014
© Australasian Society for Historical Archaeology 2014

Reproduction and Communication for Other Purposes

Except as permitted under the Copyright Act, no part of this edition may be reproduced, stored in a retrieval system, or communicated in any form or by any means without prior written permission. All requests for reproduction or communication should be made to the Australasian Society for Historical Archaeology at the address below:

Australasian Society for Historical Archaeology Inc.
PO Box 2497
North Parramatta NSW 1750
Australia

secretary@asha.org.au

National Library of Australia Cataloguing-in-Publication entry

Author:	Hayes, Sarah C. (Sarah Christie), 1979- author.
Title:	Good taste, fashion, luxury : a genteel Melbourne family and their rubbish / Sarah Hayes.
ISBN:	9781743324172 (paperback)
Series:	Studies in Australasian historical archaeology ; v.5.
Notes:	Includes bibliographical references and index.
Subjects:	Martin family.
	Immigrants--Victoria--Melbourne--Social conditions.
	Archaeology and history--Victoria--Melbourne.
	Material culture--Victoria--Melbourne.
	Melbourne (Vic.)--Social life and customs--19th century.
Other Authors/Contributors:	
	Australasian Society for Historical Archaeology, issuing body.
Dewey Number:	994.5102

Cover image by Ming Wei
Cover design by Miguel Yamin

Australasian Society for Historical Archaeology Editorial Board

Professor Eleanor Conlin Casella, University of Manchester, UK
Dr Mary Casey, Casey & Lowe Pty Ltd, NSW
Emeritus Professor Graham Connah, Australian National University, ACT
Professor Martin Gibbs, University of New England, NSW
Dr Michael Given, University of Glasgow, UK
Dr Tracy Ireland, University of Canberra, ACT
Dr Grace Karskens, University of New South Wales, NSW
Dr Susan Lawrence, La Trobe University, VIC
Professor Jane Lydon, University of Western Australia, WA
Professor Tim Murray, La Trobe University, VIC
Professor Charles Orser, New York State Museum and Illinois State University, USA
Dr Caroline Phillips, University of Auckland, New Zealand
Dr Jon Prangnell, University of Queensland, QLD
Dr Neville Ritchie, Department of Conservation, New Zealand
Dr Ian Smith, University of Otago, New Zealand
Dr Iain Stuart, JCIS Consultants, NSW

Monograph Editors

Dr Martin Gibbs
Dr Peter Davies

About the Series

The *Studies in Australasian Historical Archaeology* series is designed to make the results of high-quality research in historical archaeology available to archaeologists, other researchers, students and the public. A particular aim of the series is to ensure that the data from these studies are also made available, either within the volumes or in associated websites, to facilitate opportunities for inter-site comparison and critical evaluation of analytical methods and interpretations. Future releases in the series will include edited and revised versions of Australasian higher-degree theses, major consultancy projects and academic research, and commissioned studies on other topics of interest.

Contents

Table of Contents	v
List of Figures	vii
List of Tables	ix
Abbreviations	x
Acknowledgements	xi

1 Introduction — 1
- Urban Archaeology in Australia — 1
- Class, Material Culture and Gentilty — 2
- Theoretical Framework — 3
- Viewbank Homestead — 4
- Outline of the Study — 5

2 Early Melbourne and Viewbank Homestead — 7
- Melbourne Established — 7
- Heidelberg — 8
- Viewbank Homestead — 8

3 People at Viewbank Homestead — 11
- Dr Martin: An 'Impetuous' Gentleman — 11
- Mrs Martin: A Fiery Woman — 12
- Children — 13
- Family Roles — 14
- Servants — 15
- Moving On — 15

4 The Archaeology of Viewbank Homestead — 17
- The Excavation of Viewbank Homestead — 17
  - Dig Methods — 17
  - Excavated Areas — 18
- Artefacts — 20
  - Artefact Processing — 20
  - Artefact Cataloguing — 21

5 Artefact Analysis — 23
- Formation of the Tip — 23
- The Tip Assemblage — 24
  - Domestic — 24
  - Eating and Drinking — 25
  - Personal — 38
  - Recreational — 42

Social	44
Tools and Equipment	44
Miscellaneous	45
The Homestead Contexts	47
The Homestead Assemblage	47

6 Acquisition of Goods — 49
Markets — 49
    England: The Dominant Market — 49
    Ireland, Scotland, Continental Europe and the United States: Supplementary Goods — 51
    Asia: Exotic Goods — 52
    Australia: Rare Commodities — 52
Shopping — 53
Consumer Practice — 57

7 Daily Life at Viewbank Homestead — 59
Space — 59
Work — 62
    A Workplace for Servants — 62
    Farming Activities — 63
Leisure — 64
Genteel dining — 65
Social Events — 68
Religion — 69
Childhood — 70
Genteel Appearance — 71
    Masculine Appearance — 71
    Feminine Appearance — 71
Hygiene and Maintaining Health — 72

8 Negotiating Class — 75
Characterising the Material Culture — 75
Gentility and Class Negotiation — 76
Conclusion — 77

Appendices — 79
1. Function Key Words — 79
2. Date Ranges and Occupation Phases — 80
3. Summary of Activity and Function Groupings for Artefacts Recovered from the Tip — 85

Bibliography — 86
Archival Sources — 86
References — 86

Index — 98

Figures

1.1	Location of Viewbank homestead (Source: Ming Wei).	5
3.1	Dr Robert Martin, artist and year unknown (Source: Heidelberg Historical Society).	11
4.1	Plan of the Viewbank site showing excavated areas (Area D comprised of test trenches in various locations around the homestead) (Source: adapted from plan prepared for Heritage Victoria by the University of Melbourne).	18
4.2	Aerial view of the Heritage Victoria excavation of the homestead facing north (Source: Heritage Victoria).	18
4.3	Homestead plan showing building phases (Source: adapted from plan prepared by Heritage Victoria).	19
4.4	Homestead plan showing excavation details (Source: adapted from trench plans prepared by Heritage Victoria).	19
4.5	Satellite image of the Viewbank site showing garden terraces (Source: Google Earth, accessed 3 August 2007).	20
5.1	Candlesnuffer and wick trimmer (TS 1110).	24
5.2	Ceramic tableware forms.	26
5.3	'Summer Flowers' plate (TS 421).	27
5.4	'Bagdad' pattern plate (TS 798).	28
5.5	Robert's mug (TS 588).	35
5.6	Mustard jar (TS 872).	38
5.7	Fan fragments (TS 1143).	39
5.8	Button attachment types. From top left: one, two, three and four-hole sew-through, birdcage, hoop-shank, pin-shank and post.	40
5.9	Double oval shank clothing fastening (TS 1007).	40
5.10	Toothbrush (TS 1147).	41
5.11	Toothpaste jar (TS 953).	42
5.12	Moulded whiteware toy tea set (clockwise from top left: teacup, teapot, covered bowl and saucer).	43
5.13	Doll parts.	43
5.14	Dominoes (TS 279).	43
5.15	Die (TS 965).	44
5.16	Fish figurine (TS 779).	44
5.17	Bone netting needle (TS 780).	45
5.18	Tin-glazed earthenware vessel (TS 904).	46
5.19	Viewbank servant bell.	48
6.1	Collins Street in 1864. Briscoe and Co. Ironmongers where the Martin family purchased goods can be seen on the right side of the street (Creator: Unknown; Source: State Library of Victoria).	56
6.2	Alston and Brown, one of the drapers in Collins Street frequented by the Martin family, 1864 (Creator: Frederick Grosse 1828–1894; Source: State Library of Victoria).	56

List of Figures

7.1	Plan of Viewbank homestead showing room uses (Source: adapted from plan prepared by Heritage Victoria).	59
7.2	Detail of the plan of Viewbank from the 1875 lease showing the dwelling house, barn, stackyard and stables (Source: PROV, VPRS 460/P, Unit 1102, 1 June 1875).	64

Tables

5.1	Summary of 'Domestic' artefacts.	24
5.2	Summary of 'Eating and Drinking' artefacts.	25
5.3	Ceramic tableware forms by ware type.	26
5.4	Decorative techniques on ceramic tableware.	27
5.5	Transfer-printed decoration types on ceramic tableware.	28
5.6	Makers' marks on ceramic tableware.	29
5.7	Matching sets of ceramic tableware.	30
5.8	Complementary tableware vessels.	31
5.9	Glass tableware forms by glass colour.	31
5.10	Ceramic teaware forms by ware type.	32
5.11	Decorative techniques on ceramic teaware.	32
5.12	Matching sets of ceramic teaware in order of set size.	33
5.13	Complementary teaware vessels.	34
5.14	'Serving and Consuming' vessel forms by ware type.	34
5.15	Decorative techniques on 'Serving and Consuming' ceramics.	35
5.16	Makers' marks on 'Serving and Consuming' ceramics.	35
5.17	Storage bottle types.	36
5.18	Summary of makers' marks on glass storage bottles.	37
5.19	Summary of 'Personal' artefacts.	38
5.20	Decoration on buttons.	39
5.21	Summary of 'Recreational' artefacts.	42
5.22	Summary of 'Tools and Equipment' artefacts.	44
5.23	Summary of 'Miscellaneous' artefacts.	46
6.1	Identified country of manufacture by maker's mark.	50
6.2	Listing of unsecured debts to traders in a statement of duty regarding Dr Martin's will (PROV, VPRS 7591/P2, Unit 17, File 12-586, 11 February 1875), including details on traders from Sands and McDougall's Melbourne Directories (1874).	54

Abbreviations

GP	Graham Papers, University of Melbourne Archives
HHS	Heidelberg Historical Society
MCC	Melbourne City Council
PROV	Public Record Office of Victoria
VPRS	Victorian Public Record Series

Acknowledgements

This monograph is based on research conducted for my PhD. First and foremost I would like to thank my supervisor Susan Lawrence whose dedicated readings of this text, enthusiasm and support were a real blessing. I would also like to thank my co-supervisor Peter Davies for keeping me on track and also for his input on turning my thesis into this monograph. I am indebted to La Trobe University who supplied the scholarship that made my PhD research possible. Reconceptualising my thesis into this volume was largely done in my current role as a Research Fellow on the Australian Research Council funded *Suburban Archaeology* project held jointly by La Trobe University, Deakin University and the University of Melbourne.

I also thank all the Archaeology Department staff, particularly Katherine Katsoris, Rudy Frank, Ros Allen and Jenna Thurlow. I would also like to thank the dedicated team of volunteers from La Trobe who assisted with cataloguing the assemblage. Original maps have been produced by Wei Ming and I thank him for his work typesetting this volume.

At Heritage Victoria, I would like to thank Jeremy Smith, Leah McKenzie and Annie Muir who provided me with the necessary background to the Viewbank excavation, access to the assemblage and a place to catalogue. Thanks also to Ilka Schacht for her help with Access databases, and many detailed discussions on artefacts and cataloguing.

Particular thanks as always to Noriaki Sato for his assistance with the theoretical framework of this project, proofing drafts, and for continuing to challenge me.

1
Introduction

As 19th-century Melbourne was growing into the vibrant, global city that it would ultimately become, immigrants seeking a new way of life and prosperity were negotiating their status in the new colony. From the time of the earliest settlers to the gold rush and beyond, people from various class backgrounds with different aspirations navigated their way through fluid social structures in order to succeed and establish their position in the new colony. Class in Australia was not a fixed structure, but was flexible and often differed from the norms of British society, with which the majority of immigrants were familiar (Russell 2010:114, 126). Social mobility was possible in the colonies, and indeed was one of the drawcards for people immigrating to Australia (Fitzgerald 1987). The impact of this mobility on class structure and society has been much debated by historians (Neale 1972; Davison 1978; Connell and Irving 1980; Hirst 1988; Thompson 1994; Young 2003; Russell 2010) and is an important question for historical archaeology.

In order to examine the distinctive class structure that emerged in Melbourne in this period, this archaeological study tests the hypothesis that the material culture of different immigrant groups will be distinctive from each other. Further, by understanding gentility as a form of cultural capital, these differences can be interrogated to examine class negotiation. By doing so, it contributes to current historical archaeology in three important ways: first, by providing a detailed analysis of middle-class material culture with a view to contextualising previous historical archaeological research on Melbourne's working class; second, by providing a benchmark for further research on the diverse middle class; and third, by identifying links between material culture and class through which class negotiation can be examined.

The material culture that forms the basis of this study was recovered from the Viewbank homestead site by Heritage Victoria in 1996 and 1997. This assemblage was discarded over time by the Martin family who occupied the genteel homestead from 1843 to 1874. The family were typical of many early arrivals to Port Phillip. From a solid middle-class background, they brought with them capital and ambition. They were poised to take a role of influence in the new colony, and indeed they did. Dr Martin channelled the family wealth into pastoral pursuits with great success, while Mrs Martin set about establishing a genteel household. The Viewbank assemblage provides a unique insight into the role that material culture played in establishing the position of the Martin family in Melbourne society.

URBAN ARCHAEOLOGY IN AUSTRALIA

Research in Australian historical archaeology has steadily grown since the 1970s and has made many notable contributions in the areas of convictism, culture contact, industry and urbansim (see Connah 1993; Lawrence and Davies 2011). Notable among these studies are the large scale excavations of the inner-city 'slum' areas of The Rocks, Sydney (Lydon 1998, 1999; Consultants 1999; Karskens 1999, 2001; Crook *et al.* 2003; Crook and Murray 2004) and 'Little Lon'/Casselden Place, Melbourne (McCarthy 1989; Mayne and Lawrence 1998; Murray and Mayne 2001; Murray 2006, 2011). In both studies, material culture has been used to present a more nuanced picture of life in the 'slum' and argued for a sense of community in these areas with many residents striving for respectability (Karskens 2001; Murray and Mayne 2001). Other studies on urban working-class sites include Jane Street, Port Adelaide (Lampard 2004, 2009; Lampard and Staniforth 2011) and a number of unpublished cultural heritage management projects.

To date, no similar studies have centred on middle-class domestic occupation in the urban or suburban context, largely because such sites are located in suburban areas where commercial development is less frequent and is less likely to require excavation for cultural heritage management purposes. Although a number of studies have been conducted on stately homes (Frankel 1979; Watts 1985), rural estates (Connah 1977, 1986, 2001, 2007; Connah *et al.* 1978) and on Government Houses in Sydney (Proudfoot *et al.* 1989; Casey 2005), the middle class is underrepresented, especially in the area of material culture studies. Only three studies have involved a primary focus on middle-class material culture: Paradise in the Queensland Goldfields (Quirk 2008), Willoughby Bean's parsonage in regional Victoria (Lawrence *et al.* 2009) and the aspirational middle-class Thomas household at Port Albert (Prossor *et al.* 2012).

Since the completion of The Rocks and Little Lon projects there have been numerous calls for middle-class material culture studies (Lawrence 1998:13; Murray and Mayne 2001:103; Karskens and Lawrence 2003:100–101; Crook et al. 2005:27; Crook 2011:592; Murray 2011:578). To successfully interpret assemblages and study class differences, it is essential to study the full range of class positions and consumer behaviour (Praetzellis et al. 1988; Karskens and Lawrence 2003:101). This study represents a major contribution towards fulfilling this objective in the Australian urban context.

CLASS, MATERIAL CULTURE AND GENTILITY

The interrelations of class, material culture and gentility are at the centre of this study. Class is a key concept in the social sciences for good reason: it attempts to explain social change and stability in the past and is central in historical archaeology (Paynter 1999:184–185). It is particularly pertinent to the study of the colonial world where ideologies and social structures were being adapted to new environments, and is vital to understanding social relations in the past and ultimately society today.

Class, in spite or perhaps because of its centrality to understanding society, is a difficult and nebulous concept. This in large part is due to confusion over class as an arbitrary category or tool used by the researcher for analytical purposes, and class as a real (and reconstructable) mark of identity (Davidoff and Hall 2002:xxx; Mrozowski 2006:13; Tarlow 2007:27). The many and varied approaches to class in the social sciences are outside the scope of this study to review. Instead the focus is on class in historical archaeology.

Interest in class as a theme in historical archaeology has been growing since the 1990s. Internationally, a number of studies have addressed class in relation to capitalism (e.g. Paynter 1988; Johnson 1996; Leone 1999; Leone and Potter 1999; Mrozowski 2006), ideology (e.g. Burke 1999; Leone 2005), power (e.g. Lucas 2006), domination and resistance (e.g. Beaudry et al. 1991; Miller et al. 1995), manners (e.g. Goodwin 1999), improvement (Tarlow 2007), gender (e.g. Hardesty 1994; Wall 1994; Rotman 2009), or working-class living conditions (e.g. Mrozowski et al. 1996; Karskens 1999; Mayne and Murray 2001; Yamin 2001). In these studies, class often takes a secondary position to the theme being discussed (Wurst and Fitts 1999:1–2). A number of scholars, however, have highlighted the potential of using historical archaeology to examine class differences, social mobility and class conflict (e.g. Reckner and Brighton 1999; Praetzellis and Praetzellis 2001; Casella 2005; Griffin and Casella 2010; Brighton 2011).

Studies of class in Australian historical archaeology have generally been driven by discussions of respectability and gentility. The majority focus on the working class and view respectability as a unique and defining characteristic of that group (e.g. Lydon 1993a; Karskens 1999; Lawrence 2000; Lampard 2004). Other studies have focused on gentility (Quirk 2008; Lawrence et al. 2009), or in some cases respectability (Lampard and Staniforth 2011), as a social strategy used to project middle-class status.

Historical archaeologists have predominantly viewed class as a hierarchical scale through which people and their lifestyles can be described (Wurst and Fitts 1999:1; Wurst 2006:191, 197; Lawrence and Davies 2011:252–253). This standpoint holds that class existed in the past and through observation can be defined and reconstructed by researchers based on empirical evidence from the past. In historical archaeology, this works well at the individual site level, but has limitations for comparative studies between classes where nuanced differences between groups of people make accurate attribution to the hierarchy problematic. When seeking to compare sites, it is beneficial to treat class as a relational concept (Wurst and Fitts 1999:1; Wurst 2006:191). In doing so, such issues as social formation, class negotiation and social change can be more critically examined. While this study is not comparative, one of the major objectives of the research is to develop a framework to facilitate comparative research.

Material culture has significant potential to contribute to the study of class. The important contribution of historical archaeology to material culture studies began in the 1970s and 1980s with the formalisation of historical archaeology as a distinctive discipline within archaeology (e.g. Deetz 1977; Schlereth 1979; Hodder 1982; Miller 1985, 1987). Since the early scientific studies of artefacts (e.g. South 1977), and the structuralist search for meaning (e.g. Glassie 1975; Deetz 1977; Glassie 1982), material culture studies in historical archaeology have become increasingly interpretative and multidisciplinary (e.g. Miller 1987, 1995; Cochran and Beaudry 2006:193).

Using the early capitalist economy and emerging globalisation as the contexts for their research questions, historical archaeologists have increasingly turned to studies of consumerism. The essential principles in the anthropological study of consumerism are relevant to the present study, namely that goods can be regarded as texts that are open to multiple readings, and that consumer choices have symbolic meaning (Douglas and Isherwood 1978; McKendrick et al. 1982; Appadurai 1986; Miller 1987, 2008, 2010; Spencer-Wood 1987; McCracken 1988; Friedman 1994). Studies of consumerism have remained popular in historical archaeology and have further developed ways of viewing the social meanings of commodities in society (e.g. Orser Jr. 1994; Gibb 1996; Wurst and McGuire 1999; Majewski and Schiffer 2001).

Linked with consumer studies, the theory of social practice developed by French cultural theorist Pierre Bourdieu (1977, 1984) has become increasingly popular in historical archaeology (e.g. Wall 1992; Lawrence 1998:8; Mayne and Lawrence 1998; Shackel 2000:233; Praetzellis and Praetzellis

2001; Russell 2003; Young 2004; Rotman 2009). Bourdieu's theorisation of how goods actively pass on and structure culture has obvious appeal and application in interpreting artefacts. Further, Bourdieu suggests that a pivotal determining factor in an individual's judgement of their class is cultural capital. Webb, Shirato and Danaher (2002:x) provide a useful definition of cultural capital: 'a form of values associated with culturally authorised tastes, consumption patterns, attributes, skills and awards'. Class distinction is thus 'most marked in the ordinary choices of everyday existence, such as furniture, clothing or cooking ...' (Bourdieu 1984:77). Bourdieu (1977) argues that *habitus* is the deliberate and subconscious understanding of the behaviours and practices appropriate to one's place in society. It is not imposed, but is continually changing depending on the values and opinions of self and others. With the idea of cultural capital, Bourdieu's theory of *habitus* is a useful tool for archaeologists seeking to understand the material cultural pattern of a particular group. These ideas of practice and interaction allow interpretations to be made on how people negotiated, changed and maintained their position in society (see Casella and Croucher 2010:2).

A number of researchers in both archaeology and history have usefully linked gentility with Bourdieu's concept of cultural capital (e.g. Praetzellis and Praetzellis 2001:647; Russell 2003:168; Young 2004). The ideals associated with gentility were refinement, good taste, manners, morality, religious observance, avoidance of idleness, constructive leisure and domesticity (Russell 1994:60; Marsden 1998:2; Mitchell 2009:261–266). As an emic value, used by people of the era, genteel was a term to describe people, goods, furniture, houses, suburbs, behaviours and values according to these ideals.

It has been argued that genteel behaviour and appearance became the measure of status for the middle class (Davidoff and Hall 2002:398; Young 2003:4–5), and further that in Australia, gentility was even more important in forming and maintaining status than in Britain (De Serville 1991:2). Historian Penny Russell's (1994) study of the 'colonial Victorian gentry' argued that gentility was crucial in determining status in a situation of greater social mobility where family background was often uncertain. She emphasised genteel performance, good manners and good taste as necessary to enable those in the 'gentry' to understand who belonged (Russell 1994:14–15).

The nature of gentility is such that it leaves its mark in the archaeological record. Despite the fact that the actual practice of genteel behaviour is not represented in the archaeological record, the beliefs and values associated with gentility can be interpreted through the goods people purchased for their homes and themselves. The type, quality and quantity of domestic and personal objects purchased by a group of people can be interrogated to interpret the values, customs and position of the people who purchased them. In this way, the archaeological record can reveal something of the values, manners and behaviours associated with gentility (see Ames 1978; Goodwin 1999).

THEORETICAL FRAMEWORK

For the purpose of this study, class is treated as an arbitrary category used to examine the similarities and differences between groups of people in order to examine social formation. The terminology of working, middle and upper class is used but these groups are treated as flexible and fluid. While wealth, occupation, religious belief, ethnicity and gender are all acknowledged as contributing to class position, cultural capital is the main focus. Gentility is used here as an analytical tool which operates separately to class; as one brand of cultural capital that could be adopted, appropriated or adapted by different groups in different ways for different purposes. In this way, gentility as viewed through material culture is used to examine class structure and negotiation in Melbourne.

The approach of treating class as an arbitrary category in order to understand society has certain advantages. This way of understanding has long been espoused in social theory (Foucault 1973; Giddens 1973; Bourdieu 1977), but is rarely applied in archaeology. However, the emphasis that this approach places on the examination of the similarities and differences of the lifestyles of people using the idea of class has great potential in archaeology, particularly where comparative studies are concerned. Bourdieu's (1977, 1984) concept of cultural capital is used here as a metaphor rather than an empirical descriptor, useful for identifying the roles particular groups played in class formation (Moi 1991; Skeggs 1997:10). Further, this approach acknowledges the effect of the researcher on interpretations and the limitations of descriptions of the past which are subject to the complexities of truth, bias and interpretation, but still allows class to be used as a concept in order to contribute to knowledge of society in the past.

Another advantage of focusing on gentility as cultural capital is that it acknowledges the role of women in determining class. One limitation of the study of class is that it can overlook women, with their class position merely assumed based on the wealth or occupation of their husband or father. While this was to some degree the reality of the 19th century for many women, there are also instances where single, widowed or divorced women negotiated their class position autonomously. Women played a vital role in gentility and genteel performance (Bushman 1993:281; Russell 1994:14), and when emphasising gentility as cultural capital the class position of women, along with their role in negotiating status, can be articulated independently.

1. Introduction

The objective in this study is not to accurately attribute people to a point on the hierarchy and describe their lifestyle, but to arbitrarily group people in order to use the concept of class to understand the role of these groups in formulating and changing society. To facilitate this, immigrants to Melbourne are divided here into artificial groups based on similarities in their class backgrounds, generation, time of arrival in the colony and lifestyle once in the colony. This is not an attempt to create an alternative hierarchy, but rather to group like immigrants in order to examine the formation of class in the new colony.

The group that is the focus of this study is the 'established middle class', defined as early settlers and colonists of middle-class backgrounds who brought their gentility and privilege with them to the new colony. This group includes middle-class men, particularly those who were not in line for an inheritance, seeking adventure and independent livelihoods in the colonies. Many of the first wave of arrivals in this group included doctors, lawyers, clergy or ex-military men from good families. Most of these immigrants were English or Scottish, with smaller numbers of well-connected Irish (Broome 1984:23; De Serville 1991:3–4). Many of these men established significant wealth through business or vast pastoral properties, which brought corresponding economic and political power. Women of middle-class backgrounds immigrated to the colonies with their families or husbands, or as single women in a bid to improve their prospects for employment or marriage (Hammerton 1979:11–12; Gothard 2001:53–54). Many of the families in this group became dynasties that endured throughout the century (Broome 1984:23, 39). The 'established middle class' had a firm position of authority in the colony, however this was challenged initially by those of working-class or convict backgrounds arriving at the same time and seeking entry to their ranks, and later again by the influx of people brought by the gold rush (Russell 1994:15, 2010:113; Young 2010:136).

The assumption that social distinctions manifest in material culture is a basic premise of historical archaeological discourse (e.g. Deetz 1977; Glassie 1977; De Cunzo and Herman 1996; Leone 1999; Mayne and Murray 2001; Mrozowski 2006) and of this study. When the focus of research is on reconstructing identity or individual consumer choice, it can be difficult to distinguish class from other factors such as gender, ethnicity and socio-economic status (Wurst and McGuire 1999; Rotman 2009:1; Casella and Croucher 2010:2–3; Shackel 2010:58–60). By shifting the focus from reconstructing identity or accurately attributing people to a point on a hierarchy, however, class becomes a useful concept for articulating the distinctions between people and examining society.

Drawing on the theory of gentility as cultural capital (see Praetzellis and Praetzellis 2001:647; Young 2004:202), it is argued here that the distinctive lifestyles of the 'established middle class' and other groups of immigrants would be reflected in their material culture. Gentility formed one of the primary driving forces of consumerism at this time, and also formed an important domain of social practice to define status within society. It should not be assumed, however, that gentility was adopted by different groups of people in the same ways and for the same reasons (Praetzellis and Praetzellis 2001:647). When considering gentility as an analytical tool for research, it is useful to view it as operating separately to class, as a cultural capital that could be adopted, appropriated or adapted by different groups in different ways for different purposes. While gentility may have sometimes served as a tool in social mobility, it may not have done so in other cases (Karskens 2001:77; Praetzellis and Praetzellis 2001:647; Casella 2005:167–168).

The different uses of gentility are, therefore, indicative of changing social boundaries and class structures in 19th-century Melbourne. It is anticipated that different groups will have distinctive patterns of material culture depending on their distinctive uses of gentility, and that this can be used to interpret class structure and negotiation in the colony. For the 'established middle class' it is expected that gentility would be performed and displayed as an inherent, as opposed to learnt, behaviour and should, therefore, signal how members of this group were maintaining and defining their status in the changing social landscape of early colonial Melbourne. Such differences can be used to articulate class negotiation, particularly as more studies from more groups emerge.

The scope of this project dictates a focus on one archaeological site (Viewbank homestead) and one historical family (the Martins) as being representative of the 'established middle class'. It is important to note that while individual stories do not add up to represent the sum of colonial history, they can help us to understand it better (Russell 2010:14). When combined with the material record such stories can be used to explore the changing nature of class in society (Mrozowski 2006:1). While this study cannot fully examine class formation in 19th-century Melbourne, it emphasises the relational nature of class with a view to further research.

Viewbank Homestead

The Martin family arrived in Sydney and travelled overland to Melbourne in 1839, only four years after permanent European settlement commenced (Bride 1969:87). Dr Robert Martin, his wife Lucy and their four children lived initially at Moonee Ponds prior

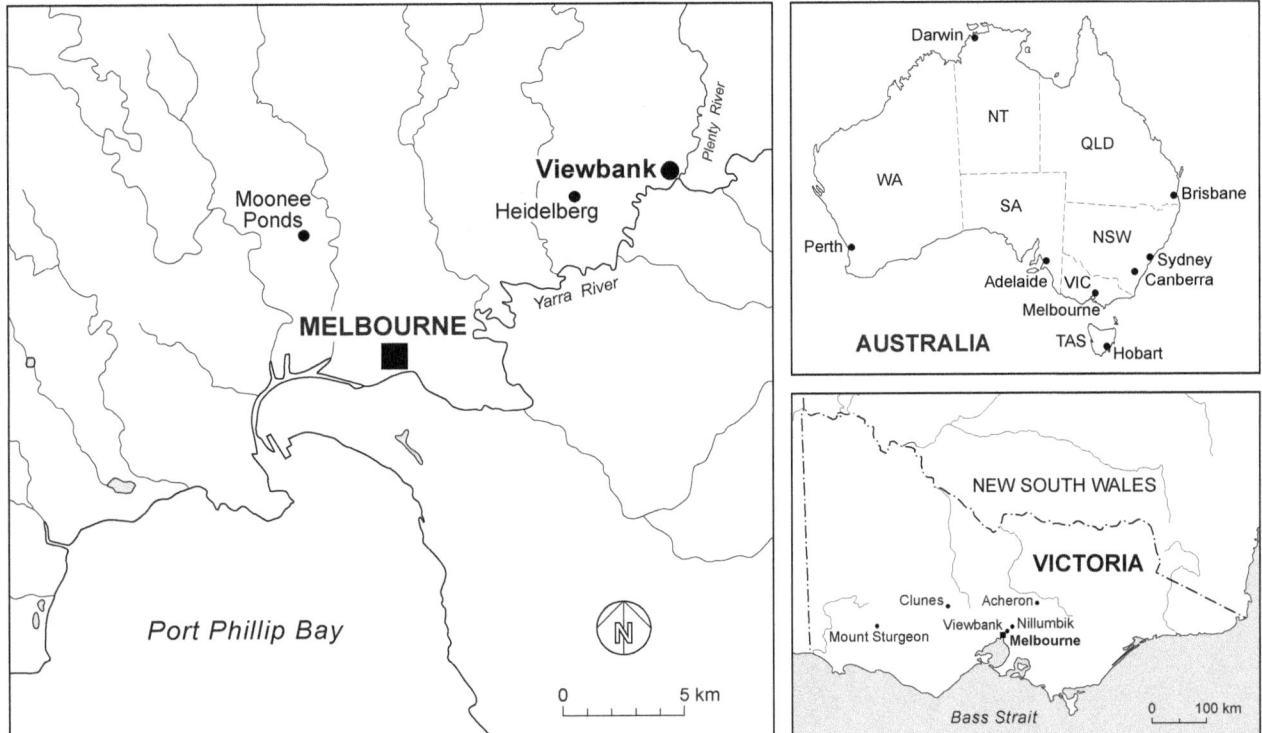

Figure 1.1: Location of Viewbank homestead (Source: Ming Wei).

to moving to Viewbank homestead in 1843 (*Port Phillip Gazette*, 22 May 1843) where two more children were born. The family occupied Viewbank (along with a number of servants) until Dr Martin's death in 1874. The grand homestead and generous allotment of land was located in the genteel settlement of Heidelberg, 15 kilometres north-east of Melbourne, Victoria (**Figure 1.1**). Dr Martin had been trained as a physician in Britain, but once in Australia he became a successful and wealthy pastoralist. The Martin family were influential and well respected in the new colony. They were typical of the 'established middle class' group and provide a compelling case study.

The Viewbank site is significant as a rare example of a middle-class archaeological site close to a city centre which has remained undeveloped and relatively undisturbed. Its location in the Melbourne Metropolitan Park along the Yarra River has ensured the relative protection of the archaeological remains. This is unusual for middle-class homes which are often in suburban areas that have been continuously occupied to the present date. Any cesspits are located in present day backyards and are generally not accessible to archaeologists. This makes Viewbank a rare opportunity to study the material culture of the middle class. Heritage Victoria excavated the homestead, adjacent tip and possible outbuildings over three seasons from **1996 to 1999**. For the purposes of this study, the artefact assemblage provides an extensive sample of middle-class material culture from the 19th century.

OUTLINE OF THE STUDY

This study uses historical and archaeological methods to examine the lives and lifestyles of the residents of Viewbank as the basis for the examination of class negotiation. The remainder of the study is comprised of three major parts: first, historical and archaeological evidence; second, interpretations on the role of gentility in the material culture and lifestyles of the Martins; and third, discussion linking this evidence to Melbourne's class structure.

The first section commences with chapter 2 which presents Melbourne's early history and the history of Viewbank homestead. This is followed by chapter 3 in which the first major component of the evidence for the study is presented, namely the personal histories of the people living at Viewbank. These histories are told for Dr Martin, Mrs Martin, their children and the servants working at Viewbank. Particular attention is paid to the background of the Martins and their success once in Melbourne. Chapter 4 follows with details of the excavations conducted by Heritage Victoria and the post-excavation artefact work undertaken by the author. This includes a discussion of the artefact processing and cataloguing methods. In chapter 5 the second major component of evidence is presented with the analysis of the material culture. Analysis focuses on domestic, kitchen, personal, recreational, work related and social items. The depositional patterns that inform the interpretation of the artefacts are also examined.

1. Introduction

The second section commences in chapter 6 with a detailed examination of the acquisition of goods at Viewbank homestead: namely, the trade networks and shopping habits that are indicated by the archaeological and historical evidence. Following this, drawing on both the archaeological and historical evidence, the lives and lifestyles of the people at Viewbank homestead are discussed in detail in chapter 7 including work, leisure, dining, social events, religion, childhood, and genteel appearance and health. The house and grounds are also considered as material culture that can inform an understanding of life at the homestead.

The discussion in chapter 8 characterises the material culture recovered from Viewbank homestead and the assemblage is examined for expressions of gentility and characterised in terms of variety, level of cohesion in public and private aspects of the assemblage, type of expensive or luxury goods and degree of fashion and good taste. It then goes on to explore how gentility can be viewed as functioning in a distinctive manner for the 'established middle class' with interpretations made on how this group was defining and maintaining their position in the new colony.

2
Early Melbourne and Viewbank Homestead

The Martin family occupied Viewbank homestead during the formative years of Melbourne. Over this period, dramatic changes took place in the settlement culminating in a 'budding metropolis' by 1880 (Davison 1978:6). This chapter provides historical background on Melbourne, the genteel Heidelberg area and Viewbank homestead.

MELBOURNE ESTABLISHED

In 1835 an unsanctioned treaty was made by John Batman and elders of the Wurundjeri to exchange yearly provision of supplies of blankets, knives, tomahawks, mirrors, axes, clothes etc. for approximately 600,000 acres of land (Broome 1984:20; Kociumbas 1992:190–191; Attwood 2009). While there had been a very limited European presence in Port Phillip prior to this, it was in 1835 that permanent settlement commenced (Boyce 2011:9–12). By this time, the Aboriginal population had already suffered from the effects of introduced diseases, particularly smallpox from Asia, and the British colonists brought tuberculosis, measles and venereal diseases (Campbell 2002:216). The Aboriginal population declined rapidly (Shaw 1996:20; Campbell 2002:xii). Disease was not the only plight of the Aboriginal people in Port Phillip. Encounters between settlers and Aboriginal people were often confused and violent (Broome 2005:14). Pastoral settlers displaced Aboriginal people from their land, particularly on Melbourne's fringe and in many cases this forced Aboriginal people to seek European food in Melbourne (Broome 2005:20–21). Displacement, exploitation and death were rife.

Following the treaty, the grab for land in the Port Phillip district commenced initially with squatters from Van Diemen's Land (now Tasmania) encouraged by Edward Henty, John Batman and the Port Phillip Association, John Fawkner and others. They were followed shortly after by 'overlanders' from New South Wales following in the footsteps of Major Thomas Mitchell who first made the journey in 1836 (Broome 1984:20). While 'overstraiters' and 'overlanders' continued to make the journey, when news of the adventure and fortune that could be had in Port Phillip reached Britain, another wave of immigrant squatters made their way to the colony (Broome 1984:22; Dingle 1984:21–22). The need for labour was initially filled by ex-convicts, but labour shortages were so severe by the mid-1840s that in Britain the working class, and in particular the agricultural poor, were actively encouraged to migrate (Broome 1984:40–41; Boyce 2011:155–156).

In England, middle-class men, although possibly influential in their profession, had little power in the political or social arena (Davidoff and Hall 2002:73). However, a middle-class man who left England for the new settlement at Port Phillip could become wealthier and more influential in society. For some, the desire to escape scandal or unhappiness functioned as a catalyst for emigration. In addition, farming families from England and Scotland were under pressure due to the recession following the end of the Napoleonic Wars in 1815 and many viewed emigration to Australia and other British colonies as a way of stretching their capital further (Broome 1984:19). These early settlers were mostly men of considerable wealth, along with their families and servants. Many were doctors, lawyers, clergy and ex-military men. Most were English, but there were also a large number of Scots and some Irish (Broome 1984:23). Arriving first in Sydney, the squatters undertook the long and hazardous overland trip from New South Wales within a short period of arriving in Australia and often with stock (Broome 1984:20–21).

Prior to the gold rush, medical men like Dr Martin far outnumbered other professionals in the colonies (Mackay 1934:476). A significant number of these doctors were Scots, as was Dr Martin himself. The universities of Edinburgh, Glasgow and Aberdeen were producing a high number of graduates, exceeding local demand. Surgeons were required on every vessel that made the voyage to Australia and many signed up for the journey, but once in the colony they found only limited opportunity for medical practice. Many turned to pastoral pursuits, and their medical background along with their good education put them in a position to take up influential roles in society such as magistrate, or president of a range of societies (Mackay 1934:476).

Conditions were hard during the first years of the Port Phillip district. Melbourne was a 'primitive village' (Davison 1978:6) and services were limited. By 1840, however, Melbourne had a population of around 4,000 and had become an administrative centre servicing the pastoral interests of the Port Phillip district (Brown-May 1998:1–2). In spite of an economic depression in the early 1840s, by 1843 shops and hotels were steadily emerging

(Dingle 1984:27; Priestley 1984:23–24). From the outset, the settlement lauded respectability and distanced itself from the 'convict stain' in spite of the undeniable presence of ex-convicts in the district (Boyce 2011:56).

In 1851, the Port Phillip district became an independent colony named Victoria. It was also at this time that the first discoveries of gold were made, bringing great upheaval and transformation to the colony (Cannon 1971:180). It also brought a fresh influx of arrivals from working-class backgrounds who sought their fortune and to establish themselves in the new society. The population of Melbourne increased from 29,000 in 1850 to 125,000 ten years later (Davison 1978:6). The gold rush continued throughout the 19th century, but was declining in influence from the 1870s (Serle 1971:1). From this time, wool, wheat, and manufacturing were the primary industries in Victoria (Serle 1971:45–85). Two periods of economic depression affected the colony while the Martins lived at Viewbank: one in the early 1840s and another in the mid-1850s (Broome 1984:35, 87). In spite of this, the legacy of the gold rush enabled Melbourne's growth into a major commercial centre, not only because of the wealth it created, but from the demand for services required by a growing population (Davison 1978:11). By 1891, Melbourne's population had expanded to 491,000 and it had become a true metropolis: a bustling, global city (Serle 1971:77; Davison 1978:7).

Heidelberg

The Woiwurrung people occupied the area drained by the Yarra River and its tributaries, including Heidelberg, at the commencement of European settlement. There were five clans of Woiwurrung speakers, and it was the Wurundjeri-willam who occupied the river flats (Barwick 1984:124; Presland 1994:36). In the early years of European settlement, Woiwurrung people in the area continued their traditional rituals. However, as European settlers took up the land along the Yarra River for farming, it became impossible for the Woiwurrung to live as they had done in the area (Presland 1994:72). There is little historical information about the experiences of the Woiwurrung people in Heidelberg, but it is likely that their experiences were much the same as elsewhere in Victoria, characterised by displacement, exploitation and violence.

Early European explorations of the Heidelberg area noted the beautiful, well-watered and fertile land. As with much of Port Phillip, the first to take up the land did so to graze sheep (Garden 1972:3–5). This was short-lived, with the first subdivisions of land for sale in Heidelberg by the Crown in 1838. The area was divided into nine portions and a village reserve. Further subdivisions continued shortly after with farms and estates being established (Garden 1972:11).

A large number of the estates in the Heidelberg area served as town residences. Advertisements for land in the area emphasised the gentlemanly estates and the prestige of the area, along with its fertility and beauty (Garden 1972:13–15). This gave Heidelberg a different character to the rest of Port Phillip. For example, one advertisement promoted the land as: '... adjoining the romantic Village of "Heidelberg", adjacent to the highly improved Estates of Joseph Hawdon, Esq., ... etc etc; and within half an hour's ride or drive of the rising and populous city of Melbourne' (*The Australian*, 5 October 1839). Hawdon's Banyule Homestead was an impressive two-storey mansion completed in 1846, which still stands today. The area was suitable for those required to go to the city on a daily basis, but also allowed for the pursuit of farming, dairying and market gardening, for which there was an increasing demand in the colony (Garden 1972:15). The area became something between suburb and country: an area of country-style residences for the influential men of Melbourne.

Heidelberg from the 1840s onwards was also home to independent and itinerant workers, employees on the estates, small farmers and those working to supply services in the growing Warringal village. From 1845, the land in the Warringal village reserve was sold and in 1848 there was a scattering of shops including a butcher, baker, wheelwright and blacksmith. The village met the basic needs of the population of Heidelberg. By the 1850s, the Old England Hotel, Church of England, Wesleyan and Roman Catholic churches had been established, along with two schools (Garden 1972:70–75). Heidelberg relied on a coach service to link it to Melbourne until 1888 when the first, albeit indirect, rail route opened. A direct rail line to Melbourne opened in 1901 (Cummins 1971:47). The area had the feel and characteristics of an English rural community. Heidelberg was also popular for day trips from the city for picnicking and leisure, and as a meeting place for Melbourne's hunt clubs (Garden 1972:74). Towards the end of the 19th century the area became increasingly popular among artists and is still renowned for the works of the Heidelberg School of Artists.

Viewbank Homestead

The first European occupation of the Viewbank land appears to have commenced in 1837 when Edward Willis occupied a run at the junction of the Plenty and Yarra Rivers (Billis and Kenyon 1932:141; Spreadborough and Anderson 1983). The first official record of ownership of the Viewbank land was when subdivision took place in Heidelberg in 1838. Richard Henry Browne purchased the portion of land on which Viewbank was to sit (PROV, VPRS 460/P, Unit 1102, 150140/16440). The land was divided into four lots and advertised for sale in *The Australian* newspaper on 7 March

1840 with the advertisement promoting the beauty of the landscape and the 'gentlemanly society' of the area.

James Williamson purchased the eastern-most 192 acres of Browne's estate in December 1839 (PROV, VPRS 460/P, Unit 1102, 31 January 1839). In 1841 the New South Wales census listed a weatherboard house at Viewbank (Peters 1996:14). Later that year Williamson was having financial difficulties and was forced to convey Viewbank under trust to pay off his debts. In August 1842, the Viewbank mortgage and Williamson's debt were conveyed to Dr Martin. In October 1842, Viewbank was advertised for sale in its entirety:

> The above beautiful and highly valuable property, situated at Heidelberg, on the banks of the Yarra, about six or seven miles from town, consisting of 192 acres, three roods, twenty-four perches, mostly alluvial flat land, with a genteel residence detached. Stables, coach-house, garden, &c., in every respect calculated for the reception of a respectable family. If not sold by the 1st September next, it will on that day be sold by auction, and parties desirous of purchasing are strongly recommended to inspect the property, which in beauty of scenery, richness of soil, elegance of its buildings, and respectability of situation, cannot be surpassed by any other in the colonies. (*Port Phillip Gazette*, 3 October 1842)

Two years later, on 23 August 1844, Robert Gear Esq. of England purchased Viewbank from Browne and conveyed the land, under the care of trustees, to his daughter, Mrs Martin (PROV, VPRS 460/P, Unit 1102, 150140/16440). Subsequent deeds refer to Dr Martin as the owner of Viewbank. The *Port Phillip Gazette* recorded on 22 May 1843 that 'Dr Martin is removing to his property at Heidelberg, his house at Moonee Ponds would be let'.

When the Martins moved to Viewbank with their children they required a larger and grander homestead than the original weatherboard house. The will of Lucy Martin states that additions were made to the homestead after 1840 (PROV, VPRS 7591/P2, Unit 87, File 26-805, 11 January 1884). The architect John Gill was employed to undertake extensions. The employment of a well-known architect indicates that substantial additions were to take place (Peters 1996:18). In 1850, a tender notice appeared in the *Melbourne Morning Herald*:

> To Carpenters and Joiners
>
> Persons willing to tender for the carpentry and joinery work (labour only) required in sundry alterations and additions to the residence of R. Martin Esq. Heidelberg. May inspect the plans and specification, and obtain all necessary information at the office of the undersigned, to whom tenders must be delivered on or before Wednesday, the 4th of December next. John Gill, Architect. (*The Melbourne Morning Herald and General Daily Advertiser*, 28 November 1850)

An earlier tender by Gill appeared in the *Port Phillip Herald* (5 August 1845) for builders and stonemasons for work on a house in Heidelberg, which may well have also been for work at Viewbank.

The house was situated on a hill with good views to the south-west. In spite of the prolific work of the Heidelberg School of Artists in the area, no drawing or painting of Viewbank homestead has been found. However, official documents and oral histories provide some information on the appearance of the house. An affidavit to Mrs Martin's will in 1884 records that on the now 195 acre Viewbank property there was a '... brick house containing 12 rooms slate roof & leaden gutters wooden out houses and stabling – fencing ...' (PROV, VPRS 7591/P2, Unit 87, File 26-805, 19 January 1884). Oral histories taken by the Heidelberg Historical Society (HHS Viewbank file) give some indication of the house at Viewbank. One records that:

> Mrs Alma White, a long time resident of Heidelberg described the house as built of handmade brick, single storey with verandas on either side of the dwelling and across the front. Windows from floor at the front of the house, and the front door had coloured glass panels on either side of door and etching on glass. (HHS Viewbank file)

Mr T. Rank, who grew up near Viewbank and was a child when the homestead was demolished, gave oral testimony in 1974 which records that the house was:

> ... a substantial residence made of handmade bricks and foundations of local stone. Where the stone was excavated on the property [sic] formed a large cellar and a big, square underground tank. The roof was slate and it was a single storied dwelling with hip roof and low gable. There were French windows opening onto a front verandah, and on either side of the front were two wings, with bedrooms on one side and living room on the other. The house contained marble fireplaces and Mr. Rank remembers his mother commenting on the beautiful wood paneling in the house. (HHS Viewbank file)

There is no direct evidence of the Martins' contact with the local Wurundjeri (Woiwurrung) people while at Viewbank, however it is possible that conflict emerged out of the competition for resources. A large Wurundjeri settlement was located at the junction of the Plenty and Yarra Rivers, not far from Viewbank (Willacy 1981). The activities at Viewbank

2. Early Melbourne and Viewbank Homestead

must have displaced these people from their land. Pastoralism certainly had a devastating impact on Aboriginal people in Victoria and Dr Martin's extensive properties would have contributed to this throughout Victoria.

Aboriginal people were often employed as stockmen by pastoralists, but probably on an unpaid basis with only food and accommodation provided. There is some suggestion in the historical records that Dr Martin employed Aboriginal people. Evelyn Pitfield Stirling Sturt of Lonsdale Street, Melbourne in a letter to Lieutenant-Governor Charles La Trobe on 20 October 1853 discussed the 'dangerous' Aboriginal population:

> I knew a fine young lad whom Dr Martin had civilized; he was a stockman, and a very intelligent lad. He accompanied a party with fat stock to Melbourne; at Buninyong he fell in with a tribe of natives, and, in the act of giving them tobacco, was basely speared, and died in the greatest agony. His only offence was that he belonged to a strange tribe. (Bride 1969:368)

This man would have worked for Dr Martin at one of his pastoral runs, and was probably travelling from Dr Martin's Mount Sturgeon pastoral property. Unfortunately there is little more that can be gleaned from the history of Viewbank on the interactions between the Martins and the Wurundjeri people.

After Dr Martin's death in 1874 (PROV, VPRS 7591/P2, Unit 17, File 12-586, 22 October 1874), Mrs Martin left Viewbank and leased 63 acres of the property, including the house, to Cecilia H. Cockburn Campbell in 1875 (PROV, VPRS 460/P, Unit 1102, 1 June 1875). The remainder of the land was leased to Joseph Bond (Peters 1996:11). The property continued to be leased for a number of years to various tenants, the last of whom was Thomas Robinson, a dairy farmer, who occupied Viewbank from 1911 to 1920 (Peters 1996:12). It is unclear whether these later tenants were occupying the homestead or just using the land.

The oral history given by Mr Rank (HHS Viewbank file) indicates that the Viewbank homestead was demolished and the materials sold off during World War I. However, Heidelberg rate books indicate that the homestead was still standing until Harold Bartram purchased the property in 1922 or 1923 (Peters 1996:12). Bartram was a dairy farmer who also owned land in Heidelberg, Bulleen and Templestowe. It appears that the Viewbank homestead was demolished when Bartram purchased the property (Peters 1996:12). Bartram farmed the land and built a house near Banyule Road in 1942 (HHS Bartram Family file). From the 1950s, Bartram began to subdivide and sell his land. In 1971, Viewbank was sold to the Melbourne Board of Works and is now part of the Yarra Metropolitan Park (HHS Bartram Family file).

Over the period that the Martin family lived at Viewbank homestead, Melbourne grew from a 'primitive village' towards a global metropolis, Heidelberg went from grazing land to a genteel village, and Viewbank from a modest, four roomed cottage to a substantial 12 roomed estate. It was a time of great opportunity and dramatic change.

3
People at Viewbank Homestead

The personal histories of the people who lived at Viewbank homestead are a vital aspect of this study as they allow for the background, aspirations and success of the residents to be examined. This information indicates that the Martin family were typical of the 'established middle class': they came from wealthy, middle class backgrounds, brought affluence with them and successfully expanded their wealth and social influence once in the colony.

Dr Martin: An 'Impetuous' Gentleman

Dr Robert Martin was born in Scotland in 1798, on the Isle of Skye, Inner Hebrides (Billis and Kenyon 1932:95) (**Figure 3.1**). There are few known facts about Dr Martin's life before coming to Australia. It is possible that he studied medicine in Scotland: the entry for Dr Martin on the online *Australian Medical Pioneers Index* (2006) suggests that he was a Licentiate of the Royal College of Surgeons in Edinburgh in 1824. The Edinburgh Royal College of Surgeons provided excellent clinical training, among the best in the world (Mitchell 2009:196). In addition, an account by his grand-daughter suggests that Dr Martin had been in the East India Service at one point and had practiced medicine in the inner London suburb of Islington (Genealogical Society of Victoria 1970:105).

The Isle of Skye suffered from social and economic collapse in the first half of the 19th century (Watson 1984:25), and wealthy farmers and landowners were forced to leave along with the workers. Many immigrated to the British colonies and it is possible that Dr Martin was among those who left for this reason. Dr Martin arrived in Melbourne in 1839 after travelling overland from Sydney (Bride 1969:87). The Martin family lived at Moonee Ponds prior to moving to Viewbank in 1843 (*Port Phillip Gazette*, 22 May 1843).

Correspondence, business records and official documents reveal something of Dr Martin's success and character once in Melbourne. He focused his attention on pastoral pursuits and established extensive pastoral properties across Victoria (see **Figure 1.1** for locations). The largest was at Mount Sturgeon in the Grampians, Western Victoria, which he took up in 1840. It comprised 112,000 acres with 1,000 cattle and 20,000 sheep, and when he sold it in 1866 it was worth more than £70,000, an enormous amount of money (Kerr's Melbourne

Figure 3.1: Dr Robert Martin, artist and year unknown (Source: Heidelberg Historical Society).

Almanac 1841; Billis and Kenyon 1932:227; Hopton 1950:378; Spreadborough and Anderson 1983:125; Niall 2004:33). Dr Martin owned another property at Acheron near the Cathedral Ranges, 120 km north-east of Melbourne, from 1872, which comprised 24,000 acres and 4,000 sheep (Billis and Kenyon 1932:95, 145; Spreadborough and Anderson 1983:149). An affidavit to Dr Martin's will records that he also owned property at Nillumbik and Clunes. The Nillumbik property north-east of Melbourne comprised 580 acres and included a three-roomed cottage (PROV, VPRS 7591/P2, Unit 17, File 12-586, 11 February 1875), while the Clunes property north of Ballarat comprised 1,400 acres and three cottages (PROV, VPRS 7591/P2, Unit 17, File 12-586, 11 February 1875). Dr Martin also had New Zealand interests: in 1857 he lent £2,000 to Melbourne Club member Arthur Hogue to establish a sheep run in Otago, and also commissioned Hogue to look for land for himself and son-in-law Dr Youl (Niall 2004:31).

Dr Martin seems to have leased these properties, or employed managers to run them, and lived at Viewbank. Letters from Charles Browning Hall and Edward Bell in 1853 recorded that Dr Martin left Mount Sturgeon under the charge of Mr Knowles (Bride 1969:266, 290). An affidavit to Dr Martin's

3. People at Viewbank Homestead

will records that the Nillumbik property, with its three-room cottage, was let to a Patrick Long, and the three cottages on the Clunes property were let to various tenants (PROV, VPRS 7591/P2, Unit 17, File 12-586, 11 February 1875).

By the standards of the day, Dr Martin was extremely wealthy. At the time of his death in 1874, his total estate was valued at £43,073.6s.3d (PROV, VPRS 7591/P2, Unit 17, File 12-586, 15 July 1874). To contextualise this, on average, business and professional men earned around £1,000 to £3,000 per annum by the 1880s (Serle 1971:91). The average income of a doctor was £250 in the 1850s rising to £800 by the late 1890s, while a well-connected doctor might have earned £3,000 per annum in the 1880s (Davison 1978:232; Pensabene 1980:82).

Dr Martin was also building a position in society and held a number of influential positions and memberships. He was a member of the Melbourne Club from 1840 (De Serville 1980:193) and the District Council of Bourke (*The Australian*, 26 December 1837), as well as being trustee of St. John's Church of England in Heidelberg (recorded on a memorial at the church), trustee of the Savings Bank of Port Phillip (Garden 1972:44), chairman of the Heidelberg Road Trust (*The Argus*, 28 October 1864), President of the Victorian Agricultural Society (*The Argus*, 6 June 1862), a member of the Board of Agriculture (*The Argus*, 16 July 1863), and a Justice of the Peace (*The Argus*, 24 April 1852; Hopton 1950:378). In the 19th century, the status of a gentleman was predominantly based on the exercise of power. This was realised in the public realm: through business ties, employment, politics and membership of social institutions (Russell 1994:1, 14, 18).

Respect in the community for Dr Martin is indicated in an 1862 news clipping that reported the wedding of his daughter Charlotte. It states:

> All classes having agreed to keep holiday in order to show their respect for Dr Martin J.P. ... for the event, and that ... the heartiness and goodwill which prevailed throughout the day unmistakably showed that the worthy Doctor had what all resident landlords should have – 'Honour, Love, Obedience and a Troop of Friends'. (HHS 1862)

It is difficult to ascertain exactly when and where Dr Martin practised medicine in Australia, if at all. Early editions of *Kerr's Melbourne Almanac* and *Port Phillip Directory* list Dr Martin as a settler, but not under 'Medical Practitioners'. *The Melbourne Commercial Directory* has a 'list of duly qualified Medical Practitioners who have received Certificates from the Medical Board up to Jan. 10 1853' which does not include Dr Martin.

There is some evidence that Dr Martin practised medicine in Heidelberg later in his life. In 1867 at the age of 69 he is listed in the *Sands and McDougall's Melbourne and Suburban Directory* as practicing at Vine Street in Heidelberg. In subsequent years, from 1868 to 1871, this directory lists Dr Robert Martin under 'Physicians, Surgeons and Medical Practitioners' and gives his location as Viewbank. This may suggest that he was practising from home at this time. It is possible that Dr Martin returned to medicine after retirement from pastoral activities. Dr Martin clearly maintained an interest in the medical profession: in 1873, just one year before he died, Dr Martin purchased three Collins Street buildings to be used by medical practitioners (MCC 1873).

Dr Martin developed business links and a close friendship with James Graham, a wealthy merchant and influential man (Graham 1998:132). Graham kept a letter book which included correspondence relating to Dr Martin, mostly concerning his business dealings. These letters provide insight into Dr Martin's character. A gentleman was expected to have manners and education (Mitchell 2009:269), however, Graham described Dr Martin as '... difficult to manage, and so impetuous that he will fly off at a tangent if anything puts him out' (GP 2 March 1866). This is hardly the ideal picture of gentility. Expressing anger was against civilised standards and showed a lack of self-control, but was more tolerable for men than for women (Young 2003:118). However, Graham was 20 years younger than Dr Martin and worked as an agent for him (essentially as an employee). Dr Martin did not need to impress Graham and, as such, may have behaved less cautiously with him.

Dr Martin's business success and secure income provided the lifestyle that the family enjoyed. This was at the heart of 19th-century masculinity – to support and order his family and household (Davidoff and Hall 2002:114). Dr Martin also invested in the future of his family providing substantial £5,000 dowries for his daughters, property for his son, and £5,000 trust funds for the eldest grandson in each family (Niall 2004:33).

Mrs Martin: A Fiery Woman

Dr Martin married Lucy Gear in London and the Genealogical Society of Victoria gives the date as 6 May 1834. However, this was one year after their first child was born so this date seems unlikely. Lucy was the daughter of Robert Gear Esq. of Lewes, Sussex and Lucy de Guzman who was the daughter of Don Dominicus de Guzman, a relative of the Spanish Marie Eugénie de Guzman y de Porto-Carrero, wife of Emperor Napoleon III of France (Genealogical Society of Victoria 1970:105; De Serville 1980:205). Genealogy, titles and heraldry were highly valued in Melbourne society (De Serville 1991:189–192; Russell 1994:38), and presumably Mrs Martin prized this connection to royalty.

Marriage, domesticity and reproduction were the dominant concepts of womanhood in 19th-century

Australia (Anderson 1992:229). Historian Penny Russell (1994:2) writes:

> Genteel femininity consisted, in its ideal form, of a series of internalised moral values, chief among which were a dislike of display, ambition or pretension and a dedication to the 'private' domestic world as a moral haven.

The dependence of women was a central concept of 19th-century Christian belief and it was also an expected part of motherhood that a woman would, in turn, provide emotional support for her children (Davidoff and Hall 2002:114, 335). Mrs Martin gave birth to her six children across a period of 13 years. Unusually, no stillbirths or infant deaths were recorded for Mrs Martin. There was a large range of family sizes in the 19th century with the number of children ranging from none to ten or more (Anderson 1985:53; Beer 1989:34, 36).

In spite of her commitment to family, it appears from historical documents that Mrs Martin was not always the demure ideal of genteel femininity. She was seen as fiery by other women in genteel society, always attributed to her being half-Spanish (Niall 2002:33).

Their Children

Viewbank was home to children from infancy to adulthood. Dr and Mrs Martin's first three children Lucy, Sarah Anne Jane (Annie) and Robert William Kirby (Willy), were born in London (Genealogical Society of Victoria 1970:105; Niall 2002:29). Their fourth child, Charlotte, was born in Victoria, but prior to the family moving to Viewbank. When the Martin family moved to Viewbank in 1843 their oldest daughter Lucy was aged 10, Annie was 6, Robert was 4 and Charlotte was 1. Emma and Edith were born at Viewbank in 1844 and 1846 respectively (Niall 2002:xxii). In the 19th century, for the first time, many children stayed at home into adulthood, partly due to the reduction of apprenticeships for middle-class professions (Flanders 2003:xxii), and this was the case for the Martin children.

The five Martin daughters ensured that the Viewbank homestead was a predominantly feminine environment. There was a 13-year age gap between the eldest, Lucy born in 1833 and youngest, Edith born in 1846. Their lives would have been closely involved with each other and their mother. In the 19th century, mother and daughters spent much time together doing handicrafts in the drawing room, attending and receiving calls, promenading and shopping, and possibly undertaking philanthropic work.

Education for girls focused on their character and behaviour in preparation for life in society. Discipline and deportment were more important than literacy and knowledge (Russell 1994:145–146). However, there are no historical records regarding any formal education of the Martin daughters. It is possible that the girls were educated by a governess, but there is no historical record of this being the case.

The historical documentation regarding the Martin daughters is almost exclusively with regard to their marriages, and reflects the significance of marriage for women in this era. It was a momentous event and shaped a woman's life completely, as her status and wealth were determined by her husband. All five of the Martin daughters married.

Attending social events was an important part of making a suitable match and would have been a large part of the daughters' lives while at Viewbank. In 1854, a year before Annie's marriage, a letter from Edward Graham to half-brother James Graham recorded that:

> The Exhibition has been a great pleasure and very good concerts have been constantly held there. One of the belles has been Annie Martin upon whom Dr Youl has got quite spoony. When she left for Heidelberg he sent her a magnificent gold watch and chain which the young lady declined. (Graham 1998:18)

Unfortunately for Annie, an arranged marriage to the middle-aged Dr Youl, coroner of Melbourne, was forced upon her (Russell 1994:38). Later, Edward expressed his dissatisfaction at not being asked to the wedding party and states that 'The marriage has been a great source of talk from everyone from Lady Hotham downwards and all pitying poor Annie' (Graham 1998:79–80).

Emma and Charlotte also made socially successful matches, marrying men of whom their father approved. Emma married Dr Youl's nephew Harry, son of pastoralist Sir James Arndell Youl, KCMG (Russell 1994). Charlotte married John Fenton Esquire in a celebration '... of unwonted gaiety and loveliness' provided by Dr Martin:

> An arch decorated with flowers and evergreens was erected at the entrance to the Church ground: the Church itself being densely crowded to witness the ceremony which was performed in an impressive manner by the Rev. J. Lyner.
> The fair Bride attracted universal attention, even in the midst of the bevy of Bridesmaids. A salvo of artillery from the Racecourse announced the tying of the Nuptual Knot and, on leaving the Church, children dressed in white scattered flowers before the happy pair. (HHS 1862)

Not all of the Martin daughters married in such grandeur. Lucy eloped when Dr Martin attempted to stop her marriage to Captain John Theodore Boyd, of whom he disapproved on grounds of his lack of fortune and inability to provide a settled home (Niall

2004:31). Lucy and John eloped to be married at Richmond on 4 February 1857 (Genealogical Society of Victoria 1970:105; Graham 1998:184). Boyd was a member of the 11th Regiment of the British Army and was military secretary to the Governor of Victoria (Genealogical Society of Victoria 1970:106).

Similarly, Dr Martin denied Edith an engagement to Mr Bradley, navigating lieutenant of the *HMS Galatea*, in 1868 because he had 'nothing at present but his pay'. However, Edith was persistent and after an engagement of two and a half years was allowed to sail to England to marry Mr Bradley in 1872 (Russell 1994:152). Dr Martin's refusal of these marriages is suggestive of the difficulties of class in Melbourne at this time. While both Boyd and Bradley were middle class, their lack of security beyond their pay clearly set them below the Martin family in Dr Martin's esteem.

The daughters were aged between 18 and 26 at the times of their marriages. They were probably significantly younger than their husbands: certainly for 18-year-old Annie with her middle-aged husband, and Lucy who was 13 years younger than John Boyd. The fact that marriage was the single most important social aspect of a woman's life in the 19th century is certainly reflected in the experiences of the Martin daughters.

The historical record reveals Willy's role in the family. For middle-class sons, education was all-important and focused on a successful career and future (Russell 1994:147). This was especially important, as a son would support the unmarried women of the family after the father died (Russell 1994:149). Willy was sent to Trinity Hall, Cambridge for his education in law (De Serville 1991:318). In a letter, James Graham, details that 'I have instructed Donaldson & Lambert [Graham's agents in London] to pay the education expenses of Dr Martin's son who is at present in England. They will advise you from time to time of the debits to our account for this purpose' (Graham 1998:85). The considerable expense involved in sending Willy to be educated in England is evidence of the importance of educating sons.

Willy was called to the English bar in 1860 (Genealogical Society of Victoria 1970:105). Although a solicitor, he, like his father, focused on pastoral pursuits. Willy took his father's place as president of the Victorian Agricultural Society in 1868 (*The Argus*, 22 October 1868) and in 1871 he became a co-founder of the Heidelberg Cheese Factory Company (Garden 1972:121).

Men could relax genteel standards to a larger extent than women. Without risking their status, men could mingle with people from other classes (particularly when it came to horse racing and gambling), attend a wider range of social functions or partake of disreputable pleasures (Russell 1994:68, 76–77). Yet Willy appears as the dutiful son. He married James Graham's daughter Minnie in 1874, a match that must have pleased Dr Martin greatly. James Graham (GP 19 May 1874) recorded in a letter that 97 guests sat down to breakfast to celebrate the wedding. He also reported that 'Dr Martin in the most liberal manner settled the whole of the property [Banyule] on Minnie'. A man had to be well established financially before he could marry, and therefore most men did not marry until they were in their thirties (Mitchell 2009:156). Willy married at 35. The couple had four daughters, Mary, Edith, Dorothy and Sylvia (Genealogical Society of Victoria 1970:105).

FAMILY ROLES

The gender divide dictated family roles, social behaviour and daily interactions in the 19th century. This began from an early age with girls viewed as pretty and boys as energetic and full of mischief (Russell 1994:142). Tightly tied in with Christian belief, the natural role of a husband was seen to be to command, and the wife, children and servants to obey (Davidoff and Hall 2002:108).

Separate spheres for men and women became part of morality and individual roles (Young 2003). The idea of male/public and female/private spheres for middle-class people is widely discussed in Australia, Britain and America (Saunders and Evans 1992:99; Russell 1994; Wall 1994; Davidoff and Hall 2002:xvi; Young 2003:18). While this pattern was generally common, there was inevitable overlap between the spheres. The private realm of women was on display to the public world, and men had private roles. In their volume on gender relations in Australia, Saunders and Evans (1992:99) state '... the private and public spheres are both co-related and interpenetrative' while also drawing attention to the fact that masculine power dominates both spheres. Davidoff and Hall (2002:13) make the important observation that:

> middle-class men who sought to be 'someone', to count as individuals because of their wealth, their power to command or their capacity to influence people, were, in fact, embedded in networks of familial and female support which underpinned their rise to public prominence.

The historical records give us some insight into family roles in the Viewbank household, particularly with regard to the Martins' interactions with their children in adulthood. In the 19th century, fathers demanded respect from their children and were also expected to provide for them. A father's authority, especially over his daughters, was not to be disputed (Russell 1994:151).

As marriages were an important and effective way of forming social alliances, Dr Martin had a particular interest in the marriages of his daughters arranging and refusing them in the interest of his family and status. In Melbourne society, marriage and kinship were crucial, and an imprudent marriage could taint many (Russell 1994:15). Three of the Martin daughters, Annie, Emma and Charlotte, married men of whom Dr Martin approved. All three men were members of the Melbourne Club; two were doctors and one a pastoralist (Niall 2002:31). However, Dr Martin was not all powerful within the family and his refusal of the marriages of both Lucy and Edith were ultimately overturned (Russell 1994:152; Graham 1998:184). Further, it appears that Mrs Martin did not share her husband's view on these marriages as she gave her daughter Lucy a Bible inscribed 'from her affectionate mother' on the day she returned from her elopement (Niall 2002:33).

Despite their defiance, Dr Martin provided financial support to Lucy and Edith, as well as his other children. It appears that he forgave Lucy, giving her a £5,000 dowry. He also provided advice suggesting that Lucy and her husband take up land in New Zealand, which they followed (Graham 1998:184). He gave Edith £500 to purchase her trousseau and a further £5,000 upon her marriage (Russell 1994:152). A letter from James Graham to Lucy Boyd (neé Martin) in 1862 states that 'Your father is anxious to raise some money previous to Charlotte's marriage...' (Graham 1998:288). Further, Dr Martin states in his will that 'I Bequeath to each of my daughters, for all of whom I have already provided on their respective marriages, the sum of One hundred pounds ... as a token of affection' (PROV, VPRS 7591/P2, Unit 17, File 12-586, 27 January 1873). In a codicil to his will Dr Martin details that his Collins Street property should be for the use of his daughter Annie and her husband, Dr Youl (PROV, VPRS 7591/P2, Unit 17, File 12-586, 15 July 1874). Also, when son Willy married James Graham's daughter Minnie, in 1874, Dr Martin settled the Banyule property at Heidelberg on Minnie. Dr Martin had purchased Banyule from Joseph Hawdon in 1867 for £7,500. Minnie continued to live there after the death of her husband in 1878 (GP 19 May 1874). Dr Martin certainly treated his children with financial generosity.

SERVANTS

A housekeeper and a contingent of domestic and general servants also worked, and possibly lived, at Viewbank homestead. Jane Warren loyally served the Martin family as housekeeper for many years. She was left £100 in Dr Martin's will and continued serving Mrs Martin after the family moved away from Viewbank (PROV, VPRS 7591/P2, Unit 17, File 12-586, 27 January 1873 and PROV, VPRS 7591/P2, Unit 87, File 26/805, 7 August 1882). The probate conducted in 1875 after Dr Martin's death lists servants' wages at £90 2s 11d, but does not detail how many or what kind of servants were employed (PROV, VPRS 7591/P2, Unit 17, File 12-586, 11 February 1875).

Although servants were remunerated primarily in board and lodging with a comparatively small amount of wages (Higman 2002:167) they were still a significant expense. A list of the servants' annual wages at Newington, Parramatta, for 1845 shows that the coachman earned the highest annual wage at £30, followed by the butler at £26, the cook at £25.10s, the gardener at £23.8s, the yardman at £20.16s, the seamstress at £20, the housemaid at £13.7s, the lady's maid at £12, and the laundress at £10.3s (Dyster 1989:146–147). This adds up to over £170 for the year. In 1849 in Port Phillip, female cooks were paid £16 to £26 per annum, while other domestic servants were paid £12 to £28 annually (Higman 2002:170). By 1872 in Victoria, the wage of a housemaid was 9s a week (or £25 per annum), and around 10s a week (or £26 pounds per annum) for a laundress or cook (Cannon 1975:244). Wages increased dramatically by the 1880s: a governess might have been paid £30 per year in Victoria, but cooks and housemaids would have considered this amount very poor (Serle 1971:84).

The amount for servants' wages in Dr Martin's probate was probably outstanding at the time of his death. It is, therefore, difficult to determine how many servants the family had from this amount as it is unknown whether it is outstanding from January or the beginning of the financial year in July. Dr Martin died on 24 September 1874, so if each servant was paid an average of £20 per annum and the amount owing is for the year-to-date then these wages would be sufficient for six servants. Upon Mrs Martin's death in December 1884 £12.1s was owed to the housekeeper; therefore, it is likely that the amounts in the probate are those outstanding from July. If the amount owing was from July for the Viewbank servants, then the £90 would have been sufficient to pay approximately 18 servants. They certainly had a housekeeper, and the presence of a housekeeper at Viewbank indicates a large contingent of indoor servants (Russell 1994:38). A groom and coachman were probably also employed at Viewbank as the presence of a stable indicates that horses were kept. Also, the extensive gardens probably required the employment of at least one gardener.

MOVING ON

In spite of their wealth and success the Martin family suffered tragedy. Charlotte, her husband John Fenton and their two children were killed in the wreck of the steamship *London* in the Bay of Biscay on 11 January 1866 (HHS 1866, GP 20 March 1866). In September 1874, Dr Martin died at the age of 76 (PROV, VPRS 7591/P2, Unit 17, File 12-586, 22 October 1874). He was buried in the Church of England section of the Warringal Cemetery in Heidelberg (HHS Viewbank file). Willy had diabetes, and died young on 14 May 1878 at the age of 39 (Genealogical Society of Victoria 1970:105; Russell 1994:38).

3. People at Viewbank Homestead

Willy and his wife had four daughters, and as such the Martin name did not continue on in Victoria. All of the Martin daughters had children, and ironically it was Lucy and John Boyd who founded one of the famous names in Australian history. Their son Arthur Merric Boyd was the first of a group of famous artists directly descended from Lucy and John Boyd.

After Dr Martin's death in 1874 (PROV, VPRS 7591/P2, Unit 17, File 12-586, 22 October 1874), Mrs Martin moved to South Yarra (PROV, VPRS 460/P, Unit 1102, 1 June 1875). The Martin's housekeeper, Jane Warren, went with her. Mrs Martin died on 10 December 1883 (PROV, VPRS 7591/P2, Unit 87, File 26/805, 9 January 1884).

The structure of the Martin family and 19th-century expectations of the roles of wives, husbands and children are apparent at Viewbank homestead. Evidence suggests that they were typical of the 'established middle class': they came from wealthy middle-class backgrounds, arrived in the earliest years after the establishment of the colony, held vast pastoral properties and were very successful in their new lives in Melbourne. They moved in the appropriate social networks and were an important part of Melbourne society.

4
The Archaeology of Viewbank Homestead

The archaeological remains of Viewbank homestead have remained relatively undisturbed. Extensive archaeological evidence uncovered at the site by Heritage Victoria provides a rare and important opportunity to study middle-class material culture from this period of Melbourne's history. This chapter provides an overview of the excavations including methods, excavated areas, outcomes and artefacts. It then goes on to discuss the post-excavation artefact work, and in particular the artefact processing and cataloguing methods used for the author's PhD research (Hayes 2008). This includes the categorisation of artefacts and analytical tools applied to the assemblage, along with limitations restricting the study.

THE EXCAVATION OF VIEWBANK HOMESTEAD

The first excavation at Viewbank homestead was undertaken in April 1980 for the Archaeological and Anthropological Society of Victoria and focused on part of the tip. There is a very brief, one page excavation report that indicates that a trench of 3 m by 1 m and 50 cm deep was dug into the tip area. The tip was interpreted as dating to sometime in the second half of the 19th century. A large number of bottles and ceramics were uncovered (Willacy 1981), but have since been lost. The report also detailed that the homestead site had been vandalised and the tip had been turned over by bottle hunters prior to the work. Further work on the site was conducted by archaeologist Fiona Weaver (1991) who undertook a survey of archaeological sites along the Plenty River for the Melbourne Metropolitan Board of Works in 1990. This included the Viewbank homestead and gardens. Viewbank was recorded as being of high significance. Weaver (1991) also notes that: 'Substantial sub-surface remains are present, and considerable erosion is occurring to the foundations and terraces from the activity of stock'.

Heritage Victoria later carried out three seasons of archaeological excavations under the direction of Dr Leah McKenzie, and this excavation is the basis of the current research. The first of these was of three weeks duration in April 1996 and uncovered three corners of the homestead and a cellar (McKenzie 1996:10, 1997:7). Staircases leading to the main entrance of the homestead were also exposed. In September 1996, resistivity, magnetometer and ground-penetrating radar surveys were carried out (Heinson *et al.* 1996). The second excavation season took place in April 1997 for two weeks, and focused on the tip area in order to uncover the material culture of the inhabitants of Viewbank. A small amount of work was also done at the homestead to establish stratigraphy. The third season was conducted in January and February 1999, and continued the work on the homestead and the tip, as well as investigating potential outbuildings associated with the homestead.

Unfortunately some of the trench books have been lost in the years since excavation was completed. Trench records are missing for two trenches in the homestead area, and for the front stairs area. For the 1996 season there were reports written by the trench supervisors, but these were not compiled for the 1997 and 1999 seasons. McKenzie (1996) presented the findings of the 1996 season at an Australasian Society for Historical Archaeology conference later that year, and has written a draft report on the 1996 and 1997 seasons (McKenzie 1997). Heritage Victoria prepared trench plans for the homestead excavation in Area A and the University of Melbourne prepared a site plan.

Dig Methods

Excavation was conducted by manual digging with hand-picks, shovels, trowels and brushes. All material excavated from the tip was sieved using nested sieves of 4 mm and 2 mm mesh. Volunteers from universities and historical societies conducted the excavations under the direction of archaeologically qualified trench supervisors.

Excavation in the homestead area was done mostly in large 10 m by 10 m trenches with finer spatial control maintained by wall footings and room spaces. The remaining trenches, dug to explore outbuildings and the tip, were smaller. For the first two seasons excavation followed the locus/level system with baulks left between trenches to highlight stratigraphy, a method originally developed by Wheeler and expanded by Kenyon (Hester *et al.* 1997:74, 89). A locus number was given to horizontal areas of the deposit and a level number to the vertical location. Level numbers are the same for that depth across loci. Use of this system varied between the trench supervisors. In the final 1999 season, the context system was used. Deposits and building features were recorded as features with sequential numbers. For all seasons of excavation

4. The Archaeology of Viewbank Homestead

there were some cases where the information in the trench books lacked sufficient description for confident interpretation.

Excavated Areas

There were four areas of excavation: the homestead (Area A), external stairs leading to the homestead (Area B), the tip (Area C), and exploratory trenches for outbuildings in various locations (Area D) (**Figure 4.1**).

Area A comprised the Viewbank homestead building, which was set into a terrace at the top of the hill (**Figure 4.1** and **Figure 4.2**). Heritage Victoria prepared trench plans for the homestead and as part of the author's PhD research, contexts included in this analysis were mapped on the plans and stratigraphic matrices were prepared.

Excavations confirmed that there were at least three periods of construction for the homestead (Heritage Victoria 2005). The initial house constructed for Williamson around 1839 was built with hand-made bricks and was single storey (see **Figure 4.3**, red section). The first extension built for the Martin family was probably built by architect John Gill in the second half of the 1840s and was of a notably better quality than the first house (see **Figure 4.3**, blue sections). Rooms in this part of the homestead were decorated with cornices and wallpaper (McKenzie 1996:10). It appears that in the 1850s or 1860s a second extension was undertaken at the rear of the homestead (see **Figure 4.3**, green

Figure 4.2: Aerial view of the Heritage Victoria excavation of the homestead facing north (Source: Heritage Victoria).

section). **Figure 4.4** provides a plan showing key details uncovered by the excavation.

Area B constituted Viewbank's stately gardens (**Figure 4.1**), which included a series of terraces following the contours of the hill to the west of the homestead, steps leading to the homestead, and a flat terrace possibly used as an outbuilding or flower garden. The garden terraces were significant earthworks and can still be seen today by satellite (**Figure 4.5**). They indicate that significant effort had been made to lay out a stately garden. The steps leading up to the homestead were constructed from brick with stone cladding and were flanked by Italian cypresses (McKenzie 1997:9). The driveway, with its curved terracing marked by pines and oaks, is also part of Area B. Excavation of the steps was undertaken, but there is no record of this work in the trench books and therefore context information for this area is not known.

Area C was a tip located approximately 100 m behind the homestead to the east (**Figure 4.1**). The surface scatter of artefacts in tip area covered approximately 10 m by 10 m. Ground-penetrating radar work revealed that the tip had a maximum depth of 1.1 m (Heinson et al. 1996). Three 5 m by 2 m trenches were excavated running north/south through the tip and this constituted only part of the total tip. Cut marks into the clay were noted at the bottom of the trench. McKenzie (1997:12) suggests that the hole may have been dug for clay to make bricks for the homestead, and subsequently used for disposing of household rubbish. This pit would not have yielded sufficient clay to build the whole homestead, but possibly part of it. A total of 27,873 artefact fragments were recovered from the tip. The deposits in the tip were fairly homogeneous, and the tip appears to have been used over a short period of time in the 19th century, probably solely by the

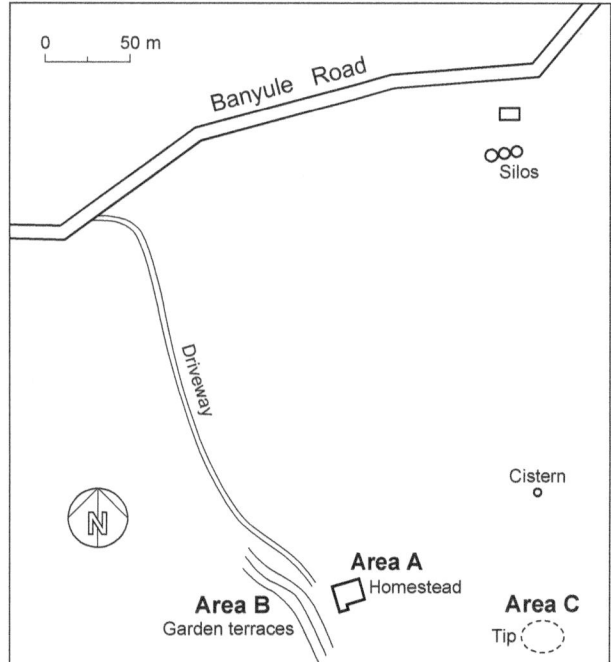

Figure 4.1: Plan of the Viewbank site showing excavated areas (Area D comprised of test trenches in various locations around the homestead) (Source: adapted from plan prepared for Heritage Victoria by the University of Melbourne).

4. The Archaeology of Viewbank Homestead

Figure 4.3: Homestead plan showing building phases (Source: adapted from plan prepared by Heritage Victoria).

Figure 4.4: Homestead plan showing excavation details (Source: adapted from trench plans prepared by Heritage Victoria).

4. The Archaeology of Viewbank Homestead

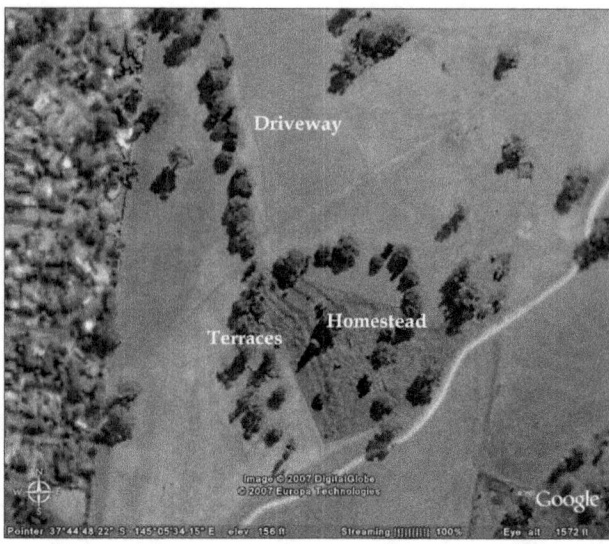

Figure 4.5: Satellite image of the Viewbank site showing garden terraces (Source: Google Earth, accessed 3 August 2007).

Martin family. This is discussed in more detail, using evidence from the assemblage, in Chapter 5.

Artefacts

Heritage Victoria's database recorded 3,754 catalogue numbers and approximately 53,800 artefact fragments for Viewbank homestead. During the excavation, artefacts were given catalogue numbers and were roughly grouped by material type. After the excavations, Heritage Victoria prepared a hand written catalogue of artefacts with the number which had been given to the artefact in the field, a brief description and the contextual location. Prior to the commencement of this current project the artefacts had been given new numbers and entered into Heritage Victoria's artefact database for curatorial purposes.

A small number of projects were conducted on the artefacts in the years following Heritage Victoria's excavation. The faunal assemblage was analysed by Howell-Meurs (2000), and Furlong (2002) examined the chemical contents of five small, clear bottles containing powders. Courtney (1998) examined the clay pipes in the assemblage and mentioned them in her Masters thesis, but no formal analysis was undertaken. Ellis (2001) catalogued and analysed approximately 80 artefacts relating to children from across the site. However, the assemblage retains much potential beyond these studies and artefacts from the tip in particular warranted the research presented here.

Additional artefact processing work was conducted on the ceramic assemblage by archaeologist Alasdair Brooks and a team of volunteers. The aim of this work was to sort the ceramics by ware and decoration and also involved labelling each individual fragment with the original number given to the artefact in the field along with the Heritage Victoria catalogue number.

The most comprehensive cataloguing and analysis of the assemblage was conducted for the author's PhD from 2005 to 2008, and this forms the basis of the present study. The Viewbank artefacts were stored at the Heritage Victoria laboratory in Melbourne at this time and all artefact work for the project was conducted there. For detailed information on methods see Hayes (2007, 2008). The remainder of this chapter discusses the artefact processing and cataloguing methods relevant to this study.

Artefact Processing

Due to the large size of the Viewbank assemblage, this study focuses on deposits that related specifically to the Martin family's occupation of the site from 1843 to 1874. There is comparatively little known about the previous and subsequent occupants of Viewbank homestead, and the majority of artefacts recovered from the site are associated with this period. Deposits were selected for analysis according to the following criteria, determined by the excavation records: they were stratified, relatively undisturbed by 20th-century impacts, and had a high potential to be related to the Martin period of occupation. The most significant deposits of interest to the current study are those from within the tip, and all contexts excavated by Heritage Victoria from within the tip are included in the analysis. Only three contexts from the homestead trenches are included here as they were the only deposits in this area that contained artefacts that could be associated with the Martins' occupation of the site. These were A-III-12, A-II-3 and A-II-3.2. A further 12 contexts from the homestead trenches where included in the initial PhD research (Hayes 2008:215–238), but are not included here as they added little to the overall interpretation of the site.

Extensive splitting, tagging, bagging and sorting of material in boxes was required at the commencement of this project. This was necessary because many of the artefacts were in bulk bags of mixed form and sometimes material. Bulk bags were sorted, and stratigraphic information was added to the labels using the original hard copy catalogue.

Artefact types related to the domestic occupation of the homestead were catalogued. Building materials and fittings were not catalogued, as the information in the Heritage Victoria database was sufficient to address the research questions for this artefact type. The faunal assemblage had already been analysed by Howell-Meurs (2000) and was not repeated for this project as reference to her work provided sufficient information.

Initially, artefacts were divided into broad fabric types: ceramic, glass, metal and organic. The ceramic artefacts were further divided by ware: bone china, coarse earthenware, porcelain, redware, stoneware, white ball clay, white granite and whiteware. Second, the ceramics were divided by decoration: transfer-printed, flown, gilded, painted, moulded, undecorated and other. The third stage in processing was to divide the ceramics by form.

Glass artefacts were sorted initially by form and then by glass colour. This was done as a second stage due to the difficulty in distinguishing variations in glass colour from the different parts of a single artefact. Colours included: aqua, black, blue, brown, cobalt blue, colourless, dark green, green, light green, purple, yellow and white. Metal artefacts were divided into aluminium, copper, gold, iron, lead, silver and composite. Organic artefacts were divided into bone, leather, textile and wood. Both were then divided by form.

Artefact Cataloguing

Cataloguing was conducted in a Microsoft® Access® database, custom designed for this project. Artefacts were catalogued in two phases: accession and type series. The advantage of this approach is that two separate (but related) catalogues were generated: one containing the formal attributes of the artefact and the other containing the interpretive aspects of each artefact type. This separation of identification and analysis allows for clarity on the inherent aspects of an artefact versus the interpretations the archaeologist has made of the artefact (Brooks 2005a:16–18). It also streamlines cataloguing as attributes common to a type only need to be recorded once (Crook et al. 2002:34).

Phase 1: The Accession Catalogue

The accession catalogue recorded the formal attributes of the artefact: object number, box number, form, material 1 and 2, quantity, minimum number of individuals (MNI), contextual information, dimensions, weight, percent complete, portion, conjoins and type series number. A team of volunteers recorded the artefacts on hard copy accession sheets, which were subsequently entered into the database by the author. This had the advantage of allowing for the records to be double-checked and standardised. A field for the integrity (high, medium or low) of the contextual information was included. This was to deal with doubt as to the provenance of some of the artefacts.

Phase 2: The Type Series Catalogue

Artefacts were grouped into types according to material, form, manufacturing technique, decoration and maker's mark, or as many of these attributes as could be identified. Types were not individual vessels or objects, but rather matching vessels or objects. Size was not considered in determining types unless this implied a different function. Due to the fragmentary nature of the collection some artefacts that were potentially related have been allocated to separate types, for example bottle finishes and bases. Details of each artefact type were recorded in the type series catalogue: type number, catalogue number of the most representative artefact, function, form, sub-form, material 1 and 2, description, dimensions, quantity, MNI, total weight, processing, decorative technique, decoration, manufacturer, retailer, place of manufacture and date.

Functional classification was included in the type series catalogue to facilitate analysis. Often artefact forms are comprised of a number of material types, therefore there is an advantage in considering an assemblage as a whole, organised by function (Miller et al. 1991). The functional categories are explicitly interpretive and treated with caution. It is acknowledged that the intended function of an object is not necessarily the actual function for which it was used, and that one object may have different functions over time (Brooks 2005a:18).

The function key words used here were adapted from those recommended in Heritage Victoria's (2004:30–35) guidelines. The Heritage Victoria key words are based on the American Getty Research Institute's Art and Architecture Thesaurus. The application of this system has been criticised because it is a museum-based system that does not consider accepted archaeological terminology (Brooks 2005b:11). However, the Viewbank assemblage is part of Heritage Victoria's collection and this system has been applied to other assemblages stored at Heritage Victoria. Maintaining some similarity to the system used by Heritage Victoria has value for comparing assemblages. The key words were adapted with archaeological systems consulted including Parks Canada (1992), Sprague (1981), Davies and Buckley (1987) and South (1977). Function key words were grouped under six broad activity categories (see Appendix 1).

Fragment counts, weights and minimum number of individual counts were all calculated in the type series catalogue. It is common for historical archaeologists to use at least one, and usually a combination, of these methods; therefore including all three facilitates comparison with other assemblages. MNI counts were calculated to be used for quantification. The calculation of MNI counts has become standard practice in historical archaeology (Miller 1986; Sussman 2000:96; Crook et al. 2002:30; Brooks 2005a:21–22; Lawrence 2006:380; Hayes 2011a:21). MNI counts were calculated for each type in the type series based on diagnostic features such as bases and finishes for bottles, and rim circumferences for ceramics. Where only the body fragments of an artefact were present the MNI was listed as one, regardless of weight. Throughout analysis MNI counts were recalculated, using the database where necessary to accommodate the problem of overestimating numbers. For example, the highest number of bottle bases or finishes was used for the MNI for a particular colour of glass.

The dating of artefacts in the type series was not carried out in order to date the site as historical records give dates for construction and occupation. Instead, dating was used to understand site formation processes and determine whether artefacts and contexts were associated with the Martin family's occupation of the site. For example, a bottle with a start date of 1920 cannot be associated with the 1843 to 1874 occupation by the Martin family. In addition, dates were important in considering the effects of time lag. Caution must be taken due to the effect of time lag, or the difference between the date of manufacture and the date of deposition. A plate manufactured in 1860 may not have been discarded until well after the Martins left the site in 1874. A variety of factors including historical events, site location, and differences in the period of time for which artefacts were used will significantly alter time lag (Adams 2003). Dates will also be used to consider consumption issues including purchasing patterns and fashion.

Start and end dates were entered in separate database fields and contained numbers only. This was to allow for searching the database for date ranges. Where makers' marks were present, these were given priority for dating. In other cases manufacture and decorative technique were helpful. Australian references were used in priority to overseas references when dating. In particular, this research has relied on Brooks' (2005a) *An Archaeological Guide to British Ceramics in Australia 1788–1901* for ceramics, and James Boow's (c.1991) *Early Australian Commercial Glass* for glass. Where references suggested dates during which an artefact was popular, this has been added to the reference field.

The Viewbank homestead excavation is among the most significant so far conducted in Victoria. With few excavations of middle-class homes, particularly in the urban or suburban context, it has great potential to contribute information on the material culture of the middle class. The methods developed for this project draw from previous archaeological work, but have been adapted to suit the aim of this study.

5
Artefact Analysis

The assemblage recovered from the site is a substantial and fascinating example of middle-class material culture from 19th-century Melbourne. The analysis focuses first on the artefacts recovered from the tip, and then artefacts from the three homestead contexts that contained accidentally lost artefacts that may relate to the Martin family. Depositional processes are presented along with a detailed quantification and description of the assemblage by functional category.

FORMATION OF THE TIP

Artefact dates for the tip support the hypothesis of the excavation director, Leah McKenzie (2005 pers. comm.), that the tip was associated with the Martin family, and almost certainly used solely by them. Appendix 2 shows artefact start and end dates grouped into the three phases of occupation for the site: pre-Martin (1843 and earlier), Martin (1843 to 1874), and post-Martin (1875 and later). Start and end dates were allocated to artefacts based on the maker's mark, material or manufacture process. The dates vary from a broad date range of manufacture to a tight period indicated by a maker's mark. Artefacts were allocated to the Martin phase if the date range for the artefact overlapped with the 1843 to 1874 time period. It is acknowledged that time lag would have greatly affected the presence of artefacts on the site. Artefacts that pre-date the arrival of the Martins at Viewbank in 1843 may in fact have been objects brought to the site by the family. Similarly, those tenants who rented the premises after the Martins' departure may have left at the site artefacts that have manufacture dates that fall within the Martin phase of occupation. The only certainty is that artefacts that have a start date post-1874 could not have belonged to the Martin family. Of the dateable artefacts, the significant majority (99.6 percent) recovered from the tip have date ranges that overlap with the Martins' occupation of the site. Only two fragments from one object pre-dated 1843. This was an overglaze transfer-printed vessel, possibly a child's mug. Three fragments representing two artefacts date to after the Martin family left Viewbank. A machine-made, crown seal bottle finish dating after 1920 was found in C-III-1 near the surface of the tip and two fragments of an internal thread jar dating from 1880 to 1920 were found in C-I-1.6 and C-III-2, which were deeper contexts. It is possible that these made their way into the tip during the later use of the site; for example, they may have been deposited by bottle hunters or other visitors to the site. The discovery of a 12 gauge shotgun shell suggests that shooting was taking place in the area in the 20th century.

The deposits in the tip were fairly homogeneous, with conjoining ceramics noted through all levels. Given the uniformity of the deposit it is possible that the tip represents a rapid deposition of household refuse as part of a major cleaning or site abandonment event (McCarthy and Ward 2000:113). It is possible, however, that the mixed deposits were the result of digging by bottle collectors. In addition, large numbers of complete vessels can be expected in 'clean-out' deposits (Crook and Murray 2004:51). About half of the ceramic tableware and teaware vessels found in the tip were part of matching sets, and although none were complete many were near complete. Parts of the Viewbank tip remain unexcavated; therefore, it is difficult to know if missing parts of near complete vessels remain. Also, the lack of complete items may be the result of the collecting practices of bottle hunters active in the area. The evidence for a 'clean-out' event at site abandonment is inconclusive; instead the tip may have been at least in part the result of a gradual accumulation of rubbish over a period of time.

The artefacts from the tip date from throughout the period that the Martins occupied the site, which may support the latter theory. Food scraps and disposable containers are likely to be the result of week-to-week refuse disposal (Crook and Murray 2004:51). The presence of a large number of condiment bottles, beverage bottles and food related faunal material in the Viewbank tip supports this pattern of disposal. The dates of both ceramic and glass bottles indicate that the goods were purchased over the entire period that the Martins lived at the site. This provides further evidence that the tip was used over time, however the effect of time lag on this is difficult to determine. It is likely that the Viewbank tip was used for week-to-week rubbish while the Martin family occupied the site and was also used in a site abandonment disposal event.

It is important to stress that the artefacts recovered from the tip do not represent the entirety of what the Martin family owned and used. Rather, the artefacts represent things that were broken, no longer needed or out of fashion, and subsequently discarded (Schiffer 1987:47–50). Generally, expensive goods that retain their value would not be discarded (Spencer-Wood 1987:14). Best sets, silverware, or valuable jewellery are unlikely to make it into the archaeological record: such items would have been kept or sold secondhand. Cutlery, metal tools and other degradable items, though discarded, may have degraded beyond the point of identification. Further, the tip was not completely excavated, and souveniring is known to have removed a number of artefacts from the site. Yet the artefacts do constitute a sample of what the Martin family used and discarded, with the assemblage representing at least some of the consumer choices of the family. Though what is absent from the assemblage can only be speculated upon, what is present can be analysed. In interpreting the assemblage, links are made between the artefacts, the reasons they were originally purchased and the ways they were used.

THE TIP ASSEMBLAGE

The assemblage recovered from the tip totalled 20,266 artefact fragments weighing 163.1 kg. For further information on artefact materials and forms see Hayes (2008). Activity and function groupings are summarised in Appendix 3 with 'Eating and Drinking' being the largest group. Note that all percentages given from here on are based on MNI counts.

Domestic

Artefacts in the 'Domestic' category are those related to life in and around the homestead. The majority of the 'Domestic' items were 'Furnishings' and 'Ornamentation', with a small number for 'Maintaining the Household' (**Table 5.1**).

Table 5.1: Summary of 'Domestic' artefacts.

Function	Form	Qty	Weight	MNI
Furnishings	cog	1	2.0	1
	knob	2	46.5	2
	lamp	2	46.1	2
	lamp chimney	175	370.8	7
	lock	5	137.1	1
Total		185	602.5	13
Maintaining the Household	bottle	50	775.7	1
	candle snuffer	2	53.6	1
Total		52	829.3	2
Ornamentation	figurine	11	102.1	1
	flower pot	23	184.4	4
	hinge	1	0.6	1
	tassel	4	1.4	1
	unidentified	2	14.4	1
	vase	16	197.1	2
Total		57	500.0	10
Total		**294**	**1,931.8**	**25**

Furnishings

A minimum number of 13 artefacts were allocated to the 'Furnishings' category, the majority of which were associated with kerosene lighting. Seven of the artefacts were colourless glass lamp chimneys. In addition, two copper alloy lamp pieces were recovered. The first was a copper alloy deflector from a vertical wick, kerosene lamp (TS 1107). It had an impressed maker's mark: 'REGISTERED/ TRADEMARK/ DIETZ/ PA...'. Robert Edwin Dietz and his brother Michael patented the first flat wick burner for use with kerosene in 1859 (Kirkman 2007). The second was the central piece from what appears to be the burner of a lamp which was decorated with moulded scrolls, although the type of lamp it was from was difficult to determine (TS 730).

Other 'Furnishing' items included two small furniture drawer or cupboard knobs, a padlock and a cog. One was whiteware (TS 963), 31 mm in diameter, with impressed lettering: 'N. / O' on the reverse and the other was copper alloy (TS 955), 19 mm in diameter, with two etched bands on the obverse. An iron alloy padlock (TS 1121) may have been used to secure a chest or gate in or around the homestead. A small copper alloy cog with iron alloy pins (TS 1027) was recovered, was identical to one found in the homestead contexts and was probably a component from a clock.

Maintaining the Household

The two artefacts belonged to the 'Maintaining the Household' category were a poison bottle and candlesnuffer. The poison bottle (TS 35) was cobalt blue with a vertical rib pattern and had incomplete embossed lettering on the body which probably read 'NOT TO BE TAKEN'. A copper alloy candlesnuffer (TS 1110) was also found (**Figure 5.1**). Candlesnuffers in the form of scissors, which trim the candlewick (or lamp wick) and collect the ashes in a box on the top blade, were common in the 18th and early 19th centuries (Woodhead *et al.* 1984:11).

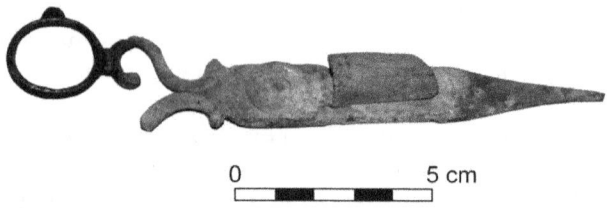

Figure 5.1: Candlesnuffer and wick trimmer (TS 1110).

Ornamentation

A minimum number of ten artefacts from the tip were attributed to the 'Ornamentation' category and included flower pots, vases, a figurine, a tassel, decorative glass and a hinge. Four unglazed terracotta flowerpots were recovered from the tip.

The pots may have been used for indoor or outdoor decoration, or possibly for growing herbs. Victorian potteries produced flowerpots, among other things, from the 1850s onwards (Ford 1995:176–293) and a variety of potted plants are identifiable in photographs of Australian interiors in the 19th century (Lawson 2004:90).

Other items would have served decorative purposes within the house. Two vases were recovered: one (TS 792) was white granite with moulded panels on the body and a scalloped rim, and the other (TS 502) was colourless glass, ovoid in section with honeycomb facets on the body and a starburst on the base. A female figurine or bust (TS 960) made from unglazed porcelain with a roughened surface to imitate marble was also a decorative item. The face had a slight smile and long hair.

Four items were components associated with decorative items. A textile and copper alloy tassel (TS 664) may have decorated a key to a wardrobe or box. The circular body of the tassel was fabric, while the threads hanging from the body were wrapped with copper alloy wire. Two purple glass disks (TS 292) with bevelled edges were recovered: one was oval and the other was a shaped rectangle. There was iron residue on the back, particularly around edges, which may indicate that the glass was mounted on a metal object such as a lamp or decorative box. Finally, a small hinge with a decorative scalloped edge (TS 1089) was possibly from a jewellery box.

Eating and Drinking

Artefacts in the 'Eating and Drinking' category were used in the preparation, serving and consuming of food and comprised a wide variety of forms (**Table 5.2**). 'Serving and Consuming Food' and 'Storing Food and Drink' were dominant in this group.

Preparing Food

A minimum of 14 artefacts from the tip were associated with 'Preparing Food'. Six of these were bowls: one (TS 835) was made from whiteware with moulded flutes on the interior and would have been used for moulding jelly or desserts, while the remainder were large utilitarian mixing bowls. Five of the mixing bowls were made from yellowware, and one from coarse earthenware. Most commonly used for utilitarian vessels, yellowware was made in Britain, America and Australia and is usually dated to post-1830 (Brooks 2005a:34). Two of the yellowware bowls had no decoration present, one (TS 906) had moulded floral decoration on the exterior and a white glazed interior, and another (TS 909) had industrial slip annular decoration in white and blue on the exterior. Annular decorated wares were in production from c1790 to the end of the 19th century (Sussman 1997). The coarse earthenware bowl (TS 869) was decorated with moulded bands at the rim.

Table 5.2: Summary of 'Eating and Drinking' artefacts.

Function	Form	Qty	Weight	MNI
Preparing Food	bowl	83	1,090.4	6
	hourglass	4	0.6	1
	milkpan	438	17,493.4	6
	unidentified	1	6.0	1
Total		526	18,590.4	14
Serving and Consuming Food	bowl	154	1,355.5	19
	corkscrew	15	20.5	1
	covered bowl	4	26.0	1
	cutlery	1	19.3	1
	dessert glass	1	82.2	1
	dish	35	299.6	7
	drainer	18	104.8	3
	egg cup	7	28.8	2
	fork	1	15.6	1
	jug	5	178.2	3
	knife	1	29.4	1
	ladle	4	89.7	1
	plate	1,178	14,092.4	71
	platter	300	8,539.1	14
	serving dish	145	2,393.6	12
	spoon	5	18.5	2
	stemware	148	1,789.1	25
	tablespoon	2	48.6	1
	tumbler	305	3,386.5	13
	tureen	145	2,499.9	7
	ui flat	77	586.5	17
	ui hollow	34	239.0	12
	unidentified	265	640.3	8
Total		2,850	36,483.1	223
Serving and Consuming Tea	jug	43	98.9	2
	mug	119	562.8	5
	saucer	574	3,419.2	41
	serving dish	4	8.6	1
	teacup	654	3,776.5	66
	teapot	3	66.7	1
	ui flat	121	214.9	4
	ui hollow	4	8.1	2
	unidentified	17	52.3	8
Total		1,539	8,208.0	130
Serving and Consuming	covered bowl	8	80.5	3
	jug	4	58.8	1
	mug	20	214.8	2
	ui flat	857	4,901.4	43
	ui hollow	332	1,358.6	54
	unidentified	1,058	2,182.6	20
Total		2,279	8,796.7	123
Storing Food and Drink	bottle	7,824	63,438.3	178
	bottle cap	7	7.5	3
	covered bowl	2	8.3	1
	crock pot	57	2,407.2	4
	jar	235	2,388.3	23
	stopper	15	507.5	13
	ui hollow	21	726.3	4
	unidentified	2	42.9	1
	wire	68	22.1	10
Total		8,231	69,548.4	237
Total		**15,425**	**141,626.6**	**727**

5. Artefact Analysis

In addition to the bowls, six milkpans were recovered from the tip, each with a flattened section of the rim for pouring and a flat base with no footring. A milkpan is a large vessel (more than 10 inches in diameter) shaped like an inverted, truncated cone. They were commonly used for cooling milk, cooking or as a washbasin (Beaudry *et al.* 2000:28). Five of the milkpans were made from redware with yellow slip-glazed interiors (TS 622 and TS 898). Brooks (2005a:42) suggests that in Australia slip-glazed coarseware vessels were probably locally made as they were becoming less popular in Britain. Vessels such as these were locally manufactured from the early days of the colony in New South Wales (Casey 1999:5), and in Victoria from the 1850s (Ford 1995:176–293). The final milkpan (TS 933) was made from undecorated whiteware and had a wide flat rim.

Two other artefacts were related to preparing food: a fine glass fragment (TS 269) which appears to be the central join of the two halves of an hourglass, possibly an egg timer, and a small copper alloy valve with a tap (TS 842) which was possibly part of a gas stove and had the lettering 'GALAN' on the tap. Gas stoves were invented early in the 19th century, but were not popular until the 1880s (Flanders 2003:70). Gas supply was not introduced to the Heidelberg area until 1889 (Garden 1972:168).

Serving and Consuming Food

A minimum number of 223 objects comprising 20 different forms related to 'Serving and Consuming Food'. Four ceramic ware types were identified in the tableware assemblage from the tip (**Table 5.3**). A significant majority was whiteware, which is not surprising as it was the dominant ware used after 1820 for almost all table and teawares (des Fontaines 1990:4; Brooks 1999:34). The next largest group was white granite. In British and Australian contexts white granite can be dated from approximately 1845 to 1890 (Brooks 2005a:73). Porcelain was also represented, the majority of which was English hard-paste porcelain produced from 1768 (Fisher 1966:229), but Chinese porcelain was also present. There was also a small amount of bone china, which was produced from 1794 (Miller 1991:11; Brooks 2005a:72). Plates and unidentified flat vessels were made from all four ware types. Smaller items, including an eggcup, were made from porcelain, while the white granite comprised larger vessels including platters and serving dishes. All of the tableware forms identified were represented in whiteware.

A wide range of artefact forms were identified within the ceramic tableware assemblage (**Figure 5.2**). Plates were the dominant form comprising 45.2 percent of the dining tableware in the tip assemblage. Staffordshire potteries used standard plate sizes: table plate (10-inch), supper plate (9-inch), twiffler (8-inch) and muffin (3 to 7-inch) (Miller 2000:96). Manufacturers did not strictly follow the sizes and often circumvented price fixing for vessel forms by producing plates between these sizes (Ewins 1997:131; Miller 2000:96). In this analysis, plates have been categorised in the closest inch measurement even if the size varied slightly from

Table 5.3: Ceramic tableware forms by ware type.

Ware	Form	MNI	%
Bone china	plate	8	
	platter	1	
	ui flat	2	
Total		11	7.0
Porcelain	bowl	3	
	egg cup	1	
	plate	6	
	spoon	1	
	ui flat	3	
Total		14	8.9
White granite	plate	9	
	platter	5	
	serving dish	2	
	ui flat	3	
Total		19	12.1
Whiteware	bowl	13	
	dish	1	
	drainer	3	
	egg cup	1	
	ladle	1	
	plate	48	
	platter	8	
	serving dish	10	
	spoon	1	
	tureen	7	
	ui flat	9	
	ui hollow	7	
	unidentified	4	
Total		113	72.0
Total		**157**	**100.0**

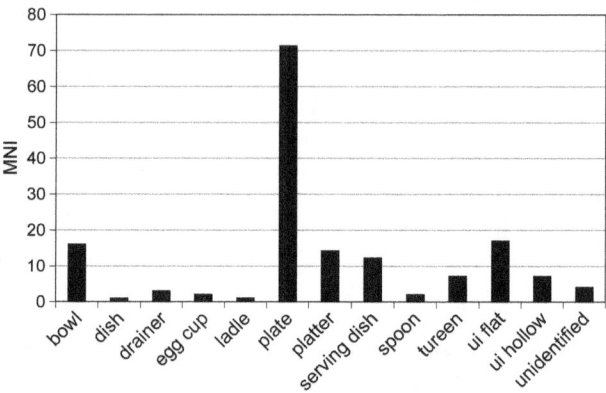

Figure 5.2: Ceramic tableware forms.

this diameter. Many of the plates, 33.8 percent, had insufficient rim fragments to determine the size. The 10-inch or table plate was the most common, closely followed by the 9-inch supper plate and 8-inch twiffler. A smaller number of soup plates and 7-inch muffin plates were represented. The larger plates would have been used for dining while the smaller plates may have been used as side or dessert plates or possibly as part of a tea service.

The next most prevalent vessel form was the bowl, while platters, serving dishes and tureens followed. Six of the tureens were soup tureens; however one (TS 754) was a smaller sauce tureen. A number of specific-use forms were also identified. These included drainers, spoons, eggcups, a dish and a ladle. Drainers had holes in the base and usually sat inside another vessel to serve boiled fish or meat, allowing the juices to drain (Coysh and Henrywood 1989:115). One of the spoons was a Chinese spoon (TS 584), while the other (TS 697) was the handle of a spoon or ladle probably for serving sauce or condiments. For the tip, 17.8 percent of the tableware was unidentified, unidentified flat and unidentified hollow, but could be related to serving and consuming food. This was based on the appearance of the vessel, or the object being part of a matching set of tableware.

A large number of decorative techniques and combinations of techniques were present within the tableware assemblage (**Table 5.4**). Only a small number of the vessels were undecorated; that is, they were complete enough to determine that there was no decoration. A slightly larger number were fragments with no decoration present and may have been decorated or undecorated.

Vessels decorated with a combination of multiple techniques were the most common decorative type. Notable among these were 16 vessels decorated with the 'Summer Flowers' pattern made by Samuel Alcock & Co., who operated in Staffordshire from 1830 to 1859 (Godden 1964:28). This was a flown black transfer-printed pattern with polychrome enamelled and gilded detail (**Figure 5.3**).

A further 11 vessels were both moulded and gilded, and had either banded or floral decoration. Moulded body and blue transfer-printed decoration were combined on eight vessels. These included three vessels decorated with a scalloped rim and the 'Asiatic Pheasants' pattern (TS 729, 746 and 753). 'Asiatic Pheasants' was one of the most commonly produced floral decorations in the 19th century (Samford 2000:69, 73). There was also a matching set of three Chinese pattern blue transfer-print plates with scalloped rims (TS 346 and 547). One of the plates had a back mark revealing that it was made by Masons, a Staffordshire pottery operating between 1820 and 1854 (Godden 1964:416–418; Coysh and Henrywood 1989:239–241). Two vessels had moulded rims combined with transfer prints in unique patterns.

Table 5.4: Decorative techniques on ceramic tableware.

Decorative Technique	MNI	%
Flow (transfer-printed black)	2	
Flow (transfer-printed blue)	20	
Total Flow	22	14.0
Gilded	15	
Total Gilded	15	9.6
Coloured glazed	1	
Total Glazed	1	0.6
Moulded	24	
Moulded (relief)	1	
Total Moulded	25	15.9
Flow (Transfer-printed blue)/enamelled	2	
Gilded/enamelled	5	
Moulded/enamelled/gilded	1	
Moulded/gilded	11	
Moulded/transfer-printed (blue)	8	
Relief/decal		
Transfer-printed (black)/enamelled	16	
Total Multiple techniques	43	27.4
Transfer-printed (blue)	19	
Transfer-printed (green)	2	
Transfer-printed (grey)	5	
Transfer-printed (purple)	1	
Total Transfer-printed	27	17.2
None present	16	
Total None present	16	10.2
Undecorated	7	
Total Undecorated	7	4.5
Unidentified	1	
Total Unidentified	1	0.6
Total	**157**	**100.0**

Figure 5.3: 'Summer Flowers' plate (TS 421).

5. Artefact Analysis

Other multiple decoration combinations included five vessels with a combination of gilt and enamel including two Chinese export porcelain bowls, two vessels with a flown transfer print and enamel detail, and a moulded, gilt and enamelled plate.

Following multiple techniques, transfer prints were the most common technique of decoration on the tableware. Of the transfer-printed ceramics recovered from the tip, 70.4 percent were blue transfers, 18.5 percent were grey, 7.4 percent were green, and one vessel was purple. While blue transfer prints date from around 1780, other colours were introduced around 1828 (Brooks 2005a:43). For the transfer-printed tableware, 28.6 percent had unidentified patterns (**Table 5.5**). The largest identified group was 'Willow' pattern, representing 25 percent of the ceramic tableware. This reflects the popularity of the Chinese inspired 'Willow' pattern, which was introduced by Josiah Spode around 1790 and subsequently produced by many different potters to this day (Samford 2000:63). The next most popular pattern at Viewbank was the 'Rhine' romantic scene. Other romantic scenes were also represented which depict landscapes usually with mountains, trees, waterfalls, castles, a body of water and small human figures. Romantic scenes were generated by the Romantic Movement in Europe and reflected the view that humans were subordinate to the forces of nature (Samford 2000:68–69). Samford (2000:69) suggests that they peaked in popularity in the United States between 1831 and 1851. Various floral decorations were present on three vessels which varied from each other. Floral decorations were popular throughout the 19th century (Samford 2000:73). One plate (TS 639) was decorated with a classical scene, including flowers and an urn with draped figures. The design also included a vignette on the rim with cartouches enclosing flowers. Classical designs inspired by archaeological excavations in Pompeii and Herculaneum were particularly popular from 1827 to 1847 (Samford 2000:67–68).

A minimum number of 24 vessels with moulded decoration alone were recovered from the tip. Of these, 75 percent were white granite, a ware type characterised by its moulded decoration. 'Berlin Swirl' and 'Girard Shape', which are common white

Table 5.5: Transfer-printed decoration types on ceramic tableware.

Decoration	MNI	%
Classical Scene	1	3.6
Floral	3	10.7
Rhine	6	21.4
Romantic Scene	3	10.7
Willow	7	25.0
Unidentified transfer print	8	28.6
Total	**28**	**100.0**

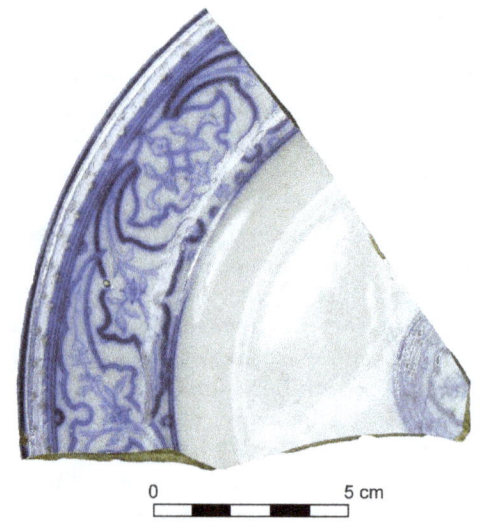

Figure 5.4: 'Bagdad' pattern plate (TS 798).

granite decorative styles, represent 29.2 percent each of the moulded vessels. Five 'Girard Shape' plates were made by John Ridgway Bates & Co. between 1856 and 1858 in Staffordshire (Godden 1964:535). Two of the 'Berlin Swirl' vessels were made by Mayer & Elliot, a Staffordshire pottery, and were impressed with the date 1860 (Godden 1964:422). Another two were made by Liddle, Elliot & Son who began operations under that name in 1862 (Godden 1964:235). White granite vessels with moulded bands on the rim, fluted face, or floral decoration were also represented. The moulded whiteware vessels had floral, banded, or fluted decoration.

Of the flown transfer-printed tableware recovered from the tip, 90 percent was blue and 10 percent black. A matching set of 'Queen's' pattern vessels represented 40 percent of the flown tableware and was made by Pinder, Bourne & Hope, of Staffordshire between 1851 to 1862 (Godden 1964:495). Further, six different floral patterns were identified representing 30 percent of the flown tableware. Three plates decorated with a flown floral and geometric pattern named 'Bagdad' [sic], also made by Pinder, Bourne & Hope were recovered (**Figure 5.4**). Also, two plates were decorated with a pattern of bluebells and leaves named 'Clematis', but the maker for this pattern could not be identified.

Other decorative techniques were represented in smaller numbers. Of the 15 gilded tableware vessels, all were banded. These vessels were plates, a drainer and unidentified forms in bone china and porcelain. A Chinese porcelain spoon (TS 584) recovered from the tip was decorated with a green 'Celadon' glaze. 'Celadon' is often found on overseas Chinese archaeological sites (Hellman and Yang 1997:156). This type of spoon was a fairly cheap Kitchen Ch'ing item, made for the Chinese market, both domestic and overseas (Muir 2003:43). Its presence at a middle-class site with no Chinese

5. Artefact Analysis

Table 5.6: Makers' marks on ceramic tableware.

Manufacturer	Makers' Mark	Place of Manufacture	MNI	Start Date	End Date
G.M. & C.J. Mason/ Charles James Mason	'MASONS' above a crown/ 'PATENT IR[ONSTONE/CHINA]'.	England - Staffordshire	1	1820	1854
John Ridgway Bates & Co.	Garter mark with crown and lettering 'J. RIDGWAY BATES & CO. CAULDON PLACE/ GIRARD SHAPE'.	England - Staffordshire	5	1856	1858
Liddle, Elliot & Son	'BERLIN IRONSTONE/ Honi Soit Qui Mal y Pense/ LIDDLE ELLIOT & SON' with the Royal Arms. Part of a diamond registration mark on one fragment and impressed 'NS'.	England - Staffordshire	2	1862	1871
Mayer & Elliot	'BERLIN IRONSTONE/ Honi Soit Qui Mal y Pense/ MAYER & ELLIOT' with the Royal Arms and diamond registration mark. Impressed: '10/60' indicating manufacture date.	England - Staffordshire	2	1860	1860
Pinder, Bourne & Hope	'QUEENS PATTERN [also BAGDAD PATTERN]/ P.B. & H.' in a circle with a wreath and crown.	England - Staffordshire	6	1851	1862
Samuel Alcock & Co.	'SUMMER FLOWERS/ S A & Co' inside a wreath of flowers.	England - Staffordshire	11	1830	1859
Thomas, Isaac & James Emberton	'RHINE' inside a cartouche with 'T.I. & J.E.' below.	England - Staffordshire	1	1869	1882
Unknown	None Present		129		
Total			**157**		

occupation is unusual: it may have been an exotic curiosity. Undecorated vessels represented 4.5 percent of the tableware assemblage. These included plates, a bowl and a serving dish. This is a fairly low percentage, indicating a preference for decorated vessels. However, it must be considered that vessel fragments with no decoration present may have in fact been undecorated.

Only 17.8 percent of the tableware had a maker's mark (**Table 5.6**). All of the identified manufacturers were Staffordshire potteries with date ranges from 1828 to 1882.

There were at least 11 matching sets (**Table 5.7**) and three complementary sets (**Table 5.8**) of tableware in the Viewbank assemblage. That is, 38.6 percent of the vessels were part of a matching set, with a further 23.4 percent part of a complementary set. For the purposes of this study matching sets were determined where two or more vessels of an identical pattern were identified. The largest set was 'Summer Flowers' with 16 vessels, followed by the 'Queen's' pattern set with ten vessels. The 'Berlin Swirl' and 'Girard Shape' white granite sets were also sizeable. A further 37 vessels may have been used as complementary vessels, giving the appearance of being sets without actually matching, including a large number of gilt banded vessels, 'Willow' vessels and undecorated vessels. Also, two banded white granite serving vessels were possibly used as complementary vessels to the white granite sets.

Sixty glass tableware items were recovered from the tip incorporating seven vessel forms (**Table 5.9**), predominantly drinking glasses. There were a minimum of 25 stemmed glasses with bowl shapes including round funnel, bucket and ovoid. At least nine of the glasses had a knop on the stem, including baluster, annular and bladed shapes. It was difficult to determine whether different decorative techniques were used on the base, stem and bowl, and how many of the glasses had some decoration present because the stemware was in highly fragmentary condition. Cut glass decoration was present on the bowls of most of the stemware. The patterns on the Viewbank stemware included cut panels, facets or flutes and alternating facets and flutes on the bodies and stems which were common decorations for 19th-century glassware (Jones 2000:174).

A minimum of 13 tumblers were recovered, far fewer than the stemmed glasses. As with the stemware, the majority of tumblers from the tip had cut decoration in panels, flutes, or alternating flutes, panels or mitres. Panels were the most common decorative motif on tumblers in the 19th century (Jones 2000:225) and were also the most common in the Viewbank tip assemblage. A minimum of two tumblers had similar decoration, but were moulded, not cut. From the 1790s, contact-moulded and pressed imitations of cut glass were a common and cheaper alternative (Jones 2000:174). Five of the tumbler bases featured a star or sunburst.

Thirteen glass vessels related to serving food were recovered, six of which were small serving dishes. Four of these (TS 161, 186, 299, and 383) were green and press-moulded with different

29

5. Artefact Analysis

Table 5.7: Matching sets of ceramic tableware.

Set Name	Type of Set	Type of Decoration	Form	MNI	Type Series Number
Bagdad	Consuming	Flow (transfer-printed blue)	9-inch plate	3	798
Clematis	Consuming	Flow (transfer-printed blue)	8-inch plate	2	783
Floral	Consuming	Flow (transfer-printed blue)	8-inch plate	2	769
Queen's	Serving and Consuming	Flow (transfer-printed blue)	side plate	1	761
			plate	3	756
			platter	2	766
			ladle	1	750
			serving dish	1	751
			tureen	1	754
			ui hollow	1	758
Berlin Swirl	Serving and Consuming	Moulded (white granite)	10-inch plate	2	935
			platter	2	1135
			platter	2	672
			ui flat	1	1136
Girard Shape	Serving and Consuming	Moulded (white granite)	plate	5	985
			serving dish	1	1006
			soup plate	1	992
Banded	Serving	Moulded (white granite)	serving dish	1	656
			platter	1	1001
Asiatic Pheasants	Serving and Consuming	Moulded/transfer-printed (blue)	10-inch plate	1	753
			platter	1	746
			bowl	1	729
Masons Chinese	Consuming	Moulded/transfer-printed (blue)	10-inch plate	2	346
			9-inch plate	1	547
Summer Flowers	Serving and Consuming	Transfer-printed (black)/enamelled	10-inch plate	4	421
			9-inch plate	1	369
			7-inch plate	3	422
			soup plate	2	424
			plate	1	293
			tureen	2	631
			meat warmer	1	632
			ui hollow	1	473
			ui hollow	1	630
Rhine	Serving and Consuming	Transfer-printed (grey)	10-inch plate	1	718
			8-inch plate	1	721
			soup plate	1	725
			platter	1	724
			ui hollow	1	727
			unidentified	1	735
Total				**61**	

detailed patterns on the exteriors. A yellow dish (TS 327) was also press-moulded with a diamond pattern. The sixth vessel was a colourless, cut glass dish (TS 524) with a scalloped rim, panelled body and a sunburst on the base. There were also three colourless, press-moulded, bowls (TS 534, 543 and 310), a small colourless glass jug (TS 491) with moulded diamonds on the body, two undecorated, colourless glass jug handles, a covered bowl (TS 523) with ovoid facets on the body, and a stemmed colourless dessert glass (TS 541) with a bladed knop. Further, there were eight unidentified glass vessels attributed to the 'Serving and Consuming Food' category most of which were body fragments that are likely to be from one of the artefacts discussed above.

Table 5.8: Complementary tableware vessels.

Set Name	Type of Set	Type of Decoration	Form	MNI	Type Series Number
Banded	Serving and Consuming	Gilded (whiteware)	drainer	1	612
			plate	1	839
			unidentified	1	592
		Gilded (bone china)	9-inch plate	2	879
			plate	2	580
			ui flat	2	888
		Gilded (porcelain)	10-inch plate	1	878
			9-inch plate	1	117
			8-inch plate	2	891
			ui flat	2	129
		Moulded/gilded (whiteware)	plate	2	886 and 948
			10-inch plate	3	825
			9-inch plate	1	840
			tureen (soup)	1	841
		Moulded/gilded (bone china)	plate	1	579
Willow	Serving and Consuming	Transfer-printed (blue)	9-inch plate	3	722
			8-inch plate	1	720
			platter	1	714
			serving dish	1	715
			ui flat	1	726
Undecorated	Serving and Consuming	(whiteware) (two variations)	plate	2	973
		(whiteware)	9-inch plate	1	931
		(whiteware)	bowl	1	916
		(whiteware)	serving dish	2	927
		(bone china)	8-inch plate	1	591
Total				37	

Table 5.9: Glass tableware forms by glass colour.

Colour	Form	MNI	%
Colourless	bowl	3	
	covered bowl	1	
	dessert glass	1	
	dish	1	
	jug	3	
	stemware	25	
	tumbler	13	
	ui hollow	5	
	unidentified	3	
Total		55	91.7
Green	dish	4	
Total		4	6.7
Yellow	dish	1	
Total		1	1.7
Total		60	100.0

Five cutlery items were recovered from the tip. A four-tang fork (TS 776) was copper alloy and appears to have been electroplated with silver, a technique introduced and patented by George Richards and Henry Elkington in 1840 (Chadwick 1958:633). A large tablespoon in the 'Fiddle' design (TS 669) was recovered and was copper alloy with silver plating. Impressed lettering on the reverse handle reads 'BP' with further illegible lettering. 'BP' stands for British Plate, a form of nickel silver (Woodhead 1991:33). The handle of a piece of nickel alloy cutlery (TS 1080) in the 'Fiddle' design had impressed lettering on the reverse of the handle, but this was illegible. Nickel silver was introduced in 1824, but became more popular after the introduction of electroplating (Chadwick 1958:608). A carbon steel knife with a scale tang (TS 1118) would have had a bone, horn or wood handle. The scale tang was generally used for kitchen cutlery (Moore 1995:28). The invention of the Bessemer converter in 1856 led to the mass production of carbon steel cutlery. For those who could afford it, blades were close-plated with silver to prevent the carbon steel from affecting the taste of food (Moore 1995:29). Type 1069, although recorded as unidentified, was probably the rectangular bone handle of a knife. In addition, a small flat non-ferrous metal handle (TS 1075) with moulded decoration may have been a mustard or condiment spoon.

5. Artefact Analysis

The final item in the 'Serving and Consuming Food' category was a corkscrew with a cylindrical wooden handle (TS 778). The handle was decorated with lathe-turned bands and had a screw-in cap at one end. This handle is typical of the Thomason corkscrew. This corkscrew was invented by Sir Edward Thomason, and patented in England in 1802. Thomason corkscrews often bore the British Royal Arms (Borrett 2007).

Serving and Consuming Tea

One hundred and thirty artefacts were related to 'Serving and Consuming Tea' and were exclusively ceramic teawares (**Table 5.10**). The majority of the ceramic teawares were teacups, representing 50.8 percent of the total. Saucers followed, representing 31.5 percent. Vessels identified as saucers were those that were flat to shallow, hollow and lacking a marly. The presence of a cup well was not considered to be necessary for diagnosis as a saucer. It is noted that saucers may have been used for a variety of functions (Brooks 2005a:51), but they were included with the teawares as this was considered to be their most likely function. A small number of mugs, a jug, a teapot and a serving dish were also identified.

Nine decorative techniques were identified for the ceramic teawares (**Table 5.11**). The predominant

Table 5.10: Ceramic teaware forms by ware type.

Ware	Form	MNI	%
Bone china	mug	1	
	saucer	14	
	teacup	41	
	unidentified	7	
Total		63	48.5
Porcelain	saucer	4	
	teacup	5	
	jug	1	
	ui flat	3	
	ui hollow	2	
Total		15	11.5
Redware	teapot	1	
Total		1	0.8
White granite	saucer	4	
	teacup	9	
Total		13	10.0
Whiteware	saucer	19	
	teacup	11	
	mug	4	
	jug	1	
	serving dish	1	
	ui flat	1	
	unidentified	1	
Total		38	29.2
Total		**130**	**100.0**

Table 5.11: Decorative techniques on ceramic teaware.

Decorative Technique	MNI	%
Enamelled	4	
Total Enamelled	4	3.1
Flow (transfer-printed black)	1	
Flow (transfer-printed blue)	8	
Flow (transfer-printed purple)	5	
Total Flow	14	10.8
Gilded	30	
Total Gilded	30	23.1
Glazed	1	
Total Glazed	1	0.8
Hand-painted	5	
Total Hand-painted	5	3.8
Moulded	17	
Moulded (relief)	5	
Total Moulded	22	16.9
Flow (transfer-printed blue)/enameled	3	
Gilded/enameled	6	
Moulded/gilded	16	
Total Multiple techniques	25	19.2
Sponged	1	
Total Sponged	1	0.8
Transfer-printed (blue)	4	
Transfer-printed (purple)	10	
Total Transfer-printed	14	10.8
None present	10	
Total None present	10	7.7
Undecorated	4	
Total Undecorated	4	3.1
Total	**130**	**100.0**

decorative technique was gilding: 56.7 percent of the gilded teawares were banded, 40 percent were decorated with the popular 'Tea leaf' design, and one vessel had a floral decoration. Vessels with moulded decoration were the next most dominant group in the teawares. The majority (40.9 percent) of the moulded teawares were white granite 'Berlin Swirl' teacups and saucers. There were also five bone china teacups with panelled bodies, a panelled porcelain saucer, a fluted bone china saucer, and bone china teacups and saucers with 'Sprigged' (applied blue) grape motifs which date to post-1820 (Brooks 2005a:43).

Multiple decorative techniques were used on 19.8 percent of the teawares and most of these had moulded bodies with gilt bands. Three saucers (TS 173 and TS 575) had panelled bodies and a gilt 'Tea leaf' in the centre. A cup (TS 620) and matching saucers (TS 641) with a flown floral transfer print in blue with enamelled detail were recovered, along with a moulded and enamelled banded hollow vessel and a gilded and enamelled banded teacup.

Fourteen teaware vessels from the tip had flown transfer prints. Of these, 11 teacups and saucers were decorated with a 'Marble' pattern in blue, purple or black. The 'Marble' pattern is a design which imitates the surface of marble. The remaining two vessels were saucers decorated with a floral pattern identified as 'Florentine' by the maker's mark. This appears to be a sheet pattern where the pattern covers the whole vessel without a different rim decoration. According to Samford (2000:73), sheet patterns were most commonly produced between 1826 and 1842.

Only 14 of the teaware vessels from the tip were transfer-printed alone. Of particular note was a matching set of purple vessels with a geometric ribbon pattern (TS 775, 741, 733, 743 and 793). Also, a matching teacup (TS 732) and saucer (TS 742) were decorated with a purple fern pattern, and a mug (TS 519) was decorated with a blue romantic scene, while the remainder had unidentified patterns.

A number of the teaware vessels were hand-painted. Three saucers and two teacups had hand-painted, banded decoration in red, blue or green. Hand-painted, stand-alone banded vessels have been dated to post-1860 (Majewski and O'Brien 1987:161). Two vessels (TS 540 and 244) were decorated with a red band on the rim and a red and green spot and leaf design on the body. Another, possibly matching, teacup (TS 572) and saucer (TS 257) set was decorated with a lustre enamel floral pattern. Lustre is a reflective metallic decoration which dates from approximately 1790 to 1850 (Brooks 2005a:40, 72). Also, a teacup handle (TS 188) appears to be decorated with spatter blue, but it was only a small fragment. A refined redware teapot lid (TS 905) with a 'Rockingham' type glaze was also found. Finally, four teaware vessels from the tip were undecorated, while a further ten vessels from the tip had no decoration present.

Only three vessels, or 2.5 percent of the teaware from the tip, had makers' marks. Two saucers (TS 987) were made between 1862 and 1871 by the Staffordshire pottery Liddle Elliot and Son and matches marks on the tableware. In addition, a saucer decorated with 'Marble' pattern (TS 790) was impressed with 'BB' on the base. This was probably the Minton mark meaning 'Best Body' used on mid-19th-century earthenwares (Godden 1964:441). Another two saucers (TS 661 and 999) had illegible impressed marks on their bases.

Of the teaware, 31.7 percent of the vessels were part of a matching set (**Table 5.12**), with a further 41.3 percent being part of a complementary set (**Table 5.13**). There were at least nine matching sets of teaware, comprising 40 vessels, recovered

Table 5.12: Matching sets of ceramic teaware in order of set size.

Set Name	Type of Set	Type of Decoration	Form	MNI	Type Series Number
Berlin Swirl	Consuming	Moulded	saucer	3	987 and 970
			teacup	6	969
Marble	Consuming	Flow (transfer-printed blue)	saucer	2	790
			teacup	1	822
Marble	Consuming	Flow (transfer-printed purple)	saucer	3	654
			teacup	2	658
Banded	Serving and Consuming	Gilded/Enamelled (blue)	teacup	1	141
			jug	1	215
			ui flat	3	190
			ui hollow	1	233
Geometric	Serving and Consuming	Transfer-printed (purple)	saucer	1	775
			jug	1	741
			serving dish	1	733
			unidentified	1	793
			ui flat	1	743
Sprigged	Consuming	Moulded (relief)	saucer	2	570
			teacup	2	569
Unidentified Floral	Consuming	Flow (transfer-printed blue)/enamelled	saucer	2	641
			teacup	1	620
Unidentified Transfer Print	Consuming	Transfer-printed (purple)	saucer	2	712
			teacup	1	711
Florentine	Consuming	Flow (transfer-printed blue)	saucer	2	820
Total				**40**	

5. Artefact Analysis

Table 5.13: Complementary teaware vessels.

Set Name	Type of Set	Type of Decoration	Form	MNI	Type Series Number
Banded	Consuming	Gilded (bone china) (three variations)	teacup	14	221
		Gilded (porcelain)	saucer	1	896
		Gilded (porcelain)	teacup	2	271 and 566
		Gilded/Moulded (bone china) (three variations)	saucer	5	245 and 599
		Gilded/Moulded (bone china) (two variations)	teacup	6	583
		Gilded/Moulded (porcelain)	saucer	1	578
Tea leaf	Consuming	Gilded (bone china)	saucer	1	575
		Gilded (bone china) (three variations)	teacup	6	560
		Gilded (bone china)	unidentified	6	586
		Gilded/Moulded (panelled)	saucer	2	173
Undecorated	Consuming	(white granite)	saucer	1	999
		(white granite)	teacup	3	1002
Marble	Consuming	Flow (transfer-printed blue)	saucer	1	661
			teacup	1	659
		Flow (transfer-printed black)	saucer	1	784
Sprigged	Consuming	Moulded (relief)/Panelled	teacup	1	234
Total				**52**	

from the tip. Matching sets were determined where two or more vessels of an identical pattern were identified. A cup and saucer were considered to be one vessel for this purpose, so either two cups or two saucers needed to be identified as matching. In most cases the sets were represented by small numbers. The largest set in the teaware assemblage was of white granite, 'Berlin Swirl'. This was also the only set to have tableware and teaware vessels. Only two of the teaware sets included vessels for serving tea in addition to those for consuming tea. A further 52 vessels may have formed part of complementary sets, giving the appearance of a set without actually matching. The 'Marble' pattern vessels listed as complementary vessels may have been used with the two matching sets of 'Marble' vessels. Similarly, the panelled, 'Sprigged' teacup may have been used with the 'Sprigged' set.

Serving and Consuming

A minimum number of 123 vessels were related to 'Serving and Consuming', but either the fragmentary nature or the form made it difficult to relate them to either food or tea service. All of the 'Serving and Consuming' artefacts were ceramic vessels. Whiteware was the most common ceramic ware type in the 'Serving and Consuming' category (**Table 5.14**). The vast majority of vessels (95.1 percent) in the 'Serving and Consuming' category were unidentified hollow, unidentified flat and unidentified. The identified vessel forms included two children's mugs that may have been used for tea or other beverages, three covered bowls that may have been for sugar or condiments, and a jug that may have been for serving milk with tea, or for gravy or sauces.

'Moralising china' is a term used by archaeologists for tableware, specifically for children, which have educational or moral phrases and decoration (Karskens 1999:141). Two such children's mugs

Table 5.14: 'Serving and Consuming' vessel forms by ware type.

Ware	Form	MNI	%
Bone china	mug	2	
	ui flat	3	
	ui hollow	8	
	unidentified	1	
Total		14	11.4
Buff-bodied earthenware	ui hollow	2	
Total		2	1.6
Porcelain	ui flat	4	
	ui hollow	5	
	unidentified	1	
Total		10	8.1
White granite	jug	1	
	ui flat	6	
	ui hollow	5	
	unidentified	5	
Total		17	13.8
Whiteware	covered bowl	3	
	ui flat	30	
	ui hollow	34	
	unidentified	13	
Total		80	65.0
Total		**123**	**100.0**

with moulded and gilded bands were found in the Viewbank tip. Gilt lettering on the body of one (TS 577) read: 'A Pres... for// A good...'. Mugs with the phrase 'A present for a good girl [boy]' were for rewarding good behaviour (Karskens 1999:141). The other (TS 588) had 'Robert' in gilt lettering and probably belonged to Dr and Mrs Martin's son, Robert (usually known as Willy) (**Figure 5.5**).

A high number of vessels in the 'Serving and Consuming' category had no decoration present (**Table 5.15**). This was in part because many of the vessels in this category were fragmentary body parts which are less likely to have decoration present. Of the 'Serving and Consuming' ceramics, 20.3 percent were transfer-printed in blue, purple, green, black or grey. Unidentified prints and floral prints were the most frequent, with geometric designs one fragment with 'Rhine' pattern also found. The next largest decorative group comprised

Table 5.15: Decorative techniques on 'Serving and Consuming' ceramics.

Decorative Technique	MNI	%
Enamelled	5	
Total Enamelled	5	4.1
Flow (transfer-printed black)	4	
Flow (transfer-printed blue)	9	
Total Flow	13	10.6
Gilded	6	
Total Gilded	6	4.9
Glazed	1	
Total Glazed	1	0.8
Hand-painted	2	
Total Hand-painted	2	1.6
Moulded	5	
Moulded (relief)	1	
Total Moulded	6	4.9
Gilded/enamelled	1	
Moulded/Flow (transfer-printed blue)	1	
Moulded/gilded	5	
Moulded/glazed	1	
Moulded/transfer-printed	1	
Transfer-printed (green)/enamelled	1	
Total Multiple techniques	10	8.1
Transfer-printed (black)	2	
Transfer-printed (blue)	13	
Transfer-printed (green)	3	
Transfer-printed (grey)	1	
Transfer-printed (purple)	6	
Total Transfer-printed	25	20.3
None present	55	
Total None present	55	44.7
Total	**123**	**100.0**

Figure 5.5: Robert's mug (TS 588).

Table 5.16: Makers' marks on 'Serving and Consuming' ceramics.

Manufacturer	Maker's Mark	Place of Manufacture	MNI	Start Date	End Date
Liddle, Elliot & Son	'BERLIN IRONSTONE/ Honi Soit Qui Mal y Pense/ LIDDLE ELLIOT & SON' with the Royal Arms.	England - Staffordshire	2	1862	1871
Pinder, Bourne & Co.	'HONI SOIT QUI MAL Y PENSE/ DIEU ET MON DROIT/ STONE CHINA/ PINDER BOURNE & CO/ BURSLEM' with the Royal Arms.	England - Staffordshire	1	1862	1882
Pinder, Bourne & Hope or Pinder, Bourne & Co.	'STO.../ PINDER.../ BUR...' and part of a diamond registration mark.	England - Staffordshire	1	1851	1882
Unidentified	'MADE IN ENGLAND'		1	1805	present
Unidentified	'IRON...'		1	1845	1890
None present	None present		121		
Total			**127**		

multiple decorative techniques most of which were moulded with a second decorative technique, most often banded. One hollow vessel (TS 911), probably a teapot, was decorated with a moulded pattern and a 'Rockingham' type glaze. 'Rockingham' glazed vessels were made both in Britain and Australia (Brooks 2005a:41). About half of the flown vessels had floral decoration, while the rest were unidentified. Also, five gilded banded vessels were recovered and one with a gilded geometric pattern. Another five vessels had moulded decoration: two were 'Berlin Swirl' and one was floral. A blue 'Sprigged' vessel was included in this category. Three vessels had enamelled floral decoration and two had enamelled banded decoration. There was also a hand-painted floral covered bowl and a hand-painted banded vessel. Finally, a buff-bodied earthenware vessel, possibly a teapot, was decorated with 'Rockingham' type glaze alone.

Makers' marks were present on 6 percent of the 'Serving and Consuming' ceramics in the tip (**Table 5.16**). As with the tableware and teaware, all of the identified makers' marks were from Staffordshire potteries. Three items had the British diamond registration mark. The marks indicate date ranges from 1845 to 1882. One partial maker's mark (TS 940) read 'MADE IN ENGLAND'. This term was usually found on 20th century English marks (Godden 1964:407).

Storing Food and Drink

The 'Storing Food and Drink' category includes bottles, jars and other vessels related to the storing of food and beverages. A minimum number of 237 artefacts were classified in this category, of which 177 were glass storage bottles. Alcohol bottles types have been included under 'Storing Food and Drink' as it cannot be assumed that the bottles always held alcohol or that alcohol was always used recreationally. There is much evidence to suggest that bottles were reused for other liquids; they may have been refilled domestically, returned by consumers to manufacturers for refilling, or redistributed by second hand bottle traders (Busch 1991:113–116; Carney 1998). For these reasons it was appropriate to group the bottles together under storage.

Alcohol bottle forms (either originally used for alcohol or commonly associated with alcohol) comprised 68.9 percent of the glass storage bottles (**Table 5.17**). The majority were dark green cylindrical bottles usually associated with beer and wine, but frequently used for other liquids. All of these cylindrical bottles were made by traditional processing methods, which here refers to both blown and moulded, non-machine, manufacture. Only one machine-made bottle was recovered from the tip: a brown beer bottle with a crown seal. A turn and paste moulded brown beer bottle (TS 17) was also recovered. Twelve wine bottles were all dark green and processed by traditional techniques.

Table 5.17: Storage bottle types.

Sub-form	MNI	%
Aerated water	5	2.8
Beer	2	1.1
Beer/wine	106	59.9
Case gin	1	0.6
Cognac	1	0.6
Condiment	5	2.8
Oil/vinegar	25	14.1
Whiskey	1	0.6
Wine	11	6.2
Unidentified	20	11.3
Total	**177**	**100.0**

String rim, ring seal, and champagne finishes were represented. A small number of spirits bottles were also recovered. A whiskey bottle (TS 111) was light green glass, traditionally manufactured with embossed lettering on the base 'SCOTCH/ WOTHE...POONS WHISKEY'. A company called Wotherspoon's of Glasgow produced jam, but it is not clear if this same company produced whiskey. Other spirits bottles included the square base of a dark green case bottle probably for gin (TS 460, and a glass seal from the shoulder of a dark green cognac bottle (TS 440). The seal read 'NEC PLURIBUS.../ COGNAC/ E FORESTIER & H SAB.../ BORDEAUX' with a logo of a sun with a face. No details could be found for this manufacturer.

Also present in the tip in significant numbers were oil/vinegar bottles. Twenty-three were light green glass with fluted decoration on the circular body (TS 106). Another oil/vinegar bottle (TS 138) had a decorative rib pattern, joining in arches on the body. A curved alternating rib and flute pattern decorated the lower body of another (TS 160). A partial maker's mark on the base indicated that the bottle was made in Liverpool. A minimum number of five condiment bottles were also recovered from the tip. Four of the bottles were light green glass pickle bottles with wide mouths. One (TS 130) had moulded 'two-tiered pickle' decoration (Roycroft and Roycroft 1979:13). A bottle with a club sauce finish (TS 150) was also recovered. Possibly part of the same item was the base of a Lea & Perrins sauce bottle (TS 204).

A small number of aerated water bottles were also recovered. All five were light green glass with blob top finishes (TS 201) and one had a wire closure in place. Twenty bottles were storage bottles of unknown use. They included light green, colourless, brown, green and dark green glass and were all made by traditional techniques.

Of the storage bottles from the tip, 22.6 percent had makers' marks present (Table **5.18**). Eighteen oil/vinegar bottles had an English diamond registration mark. These registration marks were

5. Artefact Analysis

Table 5.18: Summary of makers' marks on glass storage bottles.

Manufacturer	Retailer	Place of Manufacture	MNI	Start Date	End Date
A C B Co.	Lea & Perrins	England - Worcester	1	1838	
A.B. & Co.			1		
C W... Co			2		
Cooper & Wood		Scotland - Portobello	1	1859	1928
E Forestier & H Sab...		France - Bordeaux	1		
E.G.B.W. Co.			1		
S P & P			4		
Woolfall Man Co.		England - Manchester	1	1836	1861
Wotherspoons			1		
Diamond registration mark			1	1842	1883
Diamond registration mark			5	1842	1868
Diamond registration mark			7	1869	1883
Diamond registration mark - registered 1855			5	1855	1868
Unidentified		England - Liverpool	1		
Unidentified			8		
None present			137		
Total			**177**		

issued by the London Patent Office, usually to English manufacturers, but it must be noted that it was possible for foreign manufacturers to gain an English registration mark (Godden 1964:526). A further 13 bottles had manufacturers' marks on them, three of which could be positively identified and dated. The first was a bottle manufactured by A C B Co. for Lea & Perrins who produced their sauce in Worcester from 1838 (Godden Mackay Logan et al. 2004a:246). Another was manufactured by Cooper & Wood, a company which operated out of Portobello in Scotland from 1859 to 1928 (Boow c.1991:177). The Woolfall Co. which operated in Manchester from 1836 to 1861 was identified as the manufacturer of one bottle (Woolfall 2006). The remaining ten manufacturers' marks could not be positively associated with a company. In addition, nine bottles had illegible or incomplete marks, one of which revealed the place of manufacture of the bottle as Liverpool, England.

A number of bottle closures were also recovered from the tip. These included ten light green glass bottle stoppers of the type used for condiment or sauce bottles: four (TS 260) had circular finials and shanks and were undecorated, three more were similar in shape to these, but were decorated with moulded bands on the finial, two (TS 252) were embossed with 'LEA & PERRINS', and another (TS 236) was embossed with 'KILNER BROS DEWSBURY'. The glass works company, Kilner Brothers, operated in various locations in England during the second half of the 19th century and early 20th century (Aussie Bottle Digger 2007). Their factory in Dewsbury opened in the early 1870s. Two decanter stoppers were also recovered: one (TS 510) had a flower motif on the top and a panelled body while the other (TS 513) was a hollow ball stopper with a star top and fluted body. A number of metal bottle closures were also identified. Three of these were lead bottle caps: one (TS 958) was impressed with 'E &.../ TRADE/ EJB[D?]/ DUBLIN', another (TS 702) had an embossed 'Z' on the top, and a third (TS 27) was plain. Also, 68 fragments of copper alloy wire (TS 1072) represent an approximate minimum number of ten were identified as being wire bottle closures from champagne or other bottles.

A glass jar and two glass jar stoppers were found in the tip. The jar was a colourless glass storage jar (TS 394), with a flared finish and moulded band below the rim. The two glass jar stoppers were light green glass. One (TS 210) was embossed on the top with 'SYKES MACVAY & Co ALBION GLASSWORK [CAS]TLEFORD' and was manufactured in England after 1863 (Godden Mackay Logan et al. 2004a:243). The second was embossed with 'AIRE & CALDER BOTTLE CO. CASTLEFORD LONDON' on the top. Aire & Calder operated between 1836 and 1913 (Boow c.1991:175).

Further, 33 ceramic storage vessels were recovered from the tip, the majority of which (66.7 percent) were food and condiment jars. Eleven of these (TS 929) were straight-sided whiteware jam jars. Another (TS 872) was a polychrome underglaze transfer-printed mustard jar with a Venetian scene which dates to post-1840 (Brooks 2005a:43) (**Figure 5.6**). In addition, there were three 'Bristol' glazed buff-bodied stoneware jars and a large 'Bristol' glazed bottle with a flared rim (TS 80) which was probably a ginger beer or beverage bottle. This decorative technique was introduced by William Powell of Bristol in around 1835 (Brooks 2005a:28). Two clear glazed redware jar lids were also found

5. Artefact Analysis

Figure 5.6: Mustard jar (TS 872).

Table 5.19: Summary of 'Personal' artefacts.

Function	Form	Qty	Weight	MNI
Accessory	bead	14	11.39	14
	brooch	4	8.60	2
	earring	1	0.30	1
	fan	3	1.20	1
	jewellery	4	1.00	3
	lens	2	4.20	2
	necklace	1	1.00	1
Total		29	27.69	24
Clothing	buckle	1	2.40	1
	button	67	62.60	64
	fastening	19	19.70	10
	hook and eye	56	6.06	19
	safety pin	7	4.20	4
	shoe	120	105.00	4
	textile	2	10.54	1
Total		272	210.50	103
Grooming and Hygiene	bottle	69	1,593.70	7
	brush	5	38.20	3
	chamberpot	96	1,082.80	4
	comb	5	0.20	1
	ewer	137	1,221.60	3
	jar	8	78.40	4
	toothbrush	47	120.00	16
Total		367	4,134.90	38
Health Care	bottle	68	423.40	19
	stopper	4	52.80	4
Total		72	476.20	23
Total		**740**	**4,849.29**	**188**

in the tip, as well as a small buff-bodied stoneware jar lid with brown glaze. Four buff-bodied stoneware crock pots were also recovered. Crock pots are large open vessels with a shaped rim for holding a lid. One crock pot lid (TS 70) had a brown glazed exterior, another lid (TS 976) was salt glazed, the body of another (TS 774) had moulded bands as well as salt glaze, and the fourth (TS 755), which had both body and lid fragments, had dark brown glazed bands. Salt glaze, commonly used on stoneware storage vessels, was created by adding salt to the kiln while firing and results in a textured orange peel finish (Brooks 2005a:33). A brown glazed, buff stoneware covered bowl or jar (TS 1142), and five unidentified vessels were also recovered.

Interestingly, four Chinese food jars were found in the tip. One was a large coarse earthenware Chinese ginger jar (TS 617) with white slip glaze on the lid and body and was a cheap imitation of a porcelain ginger jar (Muir 2006 pers. comm.). A rim fragment from a similar jar (TS 991) was also recovered, as were two Chinese pickled vegetable or tofu jar lids (TS 1145). The jar lids were both rough stoneware, shaped like a saucer, commonly used for sealing wide mouthed jars containing pickled vegetables or tofu (Wegars 2007; Bowen 2012:104–105).

Personal

Within the 'Personal' category there were 740 artefact fragments representing a minimum number of 188 objects (**Table 5.19**). These include items for adornment and personal wellbeing. The 'Clothing' category was dominant in this group.

Accessory

Personal accessories were items worn by a person for adornment or convenience. Twenty-nine fragments representing 24 artefacts belong to the 'Accessory' category. Six of these were jewellery items including two brooches. One brooch (TS 997) was gold-plated copper alloy with a scroll design and an oval in the centre, which almost certainly held a gem, while the other (TS 1056) had a copper back and scalloped edge and may have been a cameo brooch. Part of a gold earring (TS 855), 10 mm in diameter, with a hinged post for a pierced ear and a fine gold chain necklace (TS 1057) were also found. Other unidentified jewellery items were also recovered including an item (TS 1031) which may have been a brooch and some small fragments in gold alloy and gold-plated copper alloy. The fact that all of the jewellery items were incomplete may indicate that they were discarded because they were broken.

In addition to these jewellery items, a total of 14 beads of eight different types were found throughout the tip. The majority of the beads (78.6 percent) were glass, in black (7), colourless (2), blue (1) and aqua (1). The two colourless beads were the only beads which were decorated. One was gilded (TS 844) while the other had etched lines (TS 1048). There were also two ceramic beads, one of which (TS 148) was made by the Prosser technique dating to post-1840 (Sprague 2002:111) and was decorated with bands. There was also one undecorated wooden bead (TS 1008). Beads varied in function, but were most commonly from necklaces, jewellery parts, rosaries, decorations on garments or lace-making bobbin spangles (Iacono 1999:42). It has been suggested that beads under 6 mm were commonly used on garments, while beads over 6 mm would be from necklace or jewellery parts (Karklins 1985:115). Twelve of the beads were between 6 and 12.6 mm and were therefore more likely to be from jewellery. The remaining two beads were tubular with diameters under 6 mm.

Two lenses (TS 183) were found in the tip: one was ovoid and convex for sight-correction, while the other was circular and did not appear to be sight-correcting. They represent two pairs of glasses, although no frame fragments were identified. They may have been from spectacles, monocles or lorgnettes. Spectacles were quite common in the 19th century, and fashionable men and women preferred folding lorgnettes. These were spectacles that folded into a short or long handle. Steel, gold and tortoiseshell frames were common. Circular and ovoid lenses were used in both spectacles and lorgnettes (Davidson and MacGregor 2002:21–24).

Fragments of a stick from a hand-held folding fan (TS 1143) were also found. The stick was bone and decorated with a carved floral motif (**Figure 5.7**). The fan was probably a brisé fan made entirely from sticks linked together at the top with a ribbon and held together at the base by a rivet. Folding fans were popular throughout the 19th century (Cheltenham Museum 2006). Type 1148 was recorded as unidentified, but may also have been part of a folding fan.

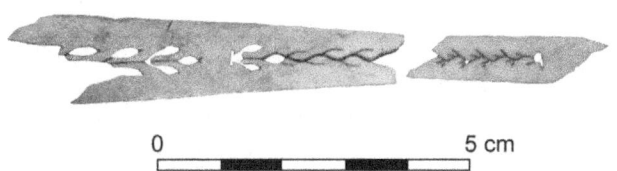

Figure 5.7: Fan fragments (TS 1143).

Clothing

A total of 272 artefact fragments representing 103 artefacts belonged to the 'Clothing' category. The majority of these were fastenings, 64 of which were buttons. The majority of the buttons were either metal or composite, but there were also shell, bone, ceramic and glass buttons. Many of the buttons, 51.6 percent, had some form of decoration (**Table 5.20**). The most common decoration type was a fabric covering. Fabric-covered buttons were factory manufactured from the early 19th century and by the 1850s inexpensive cloth covered buttons had overtaken metal buttons in popularity. Around the 1860s, it became popular to match the fabric

Table 5.20: Decoration on buttons.

Decorative Technique	Decoration	MNI	%
Applied	Floral	3	
	Prince of Wales feather	1	
Total		4	6.3
Cut	Facets	5	
Total		5	7.8
Embossed	Anchor	2	
	Bands	1	
	Rouletting	4	
	Stippling	1	
Total		8	12.5
Embossed/Japanned	Rouletting	2	
	Unidentified	1	
Total		3	4.7
Fabric covered	Fabric	9	
Total		9	14.1
Japanned	Black	1	
Total		1	1.6
Lathe-turned	Bands	1	
Total		1	1.6
Moulded	Circles	1	
	Floral	1	
Total		2	3.1
None present	None present	5	
Total		5	7.8
Undecorated	Undecorated	26	
Total		26	40.6
Total		**64**	**100.0**

on the button to that of the garment, and tailors and dressmakers purchased button moulds for this purpose (Albert and Kent 1971:46–48).

Many of the metal buttons were embossed with rouletting, stippling or bands. An embossed anchor decorated the obverse of two buttons (TS 230 and TS 1018), and another featured an applied Prince of Wales feather (TS 1023). Embossing was combined with japan decoration on three buttons and another was japanned alone. Japan decoration is a highly glossy black enamel finish popular from 1838 to 1900 (Cameron 1985:23–24). Three matching copper and iron alloy buttons (TS 1009) had an applied glass 'gem' in the centre surrounded by a copper alloy flower. These were decorative, fancy buttons 14 mm in diameter and may have been decorative buttons from women's clothing.

Five of the glass buttons (including those with metal attachments) were black and there was one each in white, yellow and dark blue. Four of the black buttons (TS 975) matched. Black buttons often adorned mourning dress and were also particularly popular in the period following Prince Albert's death in 1861 when Queen Victoria was

5. Artefact Analysis

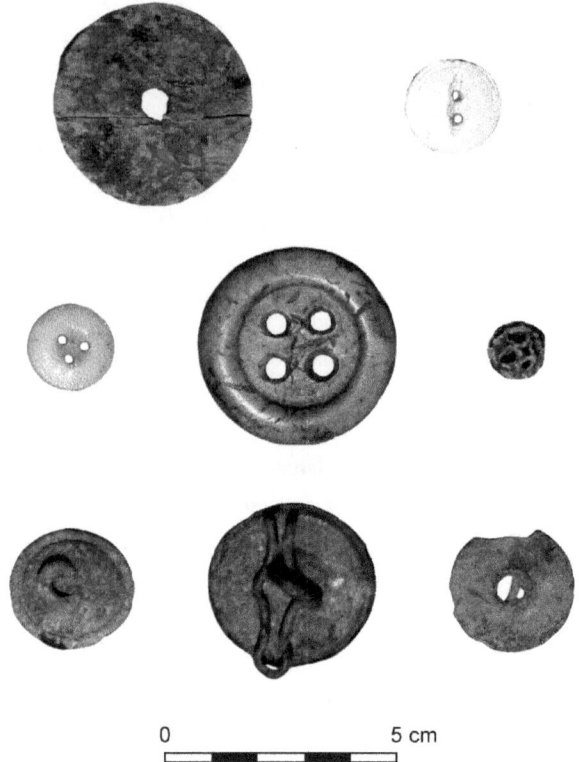

Figure 5.8: Button attachment types. From top left: one, two, three and four-hole sew-through, birdcage, hoop-shank, pin-shank and post.

in mourning (Lindbergh 1999:54). The dark blue button (TS 1024) had moulded circle indentations on the obverse and the yellow button (TS 296) had a moulded floral design. One shell button (TS 1040) was decorated with two lathe turned bands around the rim.

Eight different attachment types were identified on the Viewbank buttons (**Figure 5.8**). The most common was the four-hole sew-through type, but one, two and three-hole sew-through, as well as post sew-through types were also identified. The three bone buttons with one hole may have had a metal pin inserted through the body and twisted at the back to form a loop for sewing on to clothing (Albert and Kent 1971:25). Also common was the hoop-shank attachment, and one metal button (TS 1023) was pin-shanked. There were also three split pins, which may have belonged to other pin-shanked buttons. Four matching tiny buttons (TS 1017) had a birdcage attachment with four holes. Sew-through types were more utilitarian and cheaper than the shanked types which could be removed before washing to preserve them (Godden Mackay Logan et al. 2004b:320).

Four of the four-hole sew-through copper alloy buttons had embossed lettering; however this was illegible on two of the examples. One (TS 1029) read 'MOSES LEVY & CO. *LONDON*', but no information could be found for this maker. Another (TS 1019) read '... double ring ...' which was probably an advertisement for the quality of the button.

It is possible to use size to suggest the use of a button. Small buttons (8–15 mm) were mostly commonly used for underclothing, shirts and waistcoats, while medium buttons (16–21 mm) were used to fasten coats, jackets, pyjamas and trousers (Birmingham 1992:105). Tiny buttons (less than 8 mm) in common forms were commonly used for children's clothes, while tiny fancy buttons were more likely to be from women's garments (Lindbergh 1999:53–54; Sprague 2002:124). Of the Viewbank buttons, 64.1 percent were small, 20.3 percent medium, 10.9 percent tiny and 4.7 percent over 21 mm.

Hook and eye fastenings (TS 687) made up 16.8 percent of the 'Clothing' related artefacts and included 58 copper alloy fragments representing 19 hook and eye sets. Hook and eye fastenings were popular throughout the 19th century and continue to be used today. They were most commonly used on women's close fitting outer garments and were essential to the correct fit of bodices (Kiplinger 2004:7–8). They were not used on undergarments, which were fastened with tapes, ties or buttons (Cunnington and Cunnington 1951:18–19). Hook and eye fastenings could be purchased in large numbers relatively cheaply (Griggs 2001:81).

Three safety pins (TS 838) were recovered from the tip, each shaped from one piece of copper alloy wire. It is likely that the safety pins were used to fasten clothing or to assist with sewing. Safety pins with a cap head were first made in 1857 (Noel Hume 1969:255). It is unclear whether this open version was an earlier type or simply a more basic alternative. A fifth object (TS 1053) was in the same form as these safety pins, but had a curved copper alloy attachment. This attachment may have held a decorative element or functioned as some sort of attachment for a cloak or other item of clothing.

Further, ten fastenings associated with clothing, but of indeterminate form were recovered. Four of these were possibly men's clothing fastenings, all of which featured a circular copper alloy disk with oval feet attached on one side. One (TS 113) fastener had one foot, while three had two feet (TS 1007) (**Figure 5.9**). These feet were fixed and were not hinged like with other men's clothing fastenings

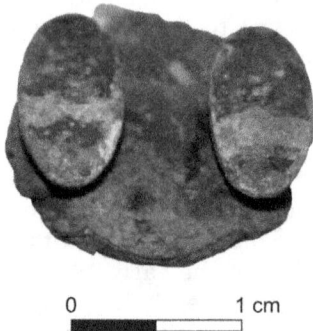

Figure 5.9: Double oval shank clothing fastening (TS 1007).

(see Eckstein and Firkins 2000). Three fastenings (TS 801 and TS 849) were possibly components from suspenders. Suspenders, which attached to the bottom of the corset as a fastener for stockings, only took the place of elastic garters in 1878 (Cunnington and Cunnington 1951:180). Another fastening (TS 623) had two slots for fabric to thread through and hold in place, while a similar item (TS 1076) was an ovoid disk with a rectangular slot in the centre. The complete form of these two artefacts is unknown, but they were possibly fastenings for undergarments. Finally, there was a square black glass cuff link or possibly button (TS 1073) measuring 20 mm by 20 mm. It had a flat obverse with cut facets on the edges. The copper alloy attachment on the reverse had been heat affected and its form was unidentifiable. Cuff links were first noted in 1824 (Cunnington and Cunnington 1951:19).

One hundred and twenty fragments representing a minimum number of four shoes or boots were recovered. Limited analysis was possible due to the fragmentary nature of the shoes. Four different sized shoelace eyelets were identified as well as one shoe lace hook. Both circular and square shoe nails were present, all of which were copper alloy. Four tightly curved sole fragments were found and appear to be from shoes with pointed toes. Gently pointed toes became particularly fashionable for men's shoes in the 1840s (Veres 2005:91). One stacked heel was recovered and was probably from a man's boot (Godden Mackay Logan *et al.* 2004b:330). A 'D' shaped iron alloy heel protector was also recovered.

Only two other artefacts were associated with clothing: a buckle and textile. The buckle was a small copper alloy slide type with two slots and no pins (TS 706) and was probably not from a belt, but rather fastened a cloth strap, possibly as part of underwear. The textile was recovered in small fragments (TS 673) and in a poor state of preservation so that the type of fabric and pattern were indiscernible.

Grooming and Hygiene

Objects related to 'Grooming and Hygiene' included those used to maintain everyday personal cleanliness and appearance. At the Viewbank site, there were 367 fragments representing a minimum of 38 objects attributed to this category, many of which were toothbrushes.

Sixteen toothbrushes were recovered from the tip, all made from bone. Ten of the unmarked toothbrushes had bristles attached by trepanning wire drawing, where the wires run through bores inside the brush head (Shackel 1993:46; Mattick 2010:12–13). A further three toothbrush heads had bristles attached by a process of wire drawing with cut grooves on the back of the brush head to accommodate the wires (Shackel 1993:45; Mattick 2010:11–12). Three of the toothbrush handles were carved with a maker's mark. One handle (TS 1041) read '4 G GURLING & CO LONDO...'. Another (TS 1147) read 'GEO...LEWIS CHEMIST// PEARL CEMENTS/ ...ENT/ LONDON' and had bristles attached by wire drawing with cut grooves (**Figure 5.10**). A third (TS 1067) read '...SFORD LONDON'. Although toothbrushes were locally available (Godden Mackay Logan *et al.* 2004b:337), all the marked examples in the Viewbank assemblage were imported from England. The large number of toothbrushes, given the relatively few occupants of the site, may represent the importance placed on oral hygiene.

Figure 5.10: Toothbrush (TS 1147).

A number of ceramic toiletware items were recovered from the tip. These included four whiteware chamberpots with flown transfer prints. Two were decorated with 'Marble' pattern: one blue (TS 653) and one black (TS 806). The black one had 'COPELAND' impressed on the base and was manufactured by W.T. Copeland and Sons between 1847 and 1867 (Godden 1964:171). Another (TS 800) had a floral pattern identified by a maker's mark as 'Royal Rose'. The initials 'J.T.' were printed below the pattern name, but the manufacturer could not be identified. The fourth was decorated with an unidentified blue pattern (TS 768). In addition, were three ewers (TS 796) all decorated with a flown black 'Marble' pattern. Two were matching, while the third varied slightly. A ewer is a large jug used to pour water into a matching basin for washing (Brooks 2005a:50).

Other artefacts were toiletry items. These included two perfume bottles (TS 93) manufactured by John Gosnell & Co. who were perfume and soap makers in London from 1834 and advertised themselves as the perfumer to the royal family (Gosnell 2006). A third colourless glass bottle (TS 313) with a flanged finish and decorative moulded neck, was also probably a perfume bottle. A colourless glass bottle (TS 376) was embossed with 'ROWLAND'S/ MACASSAR/ OIL/ THE HA.../ ...SAR AND GENUINE... CARDEN'. In the early 1800s a Londoner by the name of Rowland invented Macassar Oil and started producing it commercially (Merriam-Webster 2007). This oil was a coconut or palm oil used by men, and sometimes women and children, as a hair dressing.

Four ointment jars were included the 'Grooming and Hygiene' category. The most notable was a whiteware jar lid (TS 953) decorated with a polychrome transfer print depicting Queen Victoria in profile (**Figure 5.11**). Lettering on the print reads: '...RRY TOOTH PASTE/ ...EN/ ...FYING AND PRESERVING THE TEETH & GUMS/

5. Artefact Analysis

Figure 5.11: Toothpaste jar (TS 953).

...NDON'. Complete examples of similar toothpaste jars made by John Gosnell & Co. have been found at the Government House stables in Sydney (on exhibition at the Conservatorium of Music) and at the Dromedary convict hulk site in Bermuda (on exhibition at the Hyde Park Barracks, Sydney). From these examples, it can be surmised that the jar originally read 'Cherry Toothpaste/ Patronized by the Queen'. From the beginning of the reign of Queen Victoria in 1837, the popularity of the royal family was utilised by British manufacturers for advertising products (Pynn 2007). Common domestic products such as cloth, soap, cleanser and chocolate were sold using the Queen's image (Richards 1990:169). Cherry (a red coloured paste) and areca nut (the same formula as cherry with the addition of areca nut flavouring) were the most popular types of toothpaste (Pynn 2007). Also recovered was an undecorated whiteware ointment jar (TS 866), an undecorated whiteware lid (TS 671), and a cobalt blue glass jar lid (TS 48).

Three blacking bottles with wide necks were made from buff or grey stoneware and were salt glazed. Blacking bottles were used for leather polish, shoe polish or stove blacking (Godden Mackay Logan et al. 2004a:232). They were included in the 'Grooming and Hygiene' category as leather or shoe polish seems the most likely use.

The handle of a hand or cloth brush (TS 1065) was found in the tip. The brush had a rectangular wood backing with copper alloy nails holding a copper plate (no longer present, but green staining remains) in place. Also recovered from the tip were two brush handles (TS 1038 and 1146); however their incomplete state makes it difficult to determine whether they were hair or tooth brushes. One (TS 1038) had carved lettering '...XTRA F...' on the handle. Teeth from a vulcanite comb (TS 1061) were also recovered. A similar comb was excavated from Casselden Place in inner-city Melbourne and examples were also recovered at The Rocks site in Sydney. Vulcanite combs were mass-produced, inexpensive and readily available from the 1850s (Iacono 1999:80; Godden Mackay Logan et al. 2004b:337).

Health Care

A minimum number of 23 objects from the tip were related to 'Health Care'. All were medicine storage containers based on their shape or type of finish. Nineteen were glass bottles and none bore makers' marks or product names. The majority were colourless glass, with aqua, cobalt blue and light green also represented, and were mostly made by traditional methods. Two cobalt blue bottles were most likely used for castor oil. It is difficult to determine whether the bottles were for prescription medicines or patent medicines based on their shape alone. The remaining four 'Health Care' artefacts were four colourless glass bottle stoppers related to the medicine bottles. These were disc stoppers (TS 344 and TS 345) and flat oblong head stoppers (TS 246 and TS 343) which were commonly used for druggists' bottles (Jones and Sullivan 1989:153–156).

Recreational

A minimum of 29 objects were identified within the 'Recreational' category (**Table 5.21**). 'Children's Play' was the dominant group in this category, with smaller numbers of artefacts in the 'Competitive Activities' and 'Non-competitive Activities' categories.

Children's Play

The artefacts in the 'Children's Play' category were those that were most likely to be used by children as toys and included a minimum of 18 individual artefacts. Five of these were vessels from a matching doll's tea set decorated with press-moulded flutes (**Figure 5.12**). Toy tea sets of this kind were produced in Europe, China and Japan from c1800 to the early 20th century (Ellis 2001:178). In addition,

Table 5.21: Summary of 'Recreational' artefacts.

Function	Form	Qty	Weight	MNI
Children's Play	cartridge	5	1.8	5
	crayon	1	3.2	1
	doll	9	59.9	4
	marble	2	15.5	2
	toy saucer	2	18.7	2
	toy sugar bowl	1	1.2	1
	toy teacup	7	30.7	2
	toy teapot	2	18.5	1
Total		29	149.5	18
Competitive Activities	die	1	9.0	1
	domino	7	26.0	5
	fish figurine	1	0.6	1
Total		9	35.6	7
Non-competitive Activities	pipe	12	29.8	4
Total			12	29.8	4
Total		50	214.9	29

Figure 5.12: Moulded whiteware toy tea set (clockwise from top left: teacup, teapot, covered bowl and saucer).

a small teacup base (TS 594) with no decoration present was recovered. This teacup was probably from a child-sized toy tea set, rather than a doll-sized set.

A minimum number of four dolls were represented by limbs, feet and torsos (**Figure 5.13**). All of the doll parts were from head-and-shoulder dolls where the body parts were cast in a mould and attached to a stuffed body (White 1966:23). The dolls in the Viewbank collection were made from two types of porcelain: chinas (glazed porcelain) and parians (unglazed and untinted). Chinas were produced from around 1840 to the early 20th century, but popularity waned after the 1880s (Ellis 2001:165). Parians were made from 1850 to the 1880s and were more expensive than the chinas (Ellis 2001:166). There were five china fragments, representing a minimum of one doll, and four parian fragments representing a minimum of three dolls. One china doll leg (TS 959), with a groove for attachment to a

cloth body, had a painted black-heeled boot, with a yellow sole and a rounded toe. Two china boots (TS 964) from one doll were much smaller. Heeled boots on dolls date to after 1860 (Pritchett and Pastron 1983:332).

Two German swirl glass marbles (TS 550) with a multi-coloured swirl in the centre were recovered from the tip. These marbles were hand-made and have two irregular spots at opposite ends from the manufacturing process. They were manufactured primarily in Germany, but also in Britain and the United States (Ellis 2001:174). Manufacture in Germany began in 1846 and continued until after World War I, while in the United States, manufacture took place from 1880 to 1902. It is therefore likely that the marbles found in the Viewbank tip were from Germany. Ellis (2001:170, 174) has suggested that German swirl marbles were of a relatively higher value than other marbles.

Five small cartridge cases (TS 1081) were recovered and appear to be from a cap gun. Cap guns were introduced after 1865 when the American Civil War ended. Gun manufacturers were no longer in demand and therefore needed a new product to market and sell (Skooldays 2008). The only other possible toy recovered was an orange/red crayon (TS 1100) Lithographic and grease crayons became available in the late eighteenth century. Wax crayons, named crayolas, were introduced by Binney and Smith in 1903 (Ellis and Yeh 1997).

Competitive Activities

The artefacts in this category were all for playing board games and may have been used by children and adults. There were seven pieces recovered from the tip: five dominoes, a die and a fish-shaped gaming counter. The five dominoes (TS 279) recovered were a matching set in a European style (**Figure 5.14**). The dominoes featured a bone face with engraved circles for the numbers on each half. The bone face was pinned with copper alloy nails to a black wood backing. A stoneware die (TS 965) was also found and had a slightly irregular shape with a clear glaze on all but one side, probably where it rested when fired (**Figure 5.15**). Black, hand-painted dots represent the numbers. The

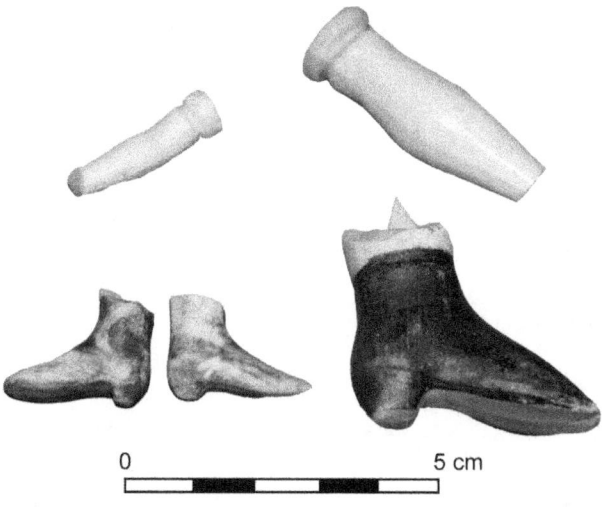

Figure 5.13: Doll parts.

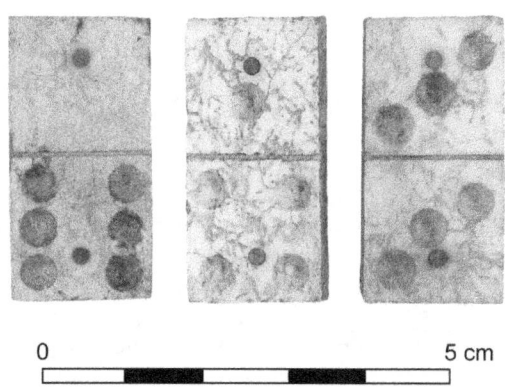

Figure 5.14: Dominoes (TS 279).

5. Artefact Analysis

Figure 5.15: Die (TS 965).

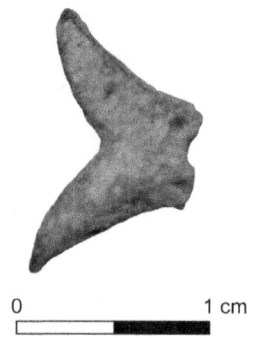

Figure 5.16: Fish figurine (TS 779).

only other artefact in this category was the tail of a broken copper alloy fish figurine (TS 779, **Figure 5.16**). Although it is possible that this was part of an ornament of some kind, it seems more likely that this was a gaming counter, similar to those made from bone in the 19th century. Bone fish counters were used as counters for games from around 1840 or earlier (Bell 2000:14).

Non-competitive Activities

The only artefacts belonging to the 'Non-competitive Activities' category were clay tobacco pipes. Although sewing equipment could be related to recreational activity it has been discussed under 'Tools and Equipment'. A minimum number of four clay pipes were recovered from the tip. All of the pipes were made from white ball clay. One of the pipe stems (TS 860) from the tip had 'T. DOUGLAS...' on one side and '...NCH BILLIARD' on the other. No information about this manufacturer was found. The length of the pipe stem was often given in inches on a pipe and this would have been present on the missing piece of stem before '...nch'. Billiard was the type of bowl shape (Davey 1987:148–153). Another pipe from the tip (TS 949) had a partial mark 'C...' with a branch of three-leaf clovers (shamrocks). The 'C...' may have read cork, again a type of bowl shape. Clovers or shamrocks were motifs used to appeal to the Irish market (Davey 1987:90). Another (TS 951) was marked with 'Yac...' on one side and '...tic' on the other with 'sideways trident' marks. This was a Baltic Yachter pipe, one of the earliest pipes to bear both the pipe name and manufacturer name on either side of the stem.

Yachting originated in Ireland and the pipe may be part of a series depicting Celtic activities (Courtney 1998:103). The Baltic Yachter appeared in the Irish Price List of Duncan McDougall in 1875, but was probably made by many manufacturers (Davey 1987:140). Only one pipe stem (TS 870) had a glazed mouthpiece, and the glaze was yellow/brown in colour.

Social

A coin was the only artefact belonging to the 'Social' category. The coin (TS 977) was fairly degraded and the lettering was illegible, but the faint outline of a king could be discerned.

Tools and Equipment

'Tools and Equipment' were objects used for work-related activities including repairs. A minimum number of 75 objects were identified in this category, the majority of which were 'Sewing' equipment (**Table 5.22**).

Sewing

Sixty-one artefacts associated with sewing and lace-making were recovered from the tip and included pins, thimbles, bobbins and a needle. Pins comprised 86.8 percent of the sewing assemblage. They were copper alloy and possibly tin-plated although this was no longer present on most of the pins. Twenty-eight of the pins were complete, while 25 were broken. The pins had solid heads, which indicates production after 1824 (Godden Mackay Logan et al. 2004b:353). Most of the pins in Australia were mass-produced in Birmingham and exported to Australia to be sold in stores (Fletcher 1989:141–142) and were relatively cheap to buy (Griggs 2001:81). No

Table 5.22: Summary of 'Tools and Equipment' artefacts.

Function	Form	Qty	Weight	MNI
Sewing	bobbin	3	4.3	3
	needle	1	0.4	1
	pin	85	5.9	53
	thimble	4	7.0	4
Total		93	17.6	61
Weapons and Ammunition	cartridge cases	7	17.2	4
Total		7	17.2	4
Work Tool	tool	23	105.1	2
	whetstone	1	30.8	1
Total		24	135.9	3
Writing and Drawing	bottle	21	97.6	1
	paper	1	56.6	1
	pen	12	15.9	3
	pencil	12	32.3	2
Total		46	202.4	7
Total		**170**	**373.1**	**75**

metal needles were identified in the assemblage; however it is possible that the points of broken pins may have in fact been needles.

All of the four thimbles (TS 885) were copper alloy with circular indentations on the top and sides, had a plain border around the base, and a rolled back edge. The thimbles ranged in height from 16 to 25 mm and had a base diameter of 14 to 18 mm. No decoration was present on the thimbles indicating that they were relatively inexpensive and utilitarian rather than keepsakes (Griggs 2001:82). Three lace-making bobbins (TS 1010) were also recovered. These were of the type used to hold threads and to add weight and tension while making lace (Beaudry 2006:155). The bobbins were made from bone and decorated with lathe-turned bands. One bobbin had a hole at one end, which may have held a spangle attachment with beads to add weight to the bobbin. As well as their practical use for making lace, bobbins could hold symbolic significance as heirlooms, gifts, prizes and love tokens (Iacono 1999:63). The final sewing item was a bone netting needle (TS 780) with a teardrop-shaped eyelet (**Figure 5.17**). Netting needles have a teardrop-shaped eyelet at each end and are used in conjunction with netting gauges (Johnson 1999:31). Similar to tatting, netting was commonly used to make doilies. The needle was 3 mm wide and 1 mm thick. The complete length was unknown as the needle was broken and may have been discarded for this reason.

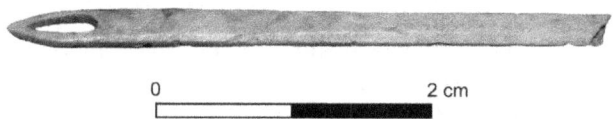

Figure 5.17: Bone netting needle (TS 780).

Weapons and Ammunition

Four cartridge cases were the only artefacts in the 'Weapons and Ammunition' category. Three copper cartridge cases 12 mm in diameter, or 0.5 calibre, with circles on the base, were recovered from the tip. They were centre fire cartridges probably used in a pistol. Brass and copper cartridge cases were introduced in 1846 (Logan 1959:5). Pepperbox pistols with manually revolved barrels appeared by the 1830s, then the revolver principle was perfected by Samuel Colt in the 1840s (Myatt 1981:9–10). The calibre of percussion revolvers varied from 0.32 in (8 mm) to 0.5 in (12.7 mm) (Myatt 1981:12–13). Also recovered from the tip was a shell case approximately 22 mm in diameter which may be a 12 gauge shotgun cartridge used for hunting. Impressed lettering on the base read: 'LONDON/ 12' and would have been a British import. Shotgun cartridges were introduced in 1850 (Logan 1959:6); however it is possible that this cartridge dated from the 20th century.

Work Tools

Artefacts in the 'Work Tools' category included those used for maintenance and repairs around the homestead and on the land. Twenty-four fragments representing a minimum of three artefacts were excavated from the Viewbank tip. One was a significantly corroded iron alloy tool (TS 1112), possibly a trowel. The second (TS 1124) was part of a tool that would have been hafted to a wooden handle. It was a black enamelled copper alloy tube with holes for attachment and was probably a gardening tool. Finally, a whetstone (TS 1103), circular in section with one flattened edge and a ground down top and bottom would have been used for sharpening implements.

Writing and Drawing

Seven objects relating to 'Writing and Drawing' were recovered. Three of these were pens represented by fragmentary components including a bone pen shaft (TS 1062) with an internal thread, which probably fastened a nib and components of two copper alloy pens, probably nib pens, with wooden handles (TS 1059). Quill pens were used until the 19th century when they were replaced by metal nib pens. A Romanian inventor created the first fountain pen in 1824, but it did not become popular until it was improved upon by L.E. Waterman in 1883 with the addition of capillary fed ink (Petrow 2007).

Other writing implements recovered were slate pencils: 12 fragments (TS 1044) were recovered representing a minimum of two pencils, but possibly more. They ranged in diameter from 5 to 6 mm and were plain pencils, some of which had facets remaining from manufacturing. Slate pencils and writing slates were cheap and durable writing implements. Slate pencils were often sold in boxes of 12 or 100 and were usually 5 ½ inches long (Davies 2005:64). While commonly associated with children's education (Iacono 1999:78; Ellis 2001), they may have been used by adults for other purposes such as shopping lists (Davies 2005:63). Ellis (2001:138) dates the use of slate pencils in Australia from the beginning of settlement to 1920, shortly after they disappeared from sales catalogues. However, there is some suggestion that they were still being used in schools and households well into the 20th century (Godden Mackay Logan et al. 2004b:357; Davies 2005:63).

A penny ink bottle (TS 42) was also found and was salt glazed, buff-bodied stoneware. Finally, multiple fragments of heavily degraded paper (TS 1119) were recovered from one context within the tip. No writing was visible on the fragments.

Miscellaneous

The 'Miscellaneous' category includes artefacts with unknown function and containers that could not be associated with one of the other categories. A

5. Artefact Analysis

Table 5.23: Summary of 'Miscellaneous' artefacts.

Function	Form	Qty	Weight	MNI
Containers	basin	2	94.9	1
	bottle	2,924	9,121.9	47
	bowl	15	59.1	2
	covered bowl	9	85.5	2
	jar	19	91.1	7
	jug	17	326.6	4
	stemware	19	91.9	1
	ui hollow	349	3,773.8	82
	unidentified	58	330.9	8
Total		3,412	13,975.7	153
Unknown Function	chain	1	1.7	1
	eyelet	4	5.2	3
	fastening	2	0.4	2
	hook	2	4.2	2
	latch	1	3.2	1
	ring	18	6.7	15
	strap	3	81.4	1
	ui hollow	6	28.1	2
	unidentified	169	764.7	35
	wire	14	17.5	4
Total		220	913.1	66
Total		**3,632**	**14,888.8**	**219**

total of 3,632 artefact fragments were catalogued in this category comprising a minimum of 220 objects (**Table 5.23**).

The majority of artefacts in the 'Miscellaneous' category were containers of unknown function: seven artefact forms were identified within this category with a total minimum number of 153. Most of the ceramic containers in this category were unidentified hollow vessels where the small size of the fragments made it hard to associate them with a particular function. There were 60 unidentified hollow ceramic vessels, most of which were whiteware, but there were also fragments of stoneware, porcelain, white granite, bone china, coarse earthenware, dyed-bodied ware and tin-glazed earthenware. The tin-glazed earthenware vessel (TS 904) had a reddish body with a glaze made white by tin oxide and was decorated with a geometric hand-painted design in yellow, black and purple (**Figure 5.18**). Tin-glazed earthenware was used for apothecary jars, ointment jars and tablewares from the 15th to 18th century (Legge 1986:12; Brooks 2005a:35). By the time Australia was settled tin-glazed earthenwares were far less common with other, higher quality wares superseding them. However, small numbers of chamberpots, ointment jars and apothecary jars were made until as late as 1830 (Brooks 2005a: 35). The Viewbank example is the only tin-glazed vessel identified in Victoria to date and was possibly an antique or replica apothecary jar (Brooks 2005a: 35). Decorative techniques on the other hollow vessels include transfer-printed (including overglazed), flown hand-painted, flown transfer-printed, glazed (including slip-glazed), gilded, hand-painted, enamelled and multiple techniques.

Other vessels of unknown function included four jugs, two covered bowls, a basin and three unidentified vessels. The jugs were transfer-printed whiteware, moulded whiteware, moulded white granite and undecorated porcelain. The covered bowls were both gilded and enamelled in floral patterns, one of which featured three leaf clovers. The basin was whiteware and decorated with gilt bands. Two jugs or vases were the only vessels with makers' marks. The first was a moulded whiteware jug or vase which bore, as part of a printed maker's mark, the national motto *E Pluribus Unum* (from many, one) which was used in the United States from 1782 to 1956. The second vase or jug had a mark which read 'PUBLISHED BY/ E. JONES/ COBRIDGE/ SEPTEMBER 1, 1838'. Elijah Jones was a Staffordshire potter (Godden 1964:358).

A number of ceramic and glass bottles and jars were also included in this category. The ceramics included nine stoneware bottles which may have been used for beverages, ink or blacking, a jar with polychrome enamelled decoration in what appears to be an oriental design, and a small jar lid possibly from an ointment or condiment jar. A further 38 glass bottles were of unknown use. Light green and colourless glass were dominant in this category, but blue, cobalt blue, aqua, green, and dark green were also represented. An additional five glass jars could not be identified as either ointment or condiment jars; four were colourless glass and one was opaque white glass. Two of these had ground rims to fit a glass lid, one had an internal thread finish, and another had a cap seat closure. A white glass jar lid (TS 351) had an embossed motif and lettering around the edge: '...N CONSOLI...'.

Bowls, hollow vessels, and unidentified vessels comprise the remainder of the items in the 'Containers' category. These were made from colourless, blue, white or green glass. Twenty-nine artefacts had an identifiable form, but 'Unknown Function' with a further 37 having an unidentifiable form.

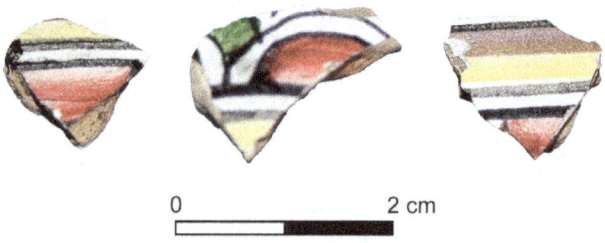

Figure 5.18: Tin-glazed earthenware vessel (TS 904).

5. Artefact Analysis

THE HOMESTEAD CONTEXTS

It is much more difficult to establish whether the artefacts recovered from the homestead contexts were associated with the Martins. It is for this reason that this study focuses predominantly on the artefacts from the tip. In contrast to the tip, a much lower 60 percent of the artefact fragments from the 14 homestead contexts selected for the original research dated from the Martin phase of occupation, in spite of focusing on sub-floor deposits or those with little disturbance (see Appendix 2). It must be noted that the majority of these artefacts had broad date ranges covering most of the 19th century. While 60 percent of the dateable artefacts overlapped with the Martin phase of occupation only two had a date range that fell only within this period or ended in this period. These were an 1873 coin, which may well have been in circulation for many years after this date, and a eucalyptus oil bottle made by J. Bosisto after 1852. All of the other artefacts had date ranges continuing to the end of the 19th century or into the 20th century. Many of these artefacts may be associated with the period of tenancy of the homestead after 1874, and/or the period after the homestead was demolished. Particularly notable in the artefacts post-dating the Martin phase was the presence of machine-made glass bottles. Many of these date to after the homestead was demolished around 1922, which suggests that the ruins were used as a bottle or rubbish dump after this time. The other artefacts that post-date the Martin phase were jars, a bowl and a 'RAAF' badge.

A much smaller number of artefacts may have been lost through the floorboards or thrown in fireplaces where they remained. It is likely that the homestead had well-built, tightly fitting floorboards and floor coverings which would have prevented artefacts falling through the floorboards. However, floor coverings in the 19th century usually left a perimeter of exposed floorboards where some artefacts may have been lost through the boards. In addition, rooms five, six, seven and eight (see **Figure 4.3**) in the Williamson dwelling had poorer construction and may have had more loosely fitting floorboards.

While it is difficult to identify from dating alone which artefacts within the homestead contexts may have belonged to the Martins, their type and location can give some idea, particularly in the case of accidental loss items. Some artefacts, such as coins, buttons, pins and clay pipes are more likely to have been lost accidentally. Within the homestead contexts these artefacts might, in some cases, be associated with the Martins. Three contexts in particular appear to have a concentration of accidentally-lost artefacts: A-III-12, A-II-3 and A-II-3.2. Context A-III-12 was in front of a fireplace in room 5 and contained a number of artefacts that were more likely to be associated with accidental loss. Contexts A-II-3 and A-II-3.2 immediately below comprised a possible sub-floor deposit in room 8 of the early-phase dwelling.

It is interesting to note that these three contexts were in rooms in the original part of the house built by Williamson. Of course this also raises the possibility that some of these objects were lost by Williamson and his family prior to the Martins' occupation. The archaeological evidence indicates that the floor was raised in these rooms at some point, probably when the Martins extended the house. The new floorboards may have been more consistent with the quality of the rest of the house. The items in the fireplace may have been lost by the Williamson family, or the Martins. In addition to the artefacts from the three included contexts, the section below will also discuss the system of servant bells recovered by the excavation.

THE HOMESTEAD ASSEMBLAGE

The assemblage recovered from the three homestead contexts totalled 35 artefact fragments weighing 80.7 g. Seventeen pins, three buttons, an 1873 coin, a slate pencil and a safety pin were recovered from context A-III-12. The 17 pins (TS 1079) recovered from this context were the only sewing related artefacts found in the homestead. These were solid head pins similar to those found in the tip and date to after 1824 (Godden Mackay Logan et al. 2004b:353). These pins were in far better condition than those found in the tip. Most still had tin-plating present. There were 14 complete pins and only three were broken.

Of the three buttons, one was a fabric covered copper alloy button, 11 mm in diameter and was missing the back (TS 731), another was a japanned button with a four-hole sew-through attachment with the lettering: 'MELBOURNE.COOKSON' (TS 1030, this maker could not be identified), and the third was a four-hole sew-through shell button lathe-turned and 8 mm in diameter (TS 1045).

The coin was a British shilling, the obverse of which read: 'ONE SHILLING/ 1873' with crown and wreath motifs. The reverse read: 'VICTORIA DEI GRATIA BRITANNIA: REG: F: D:' and had an image of the Queen in profile. This coin pre-dated the departure of the Martin family by one year.

One slate pencil fragment was also recovered from A-III-12. Slate pencils were used from the beginning of European settlement in Australia well into the 20th century. A copper alloy safety pin of the same type as those found in the tip was also recovered from A-III-12.

Aside from the 1873 coin, these artefacts had broad date ranges covering most of the 19th century. It is possible that these artefacts were swept towards the fireplace and dropped through the floorboards where the two joined. The concentration of pins, along with the buttons and safety pin, indicate that sewing was done in room 5.

5. Artefact Analysis

A sauce or condiment bottle stopper, glass and ceramic fragments were recovered from context A-II-3. Immediately below this, in context A-II-3.2, a 1697 coin and a small toy compass were found. The ceramic fragments were small, flown, floral pattern transfer-printed whiteware while the glass fragments were from colourless and aqua bottles. The glass bottle stopper (TS 260) had a circular finial and shank, was undecorated, and was of the type used for condiment bottles.

The coin recovered from A-II-3.2 is of particular interest as it dated to 1697, the reign of William III of England (1689–1702) and was probably a memento or collectible item. The obverse of the coin read: 'BRITAN.../ 1697' and had an image of Britannia. The reverse read: 'GVLIEMVS. TE[RTI]VS' and had a profile of the King. Another interesting item, a miniature compass, was excavated from this context. The compass had a circular copper case with a glass cover. A paper insert inside had a printed arrow beside an 'N'; also visible were a 'NE' and 'E'. The paper insert was possibly fixed with a pin and spun around.

In addition to the artefacts recovered from these three homestead contexts, it is worth noting the system of servant bells recovered throughout the homestead building. Four servant bells were recovered from the kitchen (room 10), and one from the south-east veranda (see **Figure 4.3**). A system of pulls was also recovered throughout the homestead: room 7, room 10, the central hall, the north-west veranda, the upper contexts of rooms 6 and 8, and the upper contexts of trenches III and IV in the centre and rear of the house. It is highly possible that the bells and bell pulls were moved from their original locations during the demolition of the homestead. It is likely that all five bells were located together in the kitchen. The bells had iron coils, which provided the spring to ring the attached bell (**Figure 5.19**). The pulls would have been in the main public and private rooms of the house. Bell pulls of this era were usually a wire with a decorative pull attached through the ceiling or wall. The pulley system would have been concealed along hallways and external walls. Servants were summoned from the rear of the house by the servant bells.

Figure 5.19: Viewbank servant bell.

While the artefacts recovered from the three homestead contexts are consistent with accidental loss, the date ranges do not conclusively allow them to be associated with the Martins. They may have been lost by the Williamson family or subsequent tenants at Viewbank.

In contrast to this, the dates of almost all of the artefacts recovered from the tip allow them to be associated with the Martin family's phase of occupation of Viewbank from 1843 to 1874. Many of the dates for artefact manufacture or decorative technique were broad, covering the entire period of the Martins' occupation of Viewbank, and in many cases, most of the 19th century. Others had tighter date ranges linking the deposit to the period that the Martins lived at Viewbank. The discarded domestic items recovered from the tip are the refuse of day-to-day living at Viewbank and the assemblage includes a large number of objects reflecting everyday practicality, as well as luxury.

6
Acquisition of Goods

Consumer practice is the behavioural pattern by which people acquire goods, both for necessity and luxury. It is influenced by a range of factors including affordability, accessibility and desirability. This chapter is informed by a number of previous archaeological studies that have focused on trade networks, consumption and shopping in Australia. Notable among these are Crook's (2000, 2011) studies of shopping in working-class Sydney and quality in consumer decision-making, Staniforth's (2003) use of evidence from shipwrecks to explore trade and social networks, Davies' work on trade networks in working-class Melbourne (Davies 2006b) and on accessing goods in remote areas (Davies 2006a:95–107), and Allison and Cremin's (2006) work on trade catalogue use in rural New South Wales.

The section on 'Markets' examines the origins of artefacts from the Viewbank assemblage in order to explore the trade networks linking Viewbank homestead to Melbourne, Australia and the world, networks which can embody the social and economic structure of the community and also changes to that structure. The following section on 'Shopping' investigates the processes of acquisition and shopping as a genteel performance. It also discusses the influence of availability and price on the choice of goods. The purchase of correct goods, in the correct taste, was central to the cultural capital of gentility, and therefore to determining class position in the new colony. The examination of consumer practice in this chapter forms the basis of the discussion on lifestyle and class to follow.

Markets

Artefact assemblages allow us to examine the economic and social networks in which people were engaged by analysing the origin of goods they purchased (Adams 1991). This engagement was facilitated by industrialised mass production and new technologies for transporting goods, which allowed for far-reaching, global trade networks in the 19th century.

Discussion of the origin of artefacts from the Martins' residence in this section is limited to those objects with makers' marks, or where possible other features, that positively identify their place of manufacture. Although this may not reveal all the sources of goods in the assemblage, it does indicate the general patterns of access to trade networks. Of the artefacts recovered from the tip, 5.9 percent could be associated with a country of manufacture (**Table 6.1**). For information regarding the origin of artefacts from the homestead contexts, see Hayes (2007:93–94).

England: The Dominant Market

The predominance of English-made goods in the tip is unsurprising because of their importance in the Australian consumer market in the 19th century. The extensive scale of production in Britain allowed these goods to dominate the market. Most notable among the positively identified English goods at Viewbank were the ceramic tableware and teaware vessels. It has been widely noted that the vast majority of ceramics found on 19th-century archaeological sites in Australia were imported from England (see Casey 1999:23; Brooks 2005a).

All of the tableware and teaware recovered from the tip with makers' marks identifying their origin were made by Staffordshire potteries. In addition, one of the chamberpots was made by a Staffordshire pottery. It is highly likely that the majority of the unmarked ceramics were also made in Staffordshire, as by the mid-19th century two-thirds of Britain's potteries were located in the region (Snyder 1997:5). The United States was the largest consumer of Staffordshire products between the end of the Napoleonic wars in 1815 and the beginning of the American civil war in 1861 (Copeland 1998:17). However, exports were also sent to South America, Canada, Australia and other countries of the British Empire (Majewski and O'Brien 1987:103; Rodriguez and Brooks 2012).

It is likely that restricted availability of goods in the Australian market influenced what was purchased by the Martin family. One example is the presence in the Viewbank assemblage of ceramics made by Staffordshire potteries, specifically for export to the United States. Many Staffordshire potteries catered exclusively for the large American market (Graham c.1979:2) with vessels which often included American national symbols and mottos, and decorations which appealed to American taste. When the American Civil War commenced in 1861 this market became restricted and the potteries quickly needed to find new markets for their wares. Newspapers documented how exports to the United States decreased, while in the subsequent years exports to Australia and New Zealand, among other countries, increased (Brooks 2005a:58–59).

49

6. Acquisition of Goods

Table 6.1: Identified country of manufacture by maker's mark.

Place of Manufacture	Form	Material	MNI	%
England	bottle	glass	18	
England	coin	metal		
England - Dewsbury	stopper	glass	1	
England - Liverpool	bottle	glass	1	
England - London	bottle	glass	2	
England - London	button	metal	1	
England - London	cartridge	metal	4	
England - London	jar	ceramic	1	
England - London	stopper	glass	1	
England - London	toothbrush	organic	3	
England - Manchester	bottle	glass	1	
England - Nottingham	bottle	ceramic		
England - Staffordshire	chamberpot	ceramic	1	
England - Staffordshire	plate	ceramic	23	
England - Staffordshire	platter	ceramic	5	
England - Staffordshire	saucer	ceramic	2	
England - Staffordshire	ui flat	ceramic	1	
England - Staffordshire	ui hollow	ceramic	2	
England - Staffordshire	unidentified	ceramic	2	
England - Worcester	bottle	glass	1	
England - Worcester	stopper	glass	1	
England - York	bottle	glass		
England - Yorkshire	stopper	glass	1	
England			72	94.7
France - Bordeaux	bottle	glass	1	
France			1	1.3
Ireland - Belfast	bottle	glass		
Northern Ireland				
Ireland - Dublin	bottle cap	metal	1	
Ireland			1	1.3
Scotland - Portobello	bottle	glass	1	
Scotland			1	1.3
America	lamp	metal	1	
America			1	1.3
Total			**76**	**100.0**

The presence of vessels clearly intended for the United States market in the Viewbank assemblage provides evidence that British exports originally intended for the United States were being sent to Australia when they could no longer be sold in the United States (Brooks 2005a:59). One such vessel was a moulded whiteware jug which bore as part of a printed maker's mark the national motto of the United States used from 1782 to 1956, *E Pluribus Unum* (from many, one).

Further evidence is the relatively large amount of white granite ware identified at Viewbank. Moulded white granite vessels were made by Staffordshire potteries in response to changes in American taste that favoured simply decorated ceramics, and to compete with popular French porcelain (Ewins 1997:46–47). In the United States the popularity of plain white or moulded white granite and ironstone from the 1850s was well established (see Majewski and O'Brien 1987:120–124; Miller 1991:6). At Viewbank, 11.9 percent of the ceramic tableware and 10.1 percent of the teaware was white granite. There were two matching sets of white granite. One was in the 'Berlin Swirl' pattern and had two vessels with the maker's mark of Mayer & Elliot, a Staffordshire pottery, and were impressed with the date 1860 (Godden 1964:422). Another two were marked with Liddle, Elliot & Son who changed to that name from Mayer & Elliot in 1862 (Godden 1964:235). The second set was 'Girard Shape' made by John Ridgway Bates & Co. between 1856 and 1858 in Staffordshire (Godden 1964:535). These dates coincide closely with the beginning of the American Civil War.

The reason for the purchase of white granite wares by the Martin family is difficult to discern. There is, to date, little evidence from other Australian sites to shed light on this. White granite has not been identified at many sites in Australia, probably to some extent because of the difficulty of distinguishing white granite from other wares, particularly when in a fragmentary condition (Brooks 2005a:25, 34–35). Brooks (2002:56) has identified white granite at sites from inner Melbourne and country Victoria. No white granite was identified, however, in the Casselden Place ceramic assemblage (Godden Mackay Logan et al. 2004a:21–22), possibly because of the different social group or the later time period.

The Martins may have purchased white granite sets because of fashion or desirability. Miller (1980, 1991) has demonstrated that in the United States white granite was relatively more expensive than other wares, such as whiteware. As such, it would have been affordable for Australia's middle class, but less accessible for working-class people. This may explain its absence on working-class sites in Australia. DiZerega Wall (1992:79) also suggests that white granite vessels in Gothic shapes became fashionable among the American middle class because of their association with the sanctity of churches, and contrast to capitalist markets. It is possible that the Australian middle class purchased white granite ware for this reason. However, it has been noted in the archaeological record that there was a trend in Britain and its colonies in the 19th century for colourful ceramics, particularly those with transfer prints (Lawrence 2003:25–26). On the whole, the Martin family were following this trend with colourful ceramics comprising the significant majority of the Viewbank assemblage.

A number of specialised items were identified as being manufactured in London: ammunition, toothbrushes, perfume bottles, a button, a cherry toothpaste jar and a food storage jar stopper. A small number of glass food storage bottles and stoppers, medicine bottles, a beer/wine bottle and an ink bottle were manufactured in other English towns (**Table 6.1**). Eighteen glass oil/vinegar bottles also bore an English registration mark. These registration marks were issued by the London Patent Office, usually to English manufacturers, but it must be noted that it was possible for foreign manufacturers to gain an English registration mark (Godden 1964:526). It is difficult to determine whether these bottles were shipped to Australia with the product inside or empty for filling by local producers. The perfume bottles were most likely shipped with their contents as the maker's mark was that of a London perfumer John Gosnell & Co.

The importance of the social and economic ties between England and Melbourne is certainly visible in the Viewbank assemblage. The relatively small population of Port Phillip, and Australia generally, relied on the strong trading system of the Empire of which they were a part. In the early to mid-19th century, local manufactures struggled to compete with British mass production. The Viewbank tip assemblage shows that household items such as tableware, condiment bottles, and also medicine bottles and personal items were being imported from England to Australia and purchased by the Martins. There is also evidence for the exploitation of the Australian market by English manufacturers for selling goods that could no longer be sold in other markets, namely the United States.

Ireland, Scotland, Continental Europe and the United States: Supplementary Goods

A small number of items had makers' marks identifying their place of origin as Ireland, Scotland, Continental Europe or the United States, implying trade links with these places. Two items were manufactured in parts of the British Isles other than England. A lead bottle cap was manufactured in Dublin, Ireland, and a beer/wine bottle was made by Cooper & Wood, Portobello, Scotland (Boow c.1991:177). Although not to the same extent as London, the manufacturing and shipping centres of Edinburgh, Glasgow and Dublin were also shipping goods directly to Australia (Nix 2005:25).

From Continental Europe there was a cognac bottle imported from Bordeaux, France. Further, four porcelain dolls were probably made in Germany, which was the main producer of porcelain doll parts until World War I. France and England also supplied doll parts, but to a much lesser extent because mass production in Germany allowed for the production of cheaper dolls (Pritchett and Pastron 1983:326). In addition to these doll parts there were two swirl marbles which were manufactured in Germany from 1846 (Ellis 2001:174). These goods may have been shipped to English or other British ports and then exported to Australia, rather than shipped directly from Europe (Nix 2005:38).

One artefact recovered from the tip was positively identified as being manufactured in the United States. This was a copper alloy deflector from a vertical wick kerosene lamp. Robert Edwin Dietz and his brother Michael patented the first flat wick burner for use with kerosene in 1859 (Kirkman 2007). This indicates that some goods were being traded from the United States to Australia after 1859.

6. Acquisition of Goods

Asia: Exotic Goods

Although not marked with makers' marks there were a number of artefacts identified as originating from China in the Viewbank tip. From the 18th century, British merchants in India were trading between ports in the Eastern seas in what was known as the 'country trade' (Staniforth and Nash 1998:7–8; Staniforth 2003:72–73). This brought Chinese export porcelain to Australia soon after European settlement in 1788. American whaling vessels also transported Chinese export porcelain to Australia until 1812 when the English/American War interrupted trade (Staniforth and Nash 1998:9). Networks expanded further after the first Opium War (1839–1842) when the British forcibly opened trade with China allowing the development of an independent trade network between Australia and China. Increasing numbers of Chinese immigrants led to the emergence of networks of Chinese trade that ultimately extended throughout Victoria (Bowen 2012:39, 123). These businesses were established to provide for Chinese communities, but inevitably served European consumers as well (McCarthy 1988:145–146). This market was utilised to some extent by the Martin family.

A 'Celadon' spoon, two Chinese ginger jars and two jar lids were part of the Viewbank tip assemblage. Such items were made in China for a Chinese market, both domestic and overseas (Muir 2003:42). From the 1850s it became increasingly common to find Chinese jars in European households (Lydon 1999:57). The contents of ginger jars, and the jars themselves, were popular among Europeans in Australia. It is possible that these Chinese objects were purchased in Melbourne for their unusual or exotic qualities or simply for their contents. Ginger jars were also often given as gifts by Chinese people to their European friends or associates (Lydon 1999:57–58). Three further items – two bowls and a jar with brightly coloured polychrome overglaze decoration – were Chinese export porcelain made for sale to Europeans (Hellman and Yang 1997:174). These objects were fragmentary and it is difficult to discern the decorative patterns, although two of the vessels include human figures.

Australia: Rare Commodities

No artefacts from the tip were marked as being manufactured in Australia. The difficulty of local producers competing with British mass production in the early to mid-19th century meant that only goods that could be produced more cheaply in the colony or were protected by tariffs were viable. These tended to be large utilitarian items that were expensive to import. The lack of goods in the assemblage marked as being Australian-made does not necessarily mean that the Martin family were not purchasing Australian-produced goods. It is known from a list of debts upon Dr Martin's death that the Martin family purchased perishable goods locally: dairy, meat, bread, grain, fruit and vegetables (VPRS 7591/P2, Unit 17, File 12-586, 11 February 1875). The only archaeological evidence of this is in the form of bones that remain from cuts of meat. Howell-Meurs' (2000:42) analysis of the faunal assemblage from the Viewbank tip indicates that much of the meat was purchased from a butcher, as indicated by the relative absence of cranial and peripheral limb elements. While the butcher was preferred, the presence of some cranial and peripheral limb bones suggests that at least some complete carcasses were processed at Viewbank.

Of the 240 glass bottles recovered from the Viewbank tip, none were marked as Australian-made, or having Australian-made contents. However, by the time the Martins arrived in Port Phillip, there were already numerous small vineyards in Melbourne, Geelong and in the Martins' local area of the Yarra Valley (Beeston 1994:38). While labour shortages during the gold rushes meant that the wine industry faltered, as the rush declined many turned to winemaking in the 1860s (Beeston 1994:47–48; Dunstan 1994:34). In addition to vineyards, by the mid-1840s there were six breweries operating in Melbourne, but the quality remained poor. In the early 1860s there were 20 breweries in Melbourne, and by 1874 there were 31 (Deutsher 1999:87). During the 1860s there were also 80 breweries operating in 34 country towns in Victoria (Deutsher 1999:88). In addition, there were 20 manufacturers of ginger beer, cordial and aerated water operating in Melbourne by 1863 (Davies 2006b:348).

It is important to consider that Australian manufacturers of beverages were using and refilling imported bottles prior to the commencement of the production of glass bottles in Australia. Many of these would have been unmarked bottles, but sometimes companies would also reuse marked imported bottles. In the 19th century, the second-hand bottle trade was a well established business with beverage manufacturers purchasing bottles from second-hand bottle dealers (Busch 1991). In Australia, there is archaeological evidence of this from a cordial factory in Parramatta which filled beer/wine bottles with its product (Carney 1998). This means that Australian-manufactured beverages are generally imperceptible in the archaeological record.

It became increasingly difficult for beverage manufacturers to obtain sufficient numbers of bottles and the demand grew for locally produced bottles. The Victorian Flint Glass Works was advertising for glassblowers in 1847, but was not a successful endeavour (Graham 1981:15–16). Demand from wine merchants for cheaply produced, locally made bottles led to the commencement of production of a small supply in Sydney from the 1860s (Graham 1981:17). However, inter-colonial tariffs prevented much trade between the colonies. It was not until 1872 that the first major glass manufacturer in Melbourne, the Melbourne Glass Bottle Works Company, opened, with other companies following (Vader 1975:14). As such, during the period the Martins lived at Viewbank there was a very limited supply of locally made glass bottles.

Stoneware bottles were produced in Sydney from early in the 19th century and in the 1850s the production of stoneware bottles began in Melbourne (Ford 1995:176–293). However, only one of the stoneware bottles from the Viewbank tip may have been for a beverage, either aerated water or ginger beer, but was unmarked.

No other artefacts recovered from the Viewbank tip had Australian makers' marks. However, a number of ceramic vessels from the Viewbank tip may have been made in Australia. Potteries had been established in New South Wales and Tasmania from the start of the 19th century (Casey 1999: 7) and in Victoria from the 1850s (Ford 1995: 176–293). From the mid-19th century onwards, Australian potters were predominantly producing utilitarian wares to avoid being in direct competition with British imports of tableware and teaware (Casey 1999:23). These potteries produced stoneware storage containers, flowerpots, cooking vessels, dairying vessels, basins, ewers, chamberpots and, frequently also, 'Rockingham' glazed teapots, and Majolica glazed kitchen and decorative wares (Birmingham and Fahy 1987:8; Ford 1995:176–293). However, very few Australian-made ceramics were marked before the later 19th century, making them difficult to positively identify in the archaeological record (Birmingham and Fahy 1987:7). In the Viewbank assemblage, a number of ceramics may have been made in Australia. These included stoneware storage containers, redware flowerpots, and two 'Rockingham' glazed vessels (probably teapots). However, 'Rockingham' glazed vessels were also produced in Britain (Brooks 2005a:41). The slip-glazed redware milkpans recovered from the Viewbank tip were probably Australian-made as they were becoming less popular in Britain by this time (Brooks 2005a:42). It seems that the Martin family were purchasing at least some Australian-made goods, although they were unmarked.

Shopping

Imported goods find their way to consumers through national, regional and local networks (Adams 1991:397). The study of shopping can provide additional insight into consumer practice and the interpretation of goods recovered from archaeological sites (Crook 2000). The method of shopping implies different social dynamics; for example, a middle-class standard of wealth was required to shop in fashionable inner-city shops, while the working class was generally restricted to open-air market shopping where goods were more affordable (Crook 2000:17). This section explores how and where the Martin family were purchasing goods.

First of all, it is possible that the Martin family brought some household goods with them from England and that these represent part of the assemblage. An overglazed, black transfer-printed and enamelled vessel dates from 1750 to 1830 (Brooks 2005a:35, 43), which is prior to the Martins' arrival in Australia. The Martins probably brought this, and a number of other items, to Australia from England.

The assemblage recovered from the tip suggests that goods were being purchased over the entire period that the Martins occupied Viewbank. The 'Summer Flowers' set and Masons plates had date ranges ending in the 1850s, a Copeland chamberpot dated from 1847 to 1867, and a set of plates with 'Bagdad' pattern dated from 1851 to 1862. The white granite vessels had start dates in the late 1850s and 1860s. Finally, a 'Rhine' plate dated from 1869 to 1882. This gives the impression that rather than purchasing ceramics all at one time upon their arrival at Viewbank, the Martins were buying goods throughout their period of occupation. Further, glass bottles with tight dates included a seal dated prior to 1850, while others dated from prior to the Martins' arrival at Viewbank to the 1870s. Other artefacts dated well into the period that the Martins lived at Viewbank. Doll parts dated from 1850 to 1880, and 1860 to 1900, and a lamp was purchased after 1859. As such, it appears that the tip included goods purchased throughout the time that the Martins occupied the site.

Some of the ways in which the family purchased goods in Victoria in the 1870s is indicated in a statement of duty after Dr Martin's death, which lists his unsecured debts to a number of traders (PROV, VPRS 7591/P2, Unit 17, File 12-586, 11 February 1875) (**Table 6.2**). Living an easy distance from inner-city Melbourne, the family would have been able to enjoy access to the full variety of goods available in the colony, which is supported by this list of debts. Fifteen of the traders to whom Dr Martin owed money were located in the inner city, ten of them located on, or adjacent, to Collins Street (**Figure 6.1**). This was the prime shopping street of the city in the 19th century where, by mid-century, traders carried a wide range of imported goods in fashionable shops, including household wares, furniture, clothes and jewellery (Priestley 1984:23–26). Generally the 'streets' were considered a moral and physical hazard, but Collins Street was elegant and refined: a respectable place for ladies (Russell 1993:29, 1994:65). According to Clara Aspinall (cited from Russell 1994:65), 'Here all things are conducted calmly, quietly, harmoniously'. Being seen on Collins Street, and spending appropriate amounts of money on fashionable goods, was an important part of genteel public performance for

6. Acquisition of Goods

Table 6.2: Listing of unsecured debts to traders in a statement of duty regarding Dr Martin's will (PROV, VPRS 7591/P2, Unit 17, File 12-586, 11 February 1875), including details on traders from Sands and McDougall's Melbourne Directories (1874).

Trader Name	Type	Location	Amount owing			Reference	Notes
			£	s	d		
Graham Bros. & Co.	Merchants	91 Little Collins St, Melbourne	728	14	5	Sands and McDougall 1874: 471	James Graham is listed as 'Graham, Hon. James'
Alston & Brown	Drapers (Silk Mercers, Drapers, Outfitters, Carpet Warehousemen & c.)	47 Collins St West, Melbourne	219	4	8	Sands and McDougall 1874: ii	
Shields & Co.	Cornfactors (Flourfactors and Grain Crushers)	corner Elizabeth and a Beckett Sts, Melbourne	104	7	4	Sands and McDougall 1874: 661	
Wm. Godfrey	Wine (and Spirit) Merchant	97 Collins St West, Melbourne	70	5	0	Sands and McDougall 1874: 470	
John Sharpe	Timber Merchant		44	19	1	Sands and McDougall 1874: 659	There is a John Sharp listed as a timber merchant at 151 Collins Street West. There is also a John Sharpe listed in Heidelberg, but no trade is given
A. (Archibald) Davidson	Grocer (and Wine) Merchant	112 Collins St East, Melbourne	44	9	0	Sands and McDougall 1874: 422	
C. (Charles) W. Watts	Butcher	Heidelberg	10	12	11	Sands and McDougall 1874: 713	
Oldfield & Lindley	Timber Merchants (and Steam Sawmills)	Elgin, Station and Nicholson Sts, Carlton, and Nicholson and Argyle Sts, Fitzroy	5	6	11	Sands and McDougall 1874: 607	
George Studley	Baker	Heidelberg	1	3	11	Sands and McDougall 1874: 683	This is the only Baker by this name
Briscoe & Co.	Ironmonger (and Iron Merchants)	11 Collins St East, Melbourne	5	10	6	Sands and McDougall 1874: 375	
Whitney, Chambers & Co.	(Wholesale) Ironmongers	7 Swanston St, and cnr. Collins and Swanston Sts, and 103 Flinders St East, Melbourne	1	11	1	Sands and McDougall 1874: 721	
By Lee	Ironmonger		1	4	0	Sands and McDougall 1874: 541	This could be Benjamin Lee, Ironmonger at 177 & 179 Bourke St. East, or Lee, E & Co. Ironmongers 71 Bourke St West
W. (William) R. Hill	Chemist (and Druggist)	63 Collins St East, Melbourne	5	1	0	Sands and McDougall 1874: 500	
Charles Ogg	Chemist (and Druggist)	117 Collins St East and Gardiners-ck Rd.	2	6	0	Sands and McDougall 1874: 606	
W.H. Lamond	Coal (and Grain) Merchant	65 Flinders St East, Melbourne	6		10	Sands and McDougall 1874: 536	
J. (John) Holmes	Saddler	72 Bridge Rd	7	2	0	Sands and McDougall 1874: 503	There is also a John Holmes, Nurseryman, in Heidelberg

(continued)

Table 6.2: (continued)

Trader Name	Type	Location	Amount owing £	s	d	Reference	Notes
Vines & Carpenter	Shoeing Smiths (and Farriers)	53 Little Collins St West, Melbourne	4	2	6	Sands and McDougall 1874: 704	
T. (Thomas) Hodgson	Blacksmith	Heidelberg	6	5	0	Sands and McDougall 1874: 502	This is the only T. Hodgson listed
E. Forster	Saddler & c.		1		6	Sands and McDougall 1874: 852	Under saddlers there is an L. Forster at 31 Post-office Place
William Lea	Saddler	34 Swanston St, Melbourne	2	13	0	Sands and McDougall 1874: 540	
E. (Edward) Ryan	Bootmaker	96 Swanston St, Melbourne	1	15	0	Sands and McDougall 1874: 649	
Dunn	Grocer		3	15	11	Sands and McDougall 1874: 438	There are many listings under Dunn. This may be Frederick Dunn, Storekeeper at Heidelberg. Alternatively it may be T. Dunn, Grocer, in High St, Wr (?) or Terence Dunn, Grocer, in Sydney Rd, Coburg
Crofts	Cheesemonger		4	6	2	Sands and McDougall 1874: 415	This is possibly the Provision Merchant at 40 Swanston St, Melbourne
Klingender & Charsley	Solicitors	Bank Place, Collins St West, Melbourne	33	4	8	Sands and McDougall 1874: 533	
(John) Stanway	Crockery (Importer of China and Glass Ware)	175 Bourke St East, Melbourne	5	19	9	Sands and McDougall 1874: 661	

women: an activity in which the Martins clearly engaged. Dr Martin would have purchased items while in the city for work, while the Martin women would have spent afternoons promenading and browsing the shops. This exclusive and fashionable area provided a pleasurable shopping experience. The city shops frequented by the Martin family in the 1870s included drapers (**Figure 6.2**), chemists, wine merchants, grocers, ironmongers, a coal merchant, shoeing smith, saddler, bootmaker and an importer of china and glass ware (**Table 6.2**). Dr Martin owed considerable sums of money to a number of these traders.

In the second half of the 19th century, the rise of shopping arcades, and later, department stores, in inner-city areas stylishly accommodated middle-class shoppers (Kingston 1994:26). Arcades and department stores catered to the middle class and were out of the price range of working-class consumers (Crook 2000:19–20). Arcades incorporated a range of elegant shops protected from the elements, and the first in Melbourne was Queen's arcade in 1853, with a number of others following. By the 1860s, window displays of tempting goods lured pedestrians from the sidewalks into the shops (Brown-May 1998:52). Around the world, in the second half of the 19th century, many general stores and draperies developed into department stores (Kingston 1994:27–28). While this process in Sydney has been well documented, little historical work has been done for Melbourne. The evolution of department stores is difficult to trace in historical records in the absence of extensive research in the area. A number of stores, such as draper and haberdasher Buckley and Nunn which was established in 1852, gradually expanded into department stores although exactly when this took place is unknown (Priestley 1984:135).

The Martins also purchased goods close to home. In Heidelberg, not far from Viewbank, there was a shopping village named Warringal which comprised a number of shops by 1848 providing the basic needs of daily life to residents in the area. Shops included a butcher, baker, miller, shoemaker, wheelwright and blacksmith, along with a brickmaker and a plasterer (Garden 1972:73). The statement of duty

6. Acquisition of Goods

Figure 6.1: Collins Street in 1864. Briscoe and Co. Ironmongers where the Martin family purchased goods can be seen on the right side of the street (Creator: Unknown; Source: State Library of Victoria).

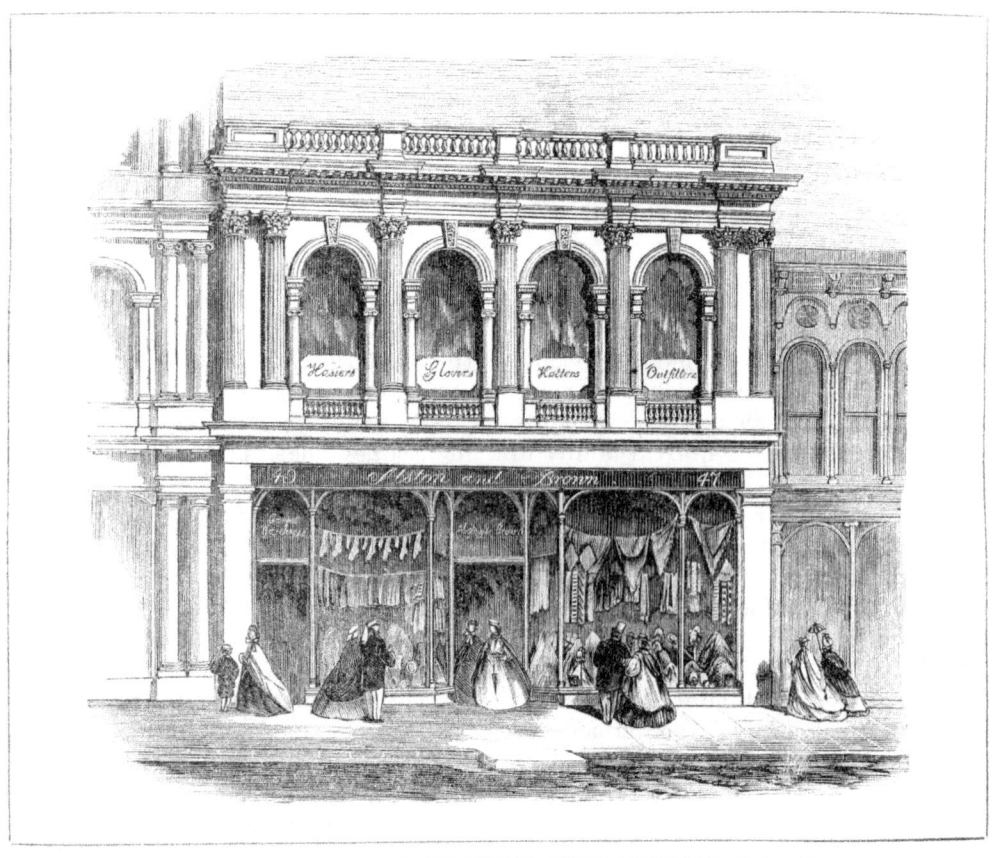

Figure 6.2: Alston and Brown, one of the drapers in Collins Street frequented by the Martin family, 1864 (Creator: Frederick Grosse 1828–1894; Source: State Library of Victoria).

indicates that Dr Martin had debts with a butcher, baker and blacksmith in Heidelberg and possibly a timber merchant, nurseryman and storekeeper (**Table 6.2**). Heidelberg was also a market-gardening area, with fresh produce including fruit, vegetables and grain crops readily available for purchase by the Martin family (Garden 1972:71–72). The Martins purchased the necessities of daily life for Viewbank from Warringal in local markets and shops, although they were probably shopped for by a servant.

Some affluent Australians ordered household goods and personal items directly from London stores to avoid the physical environment of shopping and to get the most up-to-date items (Kingston 1994:25). Also, trade catalogues were used extensively by people who lived remotely from cities and towns (Pollon 1989:233–234; Allison and Cremin 2006). It is difficult to determine from artefacts whether the item was ordered by the consumer from a trade catalogue or purchased from an Australian shop. For example, a toothbrush from the Viewbank tip bears the name of a London chemist 'GEO…LEWIS CHEMIST// PEARL CEMENTS/ …ENT/ LONDON' and was possibly ordered directly from London, but may have been purchased from a local distributor who imported the item.

Archaeological indicators of where goods were purchased are largely limited to items such as buttons or combs that have shop names marked on them. No shop names were identified on artefacts in the Viewbank assemblage. Crook (2000:24) suggests another way of using artefacts to view purchasing behaviour, namely that at a general level, the mix of luxury and poor quality items in working-class assemblages might be the result of the influence of affordability and availability of second-hand goods in market bazaars. The converse of this would be to assume that cohesion in an assemblage, such as matching sets of tableware, and a consistent level of quality across an assemblage, would indicate shopping in centralised arcades, department stores and by mail. This certainly appears to be the case for the Martin family. In the Viewbank assemblage, 11 matching sets of tableware and three complementary sets (including similar but not identical vessels), were identified along with nine matching sets of teaware and three complementary sets. This indicates that they were able to purchase a large number of vessels at one time. It would also have been possible for them to make follow-up purchases of vessels in the same patterns at a later date. A large number of high quality drinking glasses were recovered: 13 tumblers and 25 stemmed glasses. Cut glass vessels, either in simple or elaborate patterns, were a prestigious item, superior to moulded vessels (Jones 2000:174). Almost all of the stemmed drinking glasses and tumblers at Viewbank were cut glass. Also, three ewers and a chamberpot, with flown black 'Marble' decoration, were recovered from the tip. Not only were there matching toilet sets, but these sets also matched between bedrooms.

The adaptation and recycling of objects can be seen as an indicator of the necessity to make do when the availability of goods is limited, either through financial access or availability in the marketplace. Objects may be adapted from their original form to serve another purpose or repeatedly reused until worn out. For example at the remote sawmilling community of Henry's Mill in south-west Victoria, domestic recycling was identified in a variety of ways including glass bottles reshaped into storage jars, and kerosene tins adapted for various uses (Davies 2001b:161). No evidence of reuse or recycling such as this was identified in the Viewbank assemblage. This supports the notion that the Martin family had access to a wide range of goods and could afford to buy what they required for daily life.

Consumer Practice

English goods dominated the Viewbank assemblage for two reasons: first, because of their availability in the colony, and second, because of a social preference for them, or a desire for them because of their familiarity. While it is important to note that English-manufactured goods do not necessarily indicate English values or beliefs (Symonds 2003:153), the Martin family may well have sought to maintain ties to England. Trading power and dominance were not the only factors; there was a demand for goods which enabled and expressed the values, behaviours and beliefs of gentility (Young 2003:7–8).

Items from Continental Europe may well have been specialised objects not commonly available from England, or in some way superior to English products, for example French cognac and German dolls. Similarly, goods from China added some exotic items to their possessions. While some Australian goods were available to the Martin family, there is little conclusive evidence in the archaeological record for their presence on the site. It is impossible to determine whether this was because Australian-made goods were unmarked at the time or because the Martin family had a preference for imported goods, although the former seems most likely. Overall the assemblage reflects general colonial trade networks and the strong social and economic ties the colony had with England in its first 50 years.

The Martin family purchased goods in two distinct areas: near home and in the city centre. Necessity and convenience dictated that food and items for daily life be purchased nearby in Heidelberg, and occasionally in Melbourne. There is also some evidence that a garden, orchard, and dairy operated at Viewbank and may have supplied the family (see discussion in the next chapter). Household and personal goods were largely sourced from faraway places, yet purchased for the most part in the genteel atmosphere of Collins Street. There is no evidence that the Martins were shopping in the suburbs between Heidelberg and the centre of Melbourne, or any other suburbs. This implies that the social networks of the Martins, and the activities of the family, centred on these places.

The Viewbank assemblage appears to indicate that the Martins could afford the goods they wanted, imported or otherwise, and purchased them in the shopping environment they chose. The sizeable debts that Dr Martin owed to various stores suggest that price was of little hindrance to the purchasing behaviour of the family and that he had the status and wealth necessary to maintain credit at a number of stores. They shopped in ways perceived as fitting for the middle class, and shopping formed a significant part of the family's participation in 'genteel society'. Not restricted by lack of money, and with access to the full range of goods available in the colony, the Martins' consumer practice reflects their class position.

7
Daily Life at Viewbank Homestead

Gentility was expressed through various aspects of daily life. This chapter examines the lives and lifestyles of people at Viewbank via the material culture and historical records, with a view to discussing in Chapter 8 how gentility was used in class negotiation. This chapter first examines how the homestead and surrounds functioned spatially in relation to the daily happenings at Viewbank. This is followed by a discussion of work and leisure for both the Martins and their servants, perhaps the most significant aspect of daily life at Viewbank. Dining and social events were the most comprehensive aspect of daily life revealed by the material culture, and are examined here in detail along with religion, childhood, genteel appearance and health.

Space

After the two phases of extensions, the completed Viewbank homestead had 12 rooms (**Figure 7.1**). Historian Judith Flanders (2003:lii) observed that houses of the lower middle class usually had four to six rooms, while those of the upper middle class had around 12. The house was surrounded by extensive terraced gardens with plantings of European trees and was entered via a set of stairs flanked by Italian cypresses. Its position, size and grandeur communicated status. Inside, space was structured to facilitate the negotiation of daily activities both along public versus private and gender lines. Space was also organised to separate the activities of servants from those of the Martins and visitors to the house.

Figure 7.1: Plan of Viewbank homestead showing room uses (Source: adapted from plan prepared by Heritage Victoria).

The gender divide that dictated much of 19th-century life also determined the spatial arrangement of family living spaces. For the man of the house, home was a private arena where he could express his control and command. For women, the home comprised all aspects of their lives: service, reproduction and nurturing (Hourani 1990:74). Consciously or unconsciously, the spatial arrangement of a house influences its occupants, formulating and reinforcing gender relationships (Hourani 1990:70). Traditionally, in the 19th century public areas of the house were at the front, and if seen as masculine they communicated dominance over the private or feminine areas to the rear of the house. Elements of this are suggested by the spatial layout of the archaeological remains of the homestead at Viewbank.

A hall for receiving, a drawing room for entertaining, and a dining room for eating were the public rooms displayed to outsiders (Flanders 2003:xxv; Young 2003:175). These rooms communicated the success and status of the occupants, and the greatest expense was used to fit and furnish these rooms (Flanders 2003:xxviii). The floor plan revealed by excavation at Viewbank can be interpreted using historical information on typical layouts and architectural features to suggest the use of each room and layout of the homestead (**Figure 7.1**).

The many-roomed Viewbank homestead suggests there were rooms for specific functions. At the front of the homestead, room 1 appears to have been the dining room and room 4 the drawing room. Room 3, between these rooms, would have been the transitional zone of the hall. Room 2, separated by two doorways to the southeast of room 1, may have functioned as access for the servants to serve food. Other houses of the era also had a drawing room and dining room flanking a large hall (Broadbent 1995:54; Carlin 2000:94). These three public rooms served the specific functions of entertaining, eating and receiving (Young 2003:175).

Excavations have revealed that rooms 1 and 4 had marble fireplaces, wallpaper and large decorative cornices contributing to a formal atmosphere. The fragments of marble recovered from room 1 were black, some with plaster rendering still attached, while the fragments in room 4 were pale grey, black veined marble. This provides further evidence that room 1 was the dining room and room 4 the drawing room. John Claudius Loudon in his 1843 advice manual for furnishings recommended '... that a white marble chimney piece was the most elegant for a drawing room, whereas coloured stone or marble was preferable for the dining room and library' (Loudon 2000). This pattern is observable in Australian historic houses from the 19th century where dark coloured decoration was associated with men and pale colours with women (Mitchell 2009:117). These conventions were based on rules of taste that dictated feminine furnishings for the drawing room and masculine for the dining room (Flanders 2003:215; Toy and Griffin c.1990:1). This was influenced by the post-meal tradition of men remaining in the dining room for port and cigars, while the women retired to the drawing room for tea and conversation (Lawson and Carlin 2004:96). Wallpaper fragments were also excavated from the drawing room and the hall.

This front section of the homestead was quite separate from the private sleeping and service areas behind. This demarcation between the public areas and the private rooms for the family members was important, as was separation of both of these areas from the rooms for servants (Flanders 2003:xxv).

Often the segregation of men and women continued in the private areas of the house, with a private sitting room for the women and a library or office for the man of the house. The sitting room was a 19th-century addition to houses and was used for the express purpose of leisure (Bushman 1993:256). The sitting room was explicitly feminine and was busy with sewing, needlework, painting, sketching, flower arranging and music. At Viewbank, a concentration of 17 pins was recovered from the front room of the original Williamson house in the front of a fireplace (room 5, **Figure 7.1**). Fourteen of the pins were complete and only three broken. This indicates that sewing activities being carried out in this room. This may, therefore, have been the Martin's sitting room. It is possible, however, that the pins were dropped by James Williamson's mother or sister prior to the Martin's arrival.

One of the rooms at Viewbank may have functioned as Dr Martin's private library or study. A man of business would require such a room even if he had an office elsewhere. As with the sitting room, the library or study was gender defined (Young 2003:185). Women were excluded from this space, where the man of the house would set about scholarly or business activities. Traditionally the library had a strongly masculine character with furnishings that were darker in colour creating a masculine aesthetic (Lane and Serle 1990:134).

If room 5 was a sitting room and room 7 a library, it is likely that the remaining three rooms (6, 8 and 9) in the centre of the homestead were bedrooms (**Figure 7.1**). Fragments of wallpaper were excavated from room 9 and the hallway adjacent to it, which may suggest that this was a bedroom and not a service room. As the largest of the three rooms, this may have been Dr and Mrs Martin's bedroom. It is likely that the Martin children shared the remaining two rooms.

A controlled physical environment was established for servants and was perhaps an attempt to contend with the constant invasions into the private and personal space of the employers (Russell 1994:169, 172). Housework conducted by servants was largely done at the rear of the house beyond the sight of visitors (Bushman 1993:262), and the kitchen, scullery and servants' bedrooms were divided from the rest of the house (Flanders 2003:xxv). Servants' low status was clearly communicated through their relegation to cramped, badly ventilated, out-of-sight areas of the house (Hourani 1990:74).

The relegation of service areas to the back of the house, while reflecting the lower status of servants, can also be seen to indicate the comparatively lower status of the women of the house than the men (Hourani 1990:74; Yentsch 1991:207). Historical evidence suggests that middle-class wives and daughters were involved in domestic duties within the home (Hourani 1990:74). Mrs Martin would have been responsible for household management and would have spent time in the service areas of the house supervising and organising the domestic servants. Daughters would assist with domestic duties and would sometimes take over the household management duties of their mother. Wives and daughters would sometimes work together in the house alongside the servants (Russell 1994:154).

The presence of servants meant that middle-class women had to negotiate class boundaries in the home and uphold important social distinctions within the house. The threat of the influence of the lowly morals of the working class, especially on children, was a serious concern and servants were expected to maintain standards of decorum. As such, Mrs Martin's ability to take firm control was vital (Davidoff and Hall 2002:395) and the housekeeper would have helped with negotiating daily interactions with the other servants.

The service area at Viewbank was situated at the back of the homestead. The second extension to the homestead added three rooms for this purpose (rooms 10, 11 and 12, **Figure 7.1**). Room 10 appears to have been the kitchen, with small rooms at either end for the scullery and pantry. The large number of servant bells recovered in this room indicates that it was the room where the servants spent most of their time; therefore, it is most likely to have been the kitchen. Room 12 at the back of the homestead had a system of drains in place, and therefore may have functioned as a scullery. Water pipes usually ran into the scullery where water was used for kitchen and laundry duties. Piped cold water was in use in grand houses in England by the 17th century, but only made its way into middle-class homes in the 19th century depending on water supply (Flanders 2003:91). While water supply was available in many Melbourne suburbs in the 1860s it was not connected in Heidelberg until 1889. However, the area had an abundance of creeks and rivers with most big properties having a water frontage. Water could be pumped from the river and stored for use, as was the case at nearby Banyule Homestead in the 1850s, however, there is no record of how Viewbank was supplied with water (Garden 1972:105, 165).

This second extension at the back of the homestead was clearly inferior in construction to that at the front. The floor in these service rooms was concrete, in contrast to the floorboards used in the remainder of the homestead. Concrete, in use from the earliest years of the Port Phillip district, was becoming more refined in the second half of the 19th century and was readily accepted as fireproof flooring (Lewis 1988:3–5). Hardwearing surfaces such as concrete were usually confined to corridors and service areas in the 19th century (Webster 2004:37). If they had any floor covering these were usually equally hardwearing.

The large hall at the front of the Viewbank homestead which conveyed status to visitors became much narrower at the rear of the homestead. This separated the ceremonial and utilitarian areas of the house (Ames 1978:28), and also reflected and defined the status of the servants. Also, it was possible to enter each room from the hall which allowed the servants to carry out their duties without disturbing the family (Ames 1978:28). When tasks such as cleaning, making beds and bringing in firewood were required in the public and private spaces of the house, negotiation was essential to establish the times this would take place (Russell 1993:30; Griffin 2004:50). When guests were present, the occasional, appropriate appearances of servants functioned as a necessary display of wealth and gentility. Servants were expected to answer the front door to visitors, and at other times were summoned from the rear of the house by servant bells. The servant bells at Viewbank were located in the kitchen (room 10) with bell pulls throughout the house (see discussion in Chapter 5). Each of the bells was designed to make a different chime so that the servants knew where in the house they were required.

It is not clear, however, where the servants slept at Viewbank. In smaller houses domestic servants sometimes slept in the kitchen, while in larger houses they slept in rooms at the rear or upper levels of the house (Flanders 2003:1). Room 11 at the rear of the Viewbank homestead may have been the housekeeper's bedroom as it was a small room with wallpaper (**Figure 7.1**). There may have been other bedrooms at the rear of the homestead in an area not uncovered by excavations, or in an adjacent building. Servants were often housed in a separate building in grand homes of this era (Dyster 1989:102–103), and outbuildings were mentioned when the Viewbank property was leased in 1875 (PROV, VPRS 460/P, Unit 1102, 1 June 1875). It is possible that at least the male servants were housed in an adjacent building.

The spatial arrangement of the homestead at Viewbank structured and facilitated the daily undertakings of both the Martin family and their servants. It follows the norms of society at the time and reflects the values of the day in terms of the roles of women and men in the domestic environment. The activities of the servants and their daily interactions with the Martins were carefully planned and managed through the spatial layout of the homestead and the use of servant bells. Their status and position was clearly communicated through space.

WORK

For the middle class in the 19th century, not to work came to be considered poor behaviour (Young 2003:17). Middle-class men had to work to support their families; unhindered leisure was not possible. It was therefore convenient for middle-class people to view work as noble and a signifier of good character. It was nevertheless important to separate work from home, and this can be seen to distinguish the middle class from the working class. Working-class homes of early Australia were often the site of work and income generation. Women took in laundry and sewing at home to earn money. Bakeries and butchers were also run from home, and women often ran hotels and lodging houses (Karskens 1999:53–56). This was not the case for the middle class. Some work, however, if it was not dirty, noisy or requiring a large work force, could be carried out at home (Davidoff and Hall 2002:366).

Although there is little archaeological or historical evidence for exactly where Dr Martin worked, it is possible that he had an office in the city and also did some work at home. The three pens and ink bottle in the Viewbank tip may have been used by Dr Martin for his work. It is likely that, on some occasions at least, he wrote business correspondence at home. Dr Martin may have also practised medicine from Viewbank at some point. It was not unusual for doctors to see patients in a segregated room of the house, and it is possible that Dr Martin did this at Viewbank. The *Sands and McDougall's Melbourne and Suburban Directories* from 1868 to 1871 list Dr Martin under 'Physicians, Surgeons and Medical Practitioners' at Viewbank. However, there is no archaeological evidence to support this; no surgical equipment was found in the tip and medicine bottles were only in numbers adequate to supply the family.

The middle class valued work, yet it was still not appropriate for middle-class women to work for income (Young 2003:18). As a result, various activities became valued as work for women: managing the house, raising children and philanthropic volunteer work. Only the very upper levels of the middle class could afford enough servants to make domestic work unnecessary for the women of the family (Flanders 2003:xxx). It is likely that Mrs Martin's work involved managing the domestic servants employed at Viewbank and raising her children. The Martin daughters may have also undertaken some domestic work.

A Workplace for Servants

To the Martin family, Viewbank was home, but to the servants it was a workplace. Servants in larger households were employed in a range of tasks and were differentiated by their titles (Higman 2002:129). Job titles for female servants included housekeeper (who was in charge of all other female servants), general maid, housemaid, cook, laundress, lady's maid, seamstress, nursemaid, governess and dairymaid. Male servant titles included butler, manservant, coachman, groom, and gardener. Most essential to employ was a general maid, then housemaid, cook, general manservant or coachman, and another maid for sewing or attending the women (Young 2003:55).

At Viewbank, the housekeeper Jane Warren would have been in charge of a number of indoor servants. In addition, a groom and coachman were probably also employed and the extensive gardens likely required the employment of at least one gardener. As discussed in Chapter 3, a total of between 6 and 18 servants were employed.

Domestic service was the largest employer of women in Australia. Even after commerce and industry became an attractive alternative from the 1860s, in Melbourne almost half of working women were servants (Anderson 1992:231; Evans and Saunders 1992:182). However, the 'servant problem' was a common topic among Australia's middle class (Anderson 1992:231; Russell 1994:167). Servants were scarce, and those in the cities were generally recent arrivals who were highly mobile and had a frustrating propensity to marry (Anderson 1992). Melbourne's middle-class women frequently complained of expensive, unreliable and obstinate servants (Russell 1994:181–186). However, hard unpleasant work, long hours, and high expectations by employers were the plight of the servants. There was also the strain of being isolated from family and friends, and under the constant supervision of an employer who would meddle in their moral and spiritual life (Anderson 1992:235).

Some of the artefacts recovered from Viewbank may, in fact, have belonged to or have been used by the servants. The majority of artefacts, however, were recovered from the tip which would have been used by both the Martins and their servants. Therefore, the association of artefacts from the tip with the servants is difficult and somewhat speculative. The various tools and the whetstone recovered from the tip may have been used by the servants as part of their daily chores. In addition, the female servants may have used some of the sewing equipment in their work. Most housemaids were expected to do an hour and a half of needlework in the afternoon (Flanders 2003:101), and in some households a seamstress was employed.

Of the large number of matching sets of table and teaware recovered from Viewbank, some would have been used by the servants. The Martins may have purchased one or more matching sets of ceramics for their servants such as the complementary Willow and gilt banded vessels. In addition, quality ceramics may have been handed on to servants if damaged or no longer wanted (Connah 2007:259). It is difficult to determine from the archaeological record, however, which method of acquisition was used (Brooks 2007:195), and is further complicated at Viewbank by the fact that the majority of the ceramics were recovered from the tip.

Regardless of these complications it can be inferred that the servants most likely had one or possibly more sets, and that these would be the cheapest and simplest sets in the assemblage. The cheaper 'Rhine' set and complementary 'Willow' vessels are likely to have been used by the servants. In her study of hierarchy at Government House in Sydney, Casey (2005:109) suggests that one type of service was used by the servants for almost all meals.

The four clay pipes are more likely to have been used by the servants than the Martin family. In the 19th century, clay pipes became associated with the poor: labourers, Irish people and convicts; the middle and upper classes preferring briar pipes, cigarettes, cigars and snuff (Walker 1984:4; Gojak and Stuart 1999:40; McCarthy 2001:150). Walker (1984:6), when discussing smoking in Australia, suggests that while some smoking could be done while at work, for the most part it was considered a leisure activity.

Farming Activities

Viewbank was more than just a home and showplace for gentility. Some farming activities were also carried out at the homestead, and probably employed servants and farm hands. Small Australian farms in the 19th century usually had a house cow for milk and butter, and a kitchen garden (Vines 1993:4). It is interesting that Viewbank, as the residence of a wealthy pastoralist, appears to have functioned as a small farm.

Records suggest that in Victoria it was not only rural homesteads like McCrae homestead on the Mornington Peninsula that had dairies and conducted farming activities, but also properties that were of commutable distance to the city. Como House in South Yarra conducted subsistence farming including the growing of fruit and vegetables, along with dairying. Also, Hubert De Castella (1861:104), who established a grand homestead on the Yarra not far from Viewbank, recorded that 'to take full advantage of it required setting up a good dairy, bringing on thin horses which were bought cheaply in town, training bullock teams, dairy cows and so on'. He recorded that he had up to 120 cows and that dairy production supplemented his income (De Castella 1861:115). He also later turned to winemaking.

Heidelberg's fertile soil and proximity to Melbourne made it a prominent supplier of agricultural produce to Melbourne. Serious and regular floods destroyed crops in Heidelberg and competition from better-serviced producers to the south of Melbourne led to a decline in Heidelberg's agricultural success. In the 1850s and 1860s, market gardening and agricultural activities in the area decreased, and many in the area turned to pastoral activities including dairying and grazing (Garden 1972:72–73, 105, 110).

The assemblage indicates that dairying was conducted at Viewbank. A minimum of six milkpans, used for separating cream from milk, were recovered from the Viewbank tip. While this number of milkpans does not suggest large scale commercial dairying, it probably indicates that dairying was undertaken for more than home use. In his book on English dairy farmers, Fussell (1966:2) suggests that it was not unusual for a wealthy gentleman or farmer to have a small herd of cattle for milking. At Viewbank, a barn, stackyard for hay, and cattle were listed as part of the property when it was leased in 1875 (PROV, VPRS 460/P, Unit 1102, 1 June 1875). Women were usually responsible for producing dairy products (Casey 1999:3), and it is possible that dairymaids were employed at Viewbank.

In Melbourne as early as 1838, dairying and produce farming were being encouraged in Fitzroy, Collingwood and Richmond (Godbold 1989:3). Although a small number of specialised dairy farms emerged early on, dairying was predominantly left to small farmers to supply their local district (Vines 1993:8) and this may have been the role of dairying at Viewbank. As land near Melbourne became scarce, farms on the city fringe supplied dairy produce to the city (Vines 1993:7). Dairying emerged as the dominant industry in Heidelberg from the 1860s to the 1880s. The Martins' involvement in this local industry is further evidenced by Willy becoming the co-founder of the Heidelberg Cheese Factory Company in 1871 (Garden 1972:121). The Viewbank property went on to become a large scale dairy when Harold Bartram purchased it in the early 20th century.

In addition to dairying, a plan on a lease document dating to when Mrs Martin moved from Viewbank in 1875 details that there was a 'garden and orchard' established at Viewbank along with paddocks (**Figure 7.2**) and there is mention elsewhere of an orange grove beside the river (Garden 1972:44). Orchards and market gardens were needed to provide the daily needs of the early colony (Vines 1993:4). Small mixed farms often incorporated an orchard to supply fruit and jam for the household, or for additional income. Orchards were frequently combined with dairying in higher rainfall areas to the north and east of Melbourne (Vines 1993:12). In his history of Heidelberg, Donald Garden (1972:109) records that during floods in the 1860s Dr Martin lost crops at Viewbank, which supports the view that some crop farming was also undertaken.

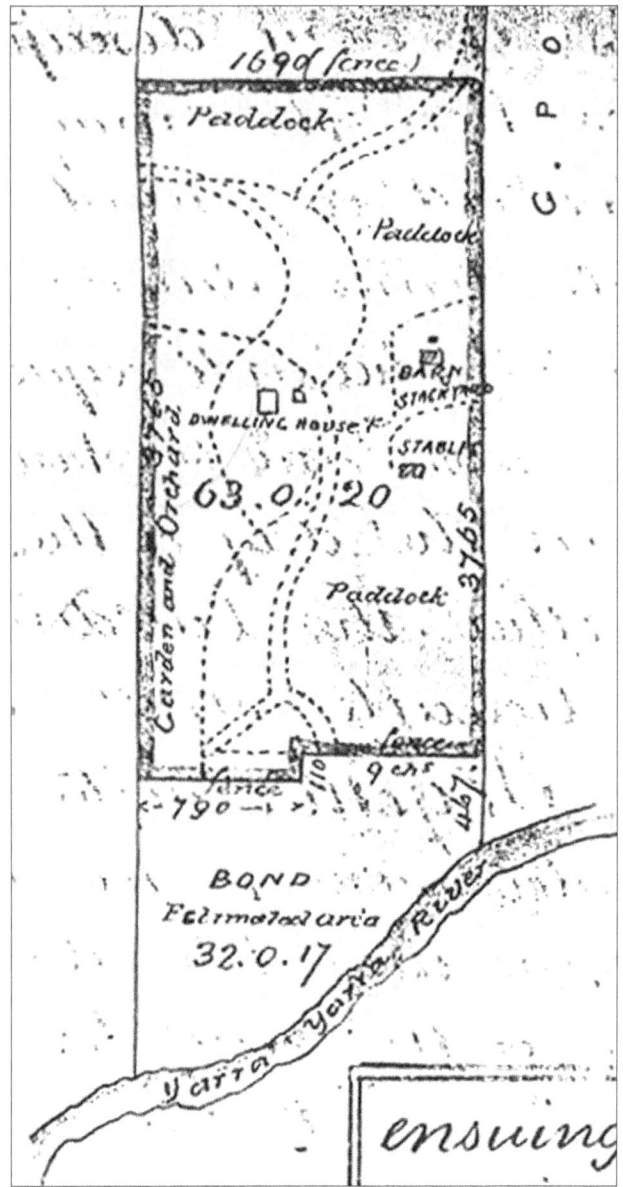

Figure 7.2: Detail of the plan of Viewbank from the 1875 lease showing the dwelling house, barn, stackyard and stables (Source: PROV, VPRS 460/P, Unit 1102, 1 June 1875).

Viewbank was as much a place of work as a home. Domestic work was conducted by both servants and the Martin women, and Dr Martin may have also carried out some incidental business or medical work. Further, Viewbank operated to some extent as a working property. It appears that both farming, food gardening and dairying activities were taking place and that these activities may have been for income as well as for home consumption. In the context of the growing settlement in Port Phillip this was not unusual. The large size of the estates at Heidelberg, and the fact that many of the occupants had extensive country pastoral runs, made farming activities a natural choice (Garden 1972:50). In the Australian context, this presented no challenge to gentility.

Leisure

Leisure for the middle class was not always about relaxation and pleasure, but also self-improvement and health. Some of the leisure activities at Viewbank homestead are suggested by the artefacts, particularly activities for shared family evenings. Such artefacts included dominoes, die and gaming counters. Domino sets come with varying numbers of tiles and it appears that the five dominoes from Viewbank are from one set. Dominoes and dice are both used to play a variety of games, with dice also sometimes used for gambling. A copper alloy fish figurine (**Figure 5.16**) may have been a gaming counter. Bone fish shaped counters were used for games from around 1840 or even earlier (Bell 2000:14).

These shared evenings were part of the refined lifestyle of the middle class and reflected ideals of domesticity. Other activities, not revealed by the assemblage, such as reading and music playing probably took place at Viewbank. Reading aloud was an important skill and was a pastime centred in education (Russell 1994:157). This was also true for playing music. In many cases reading and music were an accompaniment to the needlework of the women. Images of drawing room scenes from the era often show men reading in relaxed poses, while women sit with their needlework.

For women, it was important to keep the 'hands busy'. The primary evidence for this from the Viewbank assemblage is in the form of needlework equipment. While painting, sketching, flower arranging and music were probably also important leisure activities for the Martin women, they are less likely to be detected in the archaeological record. Such activities were a tribute to talent and leisure, but were in fact rather arduous forms of leisure (Russell 1994:97).

Sewing is often seen as a necessary source of income for working-class women in the 19th century, while in contrast it is viewed as a leisure activity for middle-class women (Lydon 1993b; Karskens 2001:80). Embroidery and decorative needlework in particular were a symbol of feminine, leisured lifestyle: an index of gentility (Lydon 1993b:129–130). However, through the 19th century increasingly more working-class women were doing needle crafts for leisure, and there is some evidence for this at Casselden Place in inner Melbourne (Porter and Ferrier 2006:387–388).

It is likely that both leisure and necessity motivated the needlework at Viewbank. The numerous pins are most likely to have been used for sewing, but could have been used for a range of needlework. It is also possible that they were used to fasten clothes (men's or women's), or fasten documents (Beaudry 2006:8). The pins and thimbles found at Viewbank may have been used by the housemaids who were expected to do some sewing each day, or a seamstress. The four thimbles were simple and undecorated indicating that they were utilitarian items. Utilitarian needlework, overseen by the woman of the house, would have included sewing, mending, and remaking garments, sheets and linens (Beaudry 2006:5). The Martin women would have done fancy needlework in the presence of guests, and when making calls on the women of other households to demonstrate their abilities in the feminine arts (Beaudry 2006:5, 106). At other times, in private, practical needlework like mending or knitting socks would be done (Mitchell 2009:230). Only less well-off women would make dresses and other large items of clothing: the well-off would do only mending (Flanders 2003:223, 265).

In the 19th century, almost all daughters, regardless of class, were taught to sew by their mothers (Beaudry 2006:105). The presence of a child-sized thimble in the Viewbank tip suggests that this was the case. Social expectations demanded it, and not doing so could bring disapproval (Parker 1984:9).

Embroidery was one of the most popular forms of fancy work and came to represent femininity as well as a genteel and leisured lifestyle from the 18th century (Beaudry 2006:4). As Parker (1984:11) explains:

> embroidery was supposed to signify femininity – docility, obedience, love of home, and a life without work – it showed the embroiderer to be a deserving, worthy wife and mother. Thus the art played a crucial part in maintaining the class position of the household, displaying the value of a man's wife and the condition of his economic circumstances.

Parker (1984:14) also draws attention to the fact that women were not passive participants in this, but drew satisfaction from embroidery.

The three lace bobbins recovered from the tip indicate that the luxury item, lace, was being made by hand at Viewbank. Although machine-made lace was available in the second half of the 19th century (Sykes 1988:3–4), it appears from archaeological evidence that hand-made lace was still popular. Beaudry (2006:151–152), in her research on needlework and sewing, suggests that while some lace was made by genteel ladies as a delicate art, lace-making was also an important cottage industry in Britain and its colonies well into the 19th century. It is difficult to determine whether the Martin women made lace as genteel leisure, or a servant was employed in this task.

The bone netting needle found in the Viewbank tip indicates that delicate items, such as doilies, were being made by netting, a similar technique to tatting. This was another form of fancy needlework for leisure. Also, decorating button moulds with fabric was a distinguished pastime for Victorian ladies (Iacono 1999:53), and had a practical outcome. Interestingly, fabric covered buttons were the most common button decoration in the Viewbank assemblage.

The only possible evidence for the leisure activities of the men from the Viewbank assemblage was in the form of hunting and shooting. These activities were considered cultivated and useful pastimes for men, much like drawing and needlework were for women (Young 2003:17). Three .50 calibre cartridges dating from 1846 and one shotgun cartridge dating from 1850 were recovered from the tip. These may be the result of hunting activity, but it is unlikely that they would have been discarded in the tip. Rather, they were probably discarded during hunting or shooting.

Of the range of possible leisure activities at Viewbank, sewing is the most visible in the archaeological record. The record also suggests that games and hunting were leisure pastimes at Viewbank, and a range of other activities not suggested by the archaeology, such as music and art, would also have formed an important part of daily life for families such as the Martins.

GENTEEL DINING

Food and tea service provided an opportunity for the display of both wealth and the subtle range of behaviours associated with gentility (Fitts 1999; Young 2003:182). In the words of Mrs Beeton (1861:905) in her book on household management: 'The rank which a people occupy in the grand scale may be measured by their way of taking their meals.' Each type of meal and each course within it required the table to be set in a genteel manner using the appropriate tableware. A well set table for genteel dining was orderly, aesthetic and fashionable and was one of the most significant platforms for displays of gentility.

A beautifully set table was part of the dining experience. Historical records tell us that Mrs Martin had inherited a Spanish mahogany dining table (Niall 2004:30). This may have been covered with a baize table cover for heat protection and a white damask cloth for the meal to be served on (Lawson and Carlin 2004:96). Each course of a meal had to be facilitated by the appropriate tableware. The breakfast table was also set in a prescribed way, and although services were smaller they also had purpose-specific vessels.

Perhaps the most important aspect of genteel dining was the use of matching sets to present an orderly meal (Wall 1994:147–158; Fitts 1999; Young 2003:182). Of the ceramic tableware vessels recovered from the tip, 38.6 percent were part of a matching set and at least 11 individual sets of tableware were represented. Nine of the sets included both consuming and serving vessels, while the white granite 'Berlin Swirl' set was the only matching set with table and teaware vessels. A further 23.4 percent of the tableware vessels were possibly part of three complementary sets. These vessels were in common decorations which were similar but not identical. Such vessels were likely purchased on an *ad hoc* basis and may or may not have subsequently been used together as a set (Lawrence *et al.* 2009:75). There were also matching sets in the teaware, with 31.7 percent of the teaware being part of at least nine matching sets. An additional 41.3 percent of the teaware vessels were possibly used in five complementary sets.

Having the appropriate set for each type of meal was an important part of genteel dining. A middle-class family would have sets for everyday use, separate sets for breakfast, lunch and dinner, and best sets (Fitts 1999:52; Young 2003:182). Wealthy households would also have cheaper ceramics for use by servants (Spencer-Wood 1987:16). The use of different sets distinguished the level of importance of each meal, for example to contrast a Sunday dinner from a weekday dinner (Wall 1994:146). While it is impossible to determine the exact type of meal that a set was used for from the archaeological record, it is possible to speculate on the use of each set in the assemblage in order to facilitate interpretation. To do so, it is useful to draw on historical accounts of what meals entailed.

In British culture, there were three major types of dinners: weeknight dinners, Sunday dinners and dinner parties (Mitchell 2009:126). On weeknights, adult members of the family generally dined alone in the dining room, children in the nursery, and servants in the kitchen. Children and servants generally received simple meat and potato meals (Flanders 2003:225), with the adult family members meals being more substantial and varied. The quantity and variety of matching sets recovered from Viewbank suggest that the Martins were indeed using different sets for different meals and possibly supplying servants with a separate set or sets.

A set such as the blue transfer print 'Queen's' pattern or the Mason's Chinese pattern may have been used for the formal weekday dinners of the adult members of the family held in the dining room. Sunday dinners were comparatively more elaborate affairs, and dinner parties more so again with the needs of all guests being accommodated by the service of numerous dishes (Flanders 2003:236). The larger and relatively more expensively decorated 'Summer Flowers' set was likely one of the Martins' best sets and may have been used for Sunday dinners or when receiving guests. It is possible that other expensive sets were taken by Mrs Martin when she left Viewbank or given to the Martin children and are not present in the archaeological record.

Breakfast and lunch were less formal affairs but still required their own tablewares. In the Victorian era, breakfast was served early and usually included one hot meat dish and toast with tea (Flanders 2003:225). The 'Bagdad' [sic] and 'Clematis' sets of plates may have been for breakfasts. Men would have lunch at the club or at work, while women and children would have a light cooked lunch at home often utilising leftovers (Flanders 2003:225; Mitchell 2009:126). The less expensive sets such as the 'Asiatic Pheasants' and 'Rhine' sets may have been used to serve lunches.

As noted above, some sets may have been for use by the servants while other sets may have been multi-purpose. Casey (2005:104) found evidence that simply decorated banded, moulded or plain vessels in tea and tableware forms were multipurpose sets not designated to lunch or dinner.

The number of tea sets also suggests their use for different purposes: when guests called, between meals and by servants. The sprigged and geometric transfer-printed sets may have been used for taking tea between meals. The gilt banded and tea leaf teawares had variations and were recorded as complementary sets, but may in fact represent a series of larger sets in these popular patterns. As with the tableware, the cheaper sets such as the 'Marble' pattern and any complementary sets were likely used by the servants.

The relative absence of tea service vessels such as teapots and creamers in the assemblage is likely because of the use of a silver tea service which would not be found in the archaeological record. As silver has an intrinsic value in spite of changing fashions it is likely that any silverware would have been retained by Mrs Martin or handed down to one of her children.

The Viewbank assemblage shows that genteel dining and tea service were part of everyday life, not just when receiving guests. Breakfasts, lunches and servants meals in the Martin household all bore the hallmark of gentility, but with a less elaborate air than when guests were in attendance.

The Viewbank dining and tea service assemblage is consistent with the use of a variety of different matching sets for different meals and occasions, but within sets genteel dining also required a wide range of vessel forms, many with specific uses (Shackel 1993:30–42; Fitts 1999:54). Different sized plates along with specialised serving vessels such as soup tureens and sauce boats can be associated with more elaborate table etiquette (Yentsch 1991:221). A standard dinner service could include 80 to 140 vessels with a range of plate sizes, sauce tureens, soup tureens, platters, serving dishes, butter dishes, pitchers and gravy boats (Fitts 1999:182; Young 2003). A large variety of forms were recovered from the Viewbank tip.

Of the 11 matching tableware sets, eight had more than one vessel form, and of the three possible complementary sets all had multiple vessel forms. The 10-inch or table plate was the most common in the Viewbank assemblage, closely followed by the 9-inch supper plate and 8-inch twiffler. A smaller number of soup plates and 7-inch muffin plates were represented. The larger plates would have been used for main courses while the smaller plates may have been used as side or dessert plates, or possibly breakfast or afternoon tea service. Single-function vessels included soup tureens, sauce tureens, ladles, drainers, serving dishes, platters and egg cups. Six vessel forms were identified in the tea service assemblage: teacup, saucer, mug, teapot, jug and serving dish. Overall, this represents a wide variety of vessel forms, many of which were purpose specific.

Good taste and therefore fashion were important aspects of gentility, and there is evidence in the Viewbank dining and tea service assemblages that the Martins were keeping up with fashions. Archaeological evidence suggests that Australians preferred colourful table settings, particularly transfer-prints, in accordance with British and British colonial tastes (Lawrence 2003:25, 26; Brooks 2010), and this is reflected in the Viewbank assemblage. Of the dining assemblage, 58 per cent of the vessels with identifiable decorations were colourful including transfer-prints and flow transfer in blue, black, green, grey, purple and with additional colourful enamelled or gilt decoration. A further 26 per cent of the assemblage had gilt decoration and 23 per cent were plain, moulded and white granite vessels. A similar pattern was represented in the tea service vessels with 53 per cent having colourful decorations including transfer-prints, hand-painted vessels, flow transfers and multiple decorations. There was a higher percentage of gilt decorated vessels at 38 per cent, and a slightly lower number of plain and moulded vessels at 18 per cent. With regard to fashionable patterns, the 'Summer Flowers' set and other vessels with enamelled decoration were the height of Victorian fashion: busy and dark toned. A number of popular patterns such as Chinese scenes, classical scenes, 'Rhine', 'Asiatic Pheasants' and 'Willow' were also represented. Further, plain or simply decorated white granite was a relatively more expensive and highly fashionable ceramic type in the United States from the 1850s (Majewski and O'Brien 1987:120–124; Miller 1991:6; Ewins 1997:46–47). Its popularity was largely the result of its association with the sanctity of churches, and contrast to capitalist markets (Wall 1992:72). However, it is not clear whether this association carried across to Australia. Many Staffordshire potteries made ceramics specifically for the United States market, and when the American Civil War commenced in 1861, had to find alternative markets for these wares (Brooks 2005:58–59). The white granite vessels in the Viewbank assemblage date tightly to the start of the Civil War. It is unclear whether white granite was marketed as the latest fashion in Australia or sold off cheaply after the United States market contracted. Without a comprehensive study for Australian preferences similar to those done by Samford (2000) or Majewski and Schiffer (2001) for the United States market, it is difficult to determine the changing fashion in patterns over time in Australia (Brooks 2005a:34).

Evidence of keeping up with fashion is, however, present in the dates of the ceramic tableware recovered from Viewbank, which indicate that they were updated regularly. Two sets may have been brought to Australia by the family or purchased in their early years in Victoria: the 'Summer Flowers' set which was manufactured between 1830 and 1859 and the Chinese transfer-printed Masons plates which were made in Staffordshire between 1820 and 1854. These two, slightly older sets, may have been discarded when the Martins left Viewbank rather than passed on to the Martin children. These were updated with 'Bagdad' pattern plates made between 1851 and 1862 and white granite vessels purchased in the early 1860s. A debt to John Stanway for crockery in 1874 indicates that they were still purchasing ceramics in their last years at Viewbank (PROV, VPRS 7591/P2, Unit 17, File 12-586, 11 February 1875). Perhaps one of their final purchases while at Viewbank was a 'Rhine' plate which dated to after 1869. Only one maker was identified on the ceramic teawares, Liddle, Elliot and Son who manufactured ceramics between 1862 and 1871, so patterns of purchasing could not be determined in the same way as for the tableware. However, the decorative techniques and purchasing patterns for the ceramic tableware indicate the Martins' interest in keeping up with fashion.

Matching sets of cutlery were also a part of genteel dining (Young 2003:181). Two of the cutlery items recovered from Viewbank were in the popular 'Fiddle' design and may have been a set. The Martins would have almost certainly had one or two silver cutlery sets. Again, cutlery items could be purpose-specific, but the small cutlery assemblage reveals little of this except for the handle of what might have been a mustard spoon.

A number of glass vessels also complemented the ceramics at the table. Six glass serving dishes and three glass bowls were found, and were probably used to serve condiments and side dishes. These were all press-moulded or cut glass and were highly decorated. Three glass jugs may also have been for serving sauces. A stemmed colourless dessert glass was a purpose-specific dessert vessel.

Drinking glasses were also an important part of a well set table. At Viewbank, a minimum of 13 tumblers were recovered from the tip, far fewer than the 25 stemmed glasses. This is unusual: as Jones (2000:224–225) argues, tumblers are usually the most common glass tableware form recovered from archaeological sites. It is difficult to determine whether tumblers as opposed to stemmed glasses have different status connotations. Stemmed drinking glasses were used for wine, champagne, claret and cordial while tumblers were used for ale, whiskey, soda water, lemonade and iced tea (Jones 2000:224–225). Wine was considered more genteel than beer or hard liquor which may explain the predominance of stemmed glasses. Alternatively, it may be the result of stemmed glasses being preferred for drinking at the table, and tumblers away from the table (Yamin 1998:83). While the pattern may simply be the result of the higher breakage rate of fragile stemware, it is likely that it represents a preference for stemmed drinking glasses.

The drinking glasses recovered from the Viewbank tip were of a high quality. Almost all of the 25 stemmed drinking glasses were cut glass. Cut glass vessels, whether in simple or elaborate patterns, were a prestigious item (Jones 2000:174). Jones (2000:224) suggests that by 1840 the variety of stemware styles began to increase, and this is reflected in the Viewbank assemblage. Patterns included cut panels, facets or flutes, and alternating facets and flutes on the bodies and stems. These were common decorations for 19th-century glassware (Jones 2000:174). As with the stemware, the majority of the 13 tumblers from the tip had cut decoration in panels, flutes, or alternating flutes, panels or mitres. Panels were the most common decorative motif on tumblers in the 19th century (Jones 2000:225) and this is reflected at Viewbank. A minimum of two tumblers have similar decorations, but were pressed imitations of cut glass. Five of the tumbler bases feature a star or sunburst. The Martins' preference for the more expensive cut glass drinking glasses is indicative of their ability to afford these items in large numbers.

Wine was readily available from the very early years of the Port Phillip district, and the Yarra Valley, the location of Viewbank, was a popular wine growing region (Beeston 1994:49). The presence of a corkscrew in the assemblage supports the drinking of wine at Viewbank. The 11 wine bottles and many of the 106 beer/wine bottles also support this, although there is no way of confirming whether the family purchased alcohol in these bottles. One bottle each of gin, cognac and whiskey indicate that at least some spirits were being consumed. Also, two decorative, colourless glass stoppers were from decanters which probably held alcohol.

The historical records present something of a contradiction on Dr Martin's attitude to alcohol. Dr Martin was one of about 100 people who signed a petition in an attempt to prevent Henry Baker, publican of the Old England Hotel in Heidelberg, from obtaining a licence in 1849. The petitioners were concerned that the hotel would promote drunkenness, immorality, disruption to the Sabbath and neighbourhood (PROV, VPRS box LD3). However, when his daughter Charlotte married, Dr Martin provided 'Barrels of Ale ... for all comers' (HHS 1862). The archaeological evidence suggests that the Martins partook of alcohol as part of their genteel dining.

A variety of matching sets with a range of vessel forms in good taste were necessary to meet the specific genteel requirements of each meal. It would appear that breakfast, lunch, afternoon tea and dinner were each catered for with the appropriate tableware, flatware and glassware at Viewbank. The appropriate use and display of table settings, in line with appropriate social protocol, was as important as its acquisition (Burley 2000:404).

Social Events

Social events were an important part of genteel performance and included calls, dinner parties, balls, parties and weddings. In the archaeological record, a large quantity of quality tableware in an assemblage indicates that the tools required for entertaining were available (Yamin 1998:82). The array of ceramic tableware and number of matching sets indicate that dinner parties would have been well within the means of the Martin family. Also, the 25 stemmed glasses in a variety of shapes and the 13 tumblers in the Viewbank assemblage are suggestive of a large enough collection of drinking glasses to host parties.

The layout of the Viewbank homestead is also suggestive of the way the Martins entertained at home. The dining room was regarded as a public space and the location for dinner parties. This room was formal and dominated by a large dining table. Further, the presence of a drawing room, such as the one at Viewbank, was an English adaptation specifically designed for social interaction (Davidoff and Hall 2002:377). This was where the family would entertain guests and gather to play games, read or have prayers.

The historical record shows that the Martins did, on occasion, throw large and lavish parties at Viewbank (Niall 2004:33). A 1933 article on Dr Martin states: 'Dr Martin entertained freely, and is well remembered by a few old residents for his famous Christmas parties' (Heidelberg Relief Organisation 1933). Hosting a party often involved rearranging the house so that more rooms could be used for the entertainment of guests (Russell 1994:74; Young 2003:74–75). Decorations and flowers would adorn the whole house, while music and food completed the event. A letter from Edward Graham to James Graham in 1855 states:

> We had merry times about New Year. A magnificent ball at Dr Martin's being the long-promised house heating. Dr Youl, the son-in-law to be, being a most efficient master of ceremonies. Then we had a ball at the McCraes', evening parties here, at the Davidsons', here and at the Butlers', and Randall's farewell bachelor party at the Port Phillip, Capel's farewell and lastly Randall's wedding (Graham 1998:46).

This was a busy schedule. Regular parties formed a central part of Melbourne society.

Paying calls, a female domain, was essential to the establishment and maintenance of networks in society. Imported from Britain, the system and etiquette of calls were rigid and important for the 'established middle class' including the Martins (Russell 1994:50). Calls were made out of courtesy to new acquaintances or as a thank you for hospitality. They were also made as congratulations, upon a birth or marriage, or condolence at the death of a family member. Tea would be served, and calls would last from 15 to 30 minutes (Mitchell 2009:151). The best matching sets of teaware, possibly the flow and enamelled floral set or the 'Florentine' set, would have been used at Viewbank when receiving calls, and probably a silver tea service. Women would often take embroidery or fancy work with them when calling on the women of other households (Beaudry 2006:106).

The correct timing and circumstance of calls was an important part of etiquette and failing in this was met with disapproval. Upon the marriage of Annie Martin, Edward Graham wrote to James Graham 'The Martins have been very odd about it. Mrs Cobham never was asked to the wedding and has received no cards. Neither have I, although except as your brother they might have been sent.' It appears that the Martin women were neglecting their social roles. The strain of constant calls could be exhausting, visiting a number of families in an afternoon two or three times a week (Russell 1994:51). This would have been particularly frantic after a celebration, but clearly disapproval was easily acquired.

Another important part of paying calls was the leaving of cards. Cards were left to issue invitations, respond to invitations, or to send condolences or congratulations. It was important that cards be left in person, and this was the responsibility of the women of the household. Therefore, this functioned as another expression of the availability of leisure time and a display of status (Ames 1978:43). The hall was the location for this ritual, and as such the size of the hall and the quality of the furnishings within conveyed status to all visitors (Ames 1978:27). At Viewbank, the hall was ample enough to accommodate the full range of hall furnishings including a hall stand, card receiver, chairs and a settee.

Weddings were another important social event and were celebrated with lavish ceremonies and parties. The elaborate celebrations for Charlotte Martin's wedding to John Fenton overtook the whole of Heidelberg:

> An arch decorated with flowers and evergreens was erected at the entrance to the Church ground: the Church itself being densely crowded to witness the ceremony which was performed in an impressive manner by the Rev. J. Lyner ...

> The fair Bride attracted universal attention, even in the midst of a bevy of Bridesmaids. A salvo of artillery from the Racecourse announced the tying of the Nuptual [sic] Knot and, on leaving the Church, children dressed in white scattered flowers before the happy pair (HHS 1862).

When Willy Martin married Minnie Graham in 1874, James Graham wrote of the lavish event to former Governor Charles La Trobe:

> We had a great gathering of old friends. Of the number invited exactly 100 accepted and we sat down 97 to breakfast. The Church was beautifully decorated ... All our friends vied with each other in sending us really cartloads of choice flowers and branches and actually trees loaded with oranges and blossoms for our decorations. The day was lovely and in a word everything passed off as well as we could possibly wish (GP 19 May 1874).

These events and social occasions were an essential part of genteel performance and the functioning of the middle class in Melbourne.

Religion

There was a strong association between the middle classes and a Christian way of life. Religious observance was necessary and included church attendance, family worship, observance of the Sabbath and interest in religious literature (Davidoff and Hall 2002:76). The absence of religious artefacts in the Viewbank assemblage does not indicate a lack of faith of the Martin family, who historical records show were practicing Anglicans.

Historical records show that Dr Martin was trustee of St. John's Church of England in Heidelberg, which he helped to establish. Work commenced on building the church in 1849 and it opened in 1851 (Garden 1972:68). The vicar complained that Dr Martin interfered with parish matters although rarely attended church (Garden 1972:97–98). Conflict arose because Dr Martin expected influence for his patronage, which displeased the vicar (Niall 2004:33). It seems his role in the church had more to do with standing in society than devout belief. Religion gave aspirational men a sense of self-respect and an air of decency (Young 2003:81). With his Scottish background it is surprising that Dr Martin was Anglican, and this suggests the power of the Church of England as an establishment church.

To a large extent, mothers were responsible for the spiritual guidance of their children. Religion was tightly connected to morality and respectability and these were important lessons for children. Suggestive of Mrs Martin's interest in the religion of her children is that she gave her daughter Lucy a

Bible upon her marriage (Niall 2002:33). Of course it is difficult to determine what this reflects in terms of devout belief versus a customary gift.

It is not surprising that symbolic religious objects were not found in the Viewbank assemblage. It was not appropriate for middle-class Anglicans to display crucifixes or other religious paraphernalia. Catholics were much more likely to display religious items and jewellery and these are often found on archaeological sites (Mezey 2005:91; Davies in press).

Religious belief could be subtly communicated through household items. Middle-class women became responsible for creating the home as a moral sanctuary suitable for raising their children with the values of gentility and Christian morality (Fitts 1999:39). There is some evidence in the Viewbank assemblage that Mrs Martin did this, in the form of fashionable tableware, matching toilet sets and flowerpots. However, it is difficult to define this as Christian belief as opposed to genteel values.

In the United States, historical archaeologists have associated Gothic style with the middle class and Christian belief. Fitts (1999:47) argues that Gothic style in architecture, furniture, perfume bottles, pickle bottles and tableware became fashionable in the United States reflecting Gothic churches (ideal places for Christian nurture). Di Zerega Wall (1992:79) suggests that white granite vessels in Gothic shapes were popular because of their association with the sanctity of churches and contrast to capitalist markets. However, there is little evidence that this association was taken up in Australia. Both pickle bottles in Gothic shapes and 'Girard' white granite vessels are present in the Viewbank assemblage. However, as discussed in Chapter 6, this is likely to be the result of the availability in Australia of goods intended for the American market.

There is no way of knowing what the Martins' religious activities were in terms of daily prayers and bible reading, or whether their servants were expected to attend church. However, what can be gathered from the historical and archaeological record is that while the Martins gave the outward appearance to those around them that they were Anglican, there is little suggestion that they were devout in their belief. For them religion may have been more about society and appearances (Young 2003:81).

CHILDHOOD

In the 19th century, childhood was seen as a precious phase of life and children were treated as individuals who were innocent and unspoiled (Davidoff and Hall 2002:343). There is some suggestion that child-centredness was even more pronounced in middle-class families in Australia than in Britain (Maynard 1994:109). In the archaeological record, child-centredness can be reflected in children having individual possessions and designated space. In the Viewbank assemblage one clear example of this was Willy's mug, gilded with his first name Robert (**Figure 5.5**).

With regard to space, it was seen as ideal that children be given their own rooms where possible (Praetzellis and Praetzellis 1992:92). In reality, the large families of the 19th century made it difficult to give each child a separate room. In this case boys and girls were separated, and ideally also older children from younger children (Flanders 2003:xxv). In addition, it was common in England to have a nursery for the use of children (Davidoff and Hall 2002:375), however this was not common in Australia (Kociumbas 1997:94, 114). Hourani's (1990:76) study of Australian middle-class homes of four to 15 rooms indicates that, generally, children's bedrooms were much smaller than the master bedroom and that there was no nursery. It is likely that the Martin children shared two or three rooms at Viewbank.

Another group of possessions for children, and part of changing attitudes to childhood in the 19th century, were 'moralising china' vessels. These were tableware and teaware items specifically for children, which had educational or moral phrases and decorations (Karskens 1999:141). At Viewbank, a mug with gilt lettering reading 'A Pres... for// A good ...' was found and was almost identical to the mug marked 'Robert'. Mugs with the phrase 'A present for a good girl [boy]' were for rewarding and encouraging good behaviour (Karskens 1999:141). The popularity of these items has been noted on many working-class Australian sites from the 19th century (Karskens 2001:76; Godden Mackay Logan *et al.* 2004a:104).

It also appears that certain expenditure was made on children's toys at Viewbank. Most of the toys dated closely to the Martin period of occupation suggesting that the toys were of the latest fashions. Also, the dolls and the matching set of dolls teaware would have been relatively expensive to purchase (Ellis 2001:48). The Martin children may well have had more expensive toys than these, as toys of significant value and expense would not have been discarded.

Toys and games became increasingly popular from the 1830s and also indicated attitudes to childhood as a separate phase of life marked by innocence and play (Karskens 2001:179). Some of the toys found at Viewbank were purely for fun, such as two marbles. Marbles were purchased in large lots and were easily lost. In her archaeological study of children's play, Wilkie (2000:102) suggests that children were more likely to make the effort to retrieve large or ornate marbles. Other toys for fun found at Viewbank were four cap gun cartridges, and a crayon.

In many cases toys were about more than play: when purchased by adults, they represent attempts to enforce and encourage certain behaviour (Wilkie 2000:101). Toys were used to teach manners, domestic duties and consumerism. For instance, toy tea sets were used to teach table manners (Fitts 1999:54), and also the correct purchasing of the tools required for genteel dining. At Viewbank, a press-moulded doll's tea set comprising a teacup, two saucers, teapot and sugar bowl were found. Toy tea items have also been recovered from working-class urban sites from the 19th century (e.g. Karskens 1999:179; Godden Mackay Logan et al. 2004b:298–299). For girls, toys were also used for learning about domestic duties like sewing and laundering (Praetzellis and Praetzellis 1992:92).

Most 19th-century dolls depicted adults, and their aim was to enforce female identity (Wilkie 2000:102). Adult dolls could also be used to educate regarding fashion and etiquette. Some of the jointed dolls at Viewbank had heeled boots and there is some suggestion that heeled boots date to after the 1860s (Pritchett and Pastron 1983: 332). This would suggest that the dolls were purchased for the Martin girls in their teenage years, the youngest daughters being 14 and 16 in 1860.

There is some archaeological evidence that the Martin children were educated at home in the form of 12 slate pencil fragments recovered from the tip. These represent a minimum of two pencils, but probably more. Slate pencils and writing slates were cheap and durable writing implements often used for educating children (Iacono 1999:78; Ellis 2001; Davies 2005:64) and again this is suggestive of investment in children (Yamin 2002:118). It is possible that the Martin family employed a governess to teach the children. Compulsory schooling was not introduced in Victoria until 1872 (Ellis 2001:17–18), but it is also possible that the Martin children were sent to the school in Heidelberg. Education was clearly important to the Martins, at least for their son. The historical records show that Willy was sent to Cambridge for his higher education (De Serville 1991:318). Both play and education were a vital part of raising children along genteel guidelines.

Genteel Appearance

Fashion and correct taste in clothes were important mechanisms in defining status and class in the new colony of Melbourne (Russell 1994:80). There is significantly more evidence of this for the women of Viewbank than the men, and this reflects the higher importance of fashion and appearance for women at this time.

Masculine Appearance

Personal appearance was a vitally important part of successfully developing connections in the genteel world of the 19th century. To play the part, a man had to look the part and men communicated their status through their clothing. Dress for middle-class men in Australia was as important, and essentially the same, as in Europe. However, a greater variety was noted by contemporary testimonies (Maynard 1994:82–83). A photograph of Dr Martin (**Figure 3.1**) shows that he wore a high stand collar and tied stock which left much of his crisp white shirt showing. Unfortunately the date that this was taken is unknown.

At Viewbank, artefacts possibly relating to masculine appearance included buttons, clothing fastenings and part of a boot. It is difficult to determine which of the buttons in Viewbank assemblage were from men's clothes and which were from women's as decorative buttons were used on the clothes of both sexes. The military buttons recovered from Viewbank with anchors and Prince of Wales feathers were most likely from military uniforms or men's clothing. Military buttons were advertised in Sears and Roebuck catalogues and used on civilian clothing (Israel 1968:320). Some of the small buttons (8–15 mm) may have been used for men's underclothing, shirts and waistcoats (Birmingham 1992:105). Other closures in the assemblage may have been cuff links or men's clothing fastenings. A stacked heel from what appears to be a man's boot may have belonged to one of the Martin men.

Feminine Appearance

When appearing in public it was vitally important for women to present and define themselves as ladies (Russell 1994:79). A number of personal items in the Viewbank assemblage suggest this: six items of jewellery, beads, possibly some of the buttons, hook and eye fastenings, possible suspender belt and undergarment fastenings, three perfume bottles, and a brisé fan. It is impossible to determine whether these items belonged to Mrs Martin or her daughters. They do, however, indicate that some, or all, of the women of the house placed particular importance on their appearance.

Many of the buttons in the Viewbank assemblage were likely to be from the clothing of Mrs Martin and her daughters. Nine fabric covered buttons were found in the Viewbank tip and one in the homestead contexts. Around the 1860s, it became popular to match the fabric on the button to that of the garment, particularly for women's dresses (Albert and Kent 1971:47–48). Three fancy buttons with a flower in the centre were also likely to be from women's clothes. The majority of the Viewbank buttons were small, possibly because undergarments and shirts had more buttons than outer garments, which frequently used hook and eyes.

Women's close fitting outer garments and bodices commonly used hook and eye fastenings (Kiplinger 2004:7–8), which were identified in the Viewbank assemblage. Women's clothing, particularly corsets, restricted mobility. Bending or picking things up was not possible while in a corset. This made it clear that others were employed to do most of the required work; as such the middle-class woman became, to some extent, an object signifying her husband's wealth (Green 1983:130). Furthermore, the complexity of women's clothes meant that it was necessary to have a maid or relative to help fasten them (Fletcher 1984:77–78). In spite of concerns about the physical damage caused by corsets and high-heeled shoes they continued to be popular throughout the 19th century (Green 1983:120–128).

A number of changes in women's fashion took place over the 30 years that the Martin family lived at Viewbank. Keeping up with changes in fashion was vitally important to displaying the correct appearance and status. Clothes for special occasions were either imported from Europe, or made locally, but still closely followed the Paris and London fashions (Maynard 1994:85).

In addition to clothing, jewellery was a way of enhancing personal appearance and displaying wealth. On a daily basis a pendant or brooch would probably be the only jewellery worn, with more elaborate pieces saved for social occasions (Young 2003:169–171). While the archaeological record indicates the importance of personal appearance, it also suggests that the Martin women did not lose or discard expensive jewellery. The brooches recovered from Viewbank were copper-alloy-based brooches, which would have been inexpensive and mass-produced. Some, more valuable, gold items were also found: a fine gold chain which may have carried a locket or watch, part of a gold earring, and a small gold loop, probably a connecting piece from a necklace or bracelet. All of the jewellery items were broken suggesting that they were discarded for this reason and none had a precious stone still in place.

The Martin women would have had more valuable jewellery than that represented in the archaeological assemblage. The lack of them in the archaeological record is likely because of care taken with precious items, and the resetting of precious stones when an item of jewellery broke or went out of fashion. Also, as suggested by historical records, valuable items were passed down through the generations. For example, the de Guzman pearls, which Mrs Martin inherited from her mother, were passed down to Lucy Boyd and then to her daughter Lucy (Niall 2004:30).

Beads can have many uses including jewellery, rosaries, clothing decoration and lace-making bobbin spangles, making their actual use difficult to confirm. However, it is possible that the eight beads recovered from Viewbank represent items of jewellery. Notable among these are seven matching black beads. Rosary beads were often made of black glass and, although predominantly associated with the Catholic Church, were sometimes used by Anglicans. Black beads were also often used for mourning jewellery.

Of the two spectacle lenses recovered from Viewbank one was oval in shape and sight-correcting and the other circular and not sight-correcting. Spectacles were often decorative, rather than functional, as they were seen as giving an air of dignity (Iacono 1999:72). Women often used long gold chains to hold spectacles, tucked in a pocket (Young 2003:171). There was a fine gold chain in the Viewbank assemblage, possibly used with one of the pairs of spectacles.

Fragments of a bone brisé folding fan carved with a floral design were found at Viewbank (**Figure 5.7**). Demure and genteel, folding fans were popular throughout the 19th century, especially at balls. In addition to their decorative purpose, fans were used to attract attention, flirt and communicate. As Beaujot (2012:63) states: 'There is little doubt ... that women used fans to their advantage as performative accessories that opened up social possibilities; the colour and design of fans that were expertly deployed could attract the interest of those around them.'

The use of scent as part of personal presentation was a luxury the Martin women could afford. Three perfume bottles were recovered from Viewbank, two of which were imported from London, made by John Gosnell & Co., a perfume and soap maker who advertised themselves as the perfumer of the royal family (Gosnell 2006).

The appropriate display of mourning was another important aspect of personal appearance. There were at least two periods of mourning at Viewbank during the Martins' time there. One period was after Charlotte, her husband John Fenton and their two children were killed in the wreck of the steamship *London* in the Bay of Biscay on 11 January 1866 (HHS 1866, GP 20 March 1866). The other was after Dr Martin died in 1874. The large proportion of black buttons, along with the seven black beads, in the Viewbank assemblage may have been from mourning clothes and jewellery. The precise details of the period and depth of mourning for various relatives were important (Russell 1994:120). In addition to mourning attire for a family member, black buttons and beads were particularly popular after 1861 when Queen Victoria went into mourning for Prince Albert (Lindbergh 1999:54).

Presenting the correct appearance in all regards was a vital part of the display of gentility for the middle class in Melbourne. The nuances of fashion required great effort to ensure that one's appearance remained genteel and not vulgar (Russell 1994).

HYGIENE AND MAINTAINING HEALTH

The immaculate body, and control of the body, were also genteel ideals (Bushman 1993:63). This included controlling physical appetites, checking emotions, hiding bodily functions and maintaining cleanliness with the goal of mental and spiritual purity (Young 2003:96). Hygiene became an important part of daily life, a fact reflected in the Viewbank assemblage.

Advisory literature in the 19th century recommended washing daily either in a bath, or a sponge bath for the face, neck, groin, hands and feet (Flanders 2003:288–289; Young 2003:97). A basin and ewer in the bedroom, accommodated on a custom-built washstand, allowed for washing in the privacy of the bedroom. Sponge baths, hip baths and shower baths became increasingly popular from the 1830s on, as interest in cleanliness and the health-giving properties of water grew (Young 2003:100–102), while bathrooms began to emerge in the later part of the 19th century (Flanders 2003:286).

Complete toilet sets of the period included: basin, ewer, soap dish, sponge bowl, toothbrush jar, and slop pail (Young 2003:98), and double toilet sets were available for shared bedrooms. Matched toiletry vessels indicate a desire for symmetry and continuity in private areas of the house as well as public (Praetzellis and Praetzellis 1992:91). At Viewbank, three ewers and a chamberpot, all with flown black marble decoration, were recovered from the tip. This suggests that the sets matched between bedrooms as well as within them. Casey's (2005:108) investigation of inventories from Government House in Sydney has revealed that high status families would have matching sets for themselves and their guests while servants would have odd sets.

Excretion was carefully managed with chamberpots. Distaste for excretion was dealt with by hiding it in a chamberpot, sometimes with a lid, in a purpose built cupboard, drawer or chair (Young 2003:109). Four chamberpots, all decorated with flown transfer-printed patterns were recovered from the Viewbank tip. In addition to the black 'Marble' printed chamberpot, other chamberpots included one with a blue 'Marble' print, another with a floral and another with an unidentified print. A further two vessels may have been chamberpots, but were too fragmentary for this to be confirmed.

In addition to washing, oral hygiene was part of the discipline of daily life. Purpose-made toothbrushes were introduced in the late 18th century and became increasingly mass-produced and widespread throughout the 19th century (Young 2003:104). This daily discipline was clearly important in the Martin family: 16 toothbrushes were found in the tip. Also recovered was a cherry toothpaste jar, one of the most popular 19th-century toothpastes (Pynn 2007). The jar depicted Queen Victoria in profile and was probably made by John Gosnell & Co.

Grooming of hair and nails were also important. Hair was not washed frequently in the 19th century because of fear of catching cold. Instead, brushing the hair for long periods of time, a number of times a day and dressing it with perfumed oils was advocated (Young 2003:104–105). A vulcanite comb was found in the Viewbank tip as were two brush handles which may have been hairbrushes. Also, a Macassar oil bottle was found: a popular treatment for healthy hair for both men and women, but most commonly used by men. Further, a rectangular wooden brush found at Viewbank was either a cloth or hand brush. Cloth brushes were used to removed dust and hair from clothes, while hand brushes were used to clean the hands and fingernails.

A small number of ointment jars were also recovered from the Viewbank tip. These included an undecorated whiteware, shallow ointment jar and lid, along with a cobalt blue glass ointment jar lid. Their exact contents were not clear, but they may have contained ointments for the skin or cosmetics.

It is likely, given Dr Martin's medical background, that both prescription and proprietary medicines were used at Viewbank. Nineteen glass bottles recovered from the Viewbank tip were identified as medicine bottles, based on their shape. None of these bottles bore a maker's mark so it is difficult to determine whether the contents were prescription medicines, or proprietary medicines, or indeed medicine bottles at all. Bottles dispensed by chemists often used paper labels and bottles were taken back to the store for re-filling usually with the same, but sometimes a different, medicine (Knehans 2005:45). Four glass bottle stoppers with disc and flat oblong heads recovered from the tip were of a type commonly used for druggists' bottles (Jones and Sullivan 1989:153–156). Two cobalt blue bottles probably held castor oil, used as a purgative or for colds and flu (Davies 2001a:71). A third cobalt blue poison bottle was embossed with 'not to be taken'. Other medicines may have been used, but have left no trace in the archaeological record. Medicines were often sold in tins, boxes and packets which are less likely to survive in the ground (Graham 2005:52).

In the mid-19th century, doctors often treated patients in perilous ways with heavy doses of drugs, bleeding and purging (Davies 2001a:63). These treatments probably did more harm than good, but it is hard to know how much the families of the sick questioned these methods. In the second half of the century there was growing concern over who could call themselves doctors. Many practitioners in fact had little or no qualifications. In 1862, the *Medical Practitioners Act* was passed to enforce controls on who could practice and how (Knehans 2005:42).

As an alternative, Australians were keen users of self-dosed proprietary medicines, many of which were imported (Davies 2006b:352). Although the Martin family probably used prescription medicines and medical techniques when required, proprietary medicines were likely used to maintain health and wellbeing. It is very difficult to distinguish between prescription medicines, proprietary medicines and others from bottle shape alone. In the 19th century, there was much blurring between the boundaries of prescription and proprietary medicines. Although medical practitioners predominantly treated patients and prescribed medicines, while chemists prepared and dispensed them, there was overlap in these roles (Knehans 2005:41). Chemists would often diagnose customers and recommend the medicines they had prepared (Hagger 1979:167). Six chemists or druggists were already open in Melbourne in 1842, and by 1860 this number had grown to 88 (Knehans 2005:42). The Martin family had accounts with two chemists in Collins Street (PROV, VPRS 7591/P2, Unit 17, File 12-586, 11 February 1875).

Such hygiene and health items are not unique to the middle class and are often present at working-class sites. It is clear, however, that the Martins could afford the necessary accoutrements to uphold the genteel values of cleanliness and refined appearance, and invest in maintaining their health.

Genteel values are clearly expressed in the daily lives and lifestyle of the Martins. For the middle class, work was highly valued and formed an important part of life. The Martin women were engaged in domestic work and running the household, while Dr Martin and Willy had business interests to tend. In addition, for the servants, Viewbank was primarily a workplace. For the Martins, leisure and social activity were equally important and genteel pursuits included fancy needlework and family games with dominoes and dice. They were also engaging with essential aspects of Melbourne social life such as entertaining, attending and hosting parties, and paying calls. Gentility also bore its mark on meals, not just when guests were present, but as part of everyday life, for breakfast, lunch and dinner. Genteel values towards religion, childhood and hygiene were also indicated by the historical and archaeological record, as was the importance of correct personal appearance. Maintenance of gentility pervaded all aspects of life from washing, dressing and eating, to leisure and work.

8
Negotiating Class

The material culture recovered from Viewbank has shown that life there in the 19th century was truly genteel. Yet the interpretation of material culture can go beyond illuminating daily life in the past. It is possible to expand on these insights by characterising the material culture in relation to gentility. This then allows for an examination of the role of material culture in negotiating class position for the 'established middle class'.

Characterising the Material Culture

The evidence from Viewbank homestead suggests that the material cultural pattern of the 'established middle class' will be characterised by three key indicators of gentility: cohesion in high quality goods across all aspects of lifestyle; consistency in goods for both public and private use; and keeping up with fashions. This pattern is markedly different from that of working-class sites previously excavated in Melbourne. For example, at the urban households of Little Lon and Casselden Place the assemblages were characterised by a smattering of expensive and luxury items among a range of cheap, utilitarian items or low quality seconds (Murray and Mayne 2001; Murray 2006). Further, higher value items were usually present in areas of life that were public as opposed to private.

It can be expected that a middle-class assemblage will have high quality goods in significant numbers, and this is certainly true for Viewbank. The assemblage included matching sets of both table and teaware, a variety of purpose-specific ceramic forms, high quality glassware, a large number of beverage bottles, expensive toys, personal items of luxury, medicine items and matching toilet sets.

When studying artefacts from working-class sites, archaeologists often particularly note the presence of high value items. Crook (2000:24) suggests that the mix of luxury and poor quality items in working-class assemblages might be the result of the influence of affordability and availability of second-hand goods in market bazaars. The presence of a small number of valuable items may also be the result of theft, gambling or heirlooms being handed down. This material cultural pattern differs significantly from that noted at Viewbank where the assemblage is suggestive of purchasing habits where desired goods could be purchased in large numbers at one time, as in the case of matching sets of ceramic or glass tableware. The purchasing of matching sets also suggests sufficient wealth to enable the family to shop in centralised arcades and specialised stores, and the list of debtors discussed in Chapter 6 shows this to be the case.

This is not to say that the Martins did not possess any cheaper items, but rather that cheaper items were purchased for particular reason such as for use by servants. There is no evidence in the assemblage of scrimping and saving, or the reuse of items. Instead, there is cohesion in the quality of the assemblage as a whole.

Another notable characteristic of the Viewbank assemblage is that it has a consistency in quality and expensive items for various aspects of daily life, not just when on display to others. A wide variety of matching sets and vessel forms for both table and tea services meant that good taste and refinement was not just for serving guests but also for private breakfasts, lunches, children's and servants meals. While marble fireplaces, elaborate cornices and wallpaper graced the public areas of the house, wallpaper was also used in the family bedrooms and housekeeper's bedroom. Matching toilet sets further suggest the importance placed on creating a harmonious and genteel environment even in the private areas of the house.

Good taste and therefore fashion were important aspects of gentility, and there is evidence in the Viewbank assemblage that the Martins were keeping up with fashions. Particularly helpful here were the table and tea service assemblages which followed the Australian preference for colourful table settings, particularly transfer-prints. Makers' marks on the ceramics allowed insight into purchasing patterns and the dates on the ceramics indicate that they were updated and purchased throughout the time that the Martins were at Viewbank. The list of debts in 1874 suggests that the Martins were continuing to update their crockery, and also drapery even in their last year at Viewbank (PROV, VPRS 7591/P2, Unit 17, File 12-586, 11 February 1875). Other artefacts also suggest keeping up with fashion including costume jewellery, dolls in fashionable styles, fashionable fabric covered buttons, and non-sight-correcting spectacles for appearance only.

Along with cohesion in value and consistency in goods for public and private use, fashion also indicates the gentility that characterises the Viewbank assemblage. Genteel performance and display were likely part of the rationale behind the acquisition of goods for the Martin family, however the genteel nature of the goods clearly extended beyond those that would form public display. Gentility pervaded all aspects of life from washing, dressing, eating and shopping, to religion and leisure.

GENTILITY AND CLASS NEGOTIATION

While gentility can be used as a descriptor to characterise material culture and daily life, it can go beyond this when used as an analytical tool. It can be used to examine similarities and differences between people, and in turn society as a whole. By focusing on one family as representative of one group of immigrants in early colonial Melbourne, this study seeks to understand how this group were negotiating their position within, and also shaping, colonial society.

Gentility established a value system within which all social practice took place, akin to cultural capital as defined by Bourdieu (1977, 1984). Gentility dictated the tastes, behaviours and rituals of the middle class in Australia. It provided middle-class individuals with a means to locate themselves within the social organisation of 19th-century Australia and their choice of goods and their practices were vital in this.

The cultural capital of the upper middle class in Victoria was adopted and appropriated from British social standards. Russell's (1994:50, 61) work on the colonial gentry in Victoria highlights that the Martin family were a part of exclusive society in Melbourne that relied on social standards and etiquette imported directly from Britain. Social practices, such as the complex system of social calls and genteel dining habits, were brought to Australia.

As society in early colonial Melbourne came to incorporate more and more people over the 19th century, it became increasingly difficult to tell people apart. The middle class became a large and diverse group incorporating many people with different class backgrounds and lifestyles. Young (2010:136) argues that 'the range of internal variations set up hurdles of snobbery that generated a tension within the middle class in asserting and maintaining genteel status'. Social mobility and the difficulty of determining hierarchy in the colonial context meant that it was vitally important for middle-class individuals to define their status (Russell 1994; Waterhouse 1995:101), but gentility was more subjectively determined in Melbourne than in Britain and caused much anxiety.

Familial connections could not always be proven in the colony and were thus not as relevant as in Britain. The middle class feared that working-class interlopers would invade their group if they were not vigilant about maintaining boundaries. The Australian middle class imposed strict tests on educational and behavioural standards for admission to their ranks (Cannon 1975:214). Material culture became an important element in determining position (see Cohen 2006:xi), and gentility a key indicator of class (Davidoff and Hall 2002:398; Young 2003:4–5).

Women became central to demonstrating class: they were responsible for domestic affairs and gentility was increasingly enacted on a domestic stage (Bushman 1993:281). The emergence of a 'cult of domesticity' in the early 19th century created a shift in the role of women (Sklar 1973; Clark 1986; Marsh 1990): they became influential consumers, purchasers, users, and discarders (Klein 1991:78; Young 1998:134–135). The selection of goods and associated genteel performance was the domain of women (Bushman 1993:281) and was a vital determinant of class in the colonial context. Women negotiated their status through the social networks they established with other women in ways that were just as important, if not more so, than men (Russell 1994:14). The Viewbank assemblage suggests that Mrs Martin embraced her domestic role. Carefully chosen tableware in matching sets, expensive glassware, efforts to keep up with fashion, matching toiletware, appropriate jewellery and equipment for fancy needlework were all tools in genteel performance.

The characteristics of the Viewbank assemblage can be interpreted as the result of the particular and unique way that gentility was employed by the 'established middle class' (Hayes 2011b:40–41). For this group maintaining their rightful position meant that gentility had to appear to be inherent, coming naturally and seemingly without effort (Russell 1994:60). The assemblage recovered from Viewbank indicates that the Martins had the required equipment in the correct, up-to-date fashions for this to be achieved. With gentility pervading all aspects of their lives, the Martins can be seen as truly genteel and maintaining a superior position within society. Gentility manifests itself as inherent for the Martin family: it was a cultural capital with which they were seemingly born.

The material culture from Viewbank homestead also suggests that the inherent nature of gentility for the 'established middle class' can be seen as taking on a distancing aspect. Only the truly genteel could display the full repertoire of correct goods and behaviours. This allowed this group to be distinguished from socially mobile people of different class backgrounds. The Martin family, and others equal to their rank, could therefore claim a firm class position at the top of colonial society. For the 'established middle class' maintaining this position meant the display of gentility was all the more important, and it can be argued that maintaining delineation from those of lower-class backgrounds became an activity with which this group had to become fully engaged (see Russell 1994:14–15).

While the inherent and distancing nature of gentility for this group acted to exclude some, it also served the vital role of creating a sense of inclusion for those who did belong. Gentility allowed people of the same group to impress each other, but subtly and with seeming indifference (Russell 1994).

It was, however, necessary to allow entry to some. While it is beyond the scope of this study to examine how material culture was used to negotiate this, it likely played a key role in determining entry along with behaviour, networks and marriages (Russell 1994:9, 18). It is worth noting here that Dr Martin used the marriage of his children strategically to forge alliances in society, and was enraged when two of his daughters married 'beneath them'.

The Martins' brand of gentility suggests that they were negotiating a position of superiority in the colony, but without giving the impression of doing so. They capitalised on their middle-class background to give themselves an air of establishment, of having always been superior, once in the colony. Social and economic mobility was a threat to their position, but they too achieved higher status in Melbourne than at home.

While the Martins' move from England to the colony afforded them greater wealth and status, it did not facilitate a significant move up the social ladder. Although their lifestyle was to some degree modelled on the British landed gentry, they did not in fact possess the power and control of the ruling class. Instead they appropriated characteristics of the British ruling class in a distinctive middle-class way. Though they remained middle class by British standards, they were near the top of Melbourne society. Their brand of gentility, as revealed by their material culture, set them apart within the middle class. It allowed them to negotiate a position of superiority and to attempt to control the boundaries of their group.

To some degree it was families like the Martins who ensured that class structure was transported to Melbourne. While it is not possible to know what the Martins thought of their class position, by using material culture and the cultural capital of gentility, it can be argued that class benefitted this group. They used gentility and its expression through prestigious goods to define themselves within their group, and to maintain their position in the face of great social mobility. They engaged with gentility to a significant extent throughout all facets of their lives. They communicated their class through their behaviours and consumer choices. Importantly, they also challenged those seeking entry to the middle class to grapple with the nuances of gentility.

Conclusion

Class structure in early Melbourne was both a recreation of British standards and a carefully contested adaptation that served to benefit some, but not others. Those who benefitted were families like the Martins: the 'established middle class'. By focusing on the material culture of this group and treating class as an arbitrary category for analysis it has been possible to go beyond describing the Martins' lifestyle and class position to examine class negotiation. By doing so, this study has demonstrated the potential of the archaeological record to examine the unique ways in which different groups of people engaged with gentility as the cultural capital through which they could define and maintain their position.

Arriving wealthy, the Martin family obtained significant property and expanded their wealth and influence once in Melbourne. Although the move from England to the colony afforded the family greater wealth, it did not facilitate a significant move up the social ladder. However, they did hold a position of superiority in the colony, one that they communicated through material culture.

The Viewbank homestead itself was in a situation that communicated status. Beautiful views, attractive gardens, a grand dwelling and desirable neighbourhood portrayed gentility. Inside, the house conveyed status to visitors through grand, purpose-specific public rooms and a large number of private rooms also catered to the needs of the household.

The material culture recovered from Viewbank homestead provides insight into the genteel lifestyle conducted by the Martins. Genteel dining was not just for guests but was also an important part of daily life with different sets of tableware for breakfasts, lunches and dinners. The Martins also had the necessary equipment to host parties and receive calls. Leisure involved family games, but there was also importance placed on constructive leisure such as sewing. Childhood was a valued phase of life as suggested by moralising china and expensive toys. Spending appropriate amounts of money shopping on Collins Street functioned as genteel performance for the women. Effort was taken with personal appearance and hygiene as suggested by jewellery, matching toilet sets, toothbrushes and ointment jars. Gentility was integral to all aspects of life.

While Viewbank was a place for private family time and the receiving of guests for the Martin family, it was a workplace for the servants employed there. The constant negotiation of class within the household was a daily issue at Viewbank and a characteristic experience of the middle class. The physical space at Viewbank was structured in such a way as to segregate servants from the family. They have left their own small trace in the archaeological record in the form of clay tobacco pipes, at least one dinner service, milkpans, and a small number of garden and sewing tools.

It has been possible to expand on these insights into daily life and lifestyle by characterising the assemblage in relation to gentility. The Viewbank assemblage can be characterised by cohesion in high quality goods across all aspects of lifestyle, consistency in goods for both public and private use, and keeping up with fashions. These characteristics can be interpreted as the result of the unique way in which the 'established middle class' used gentility as cultural capital.

For the 'established middle class', gentility had to appear to be inherent, a cultural capital with which they were seemingly born. This in turn enabled gentility to serve a distancing function to delineate this group from those seeking entry to their ranks. This also created a sense of inclusion for those who did belong. For the 'established middle class' to maintain their class position under the threat of social mobility, the cultural capital of gentility was a vital tool. The Martin family were defining and defending their class position in the new society that was coming in to being in Melbourne, and by this very action were at the same time imposing the class system that benefitted them.

Appendix 1
Function Key Words

Domestic

Artefacts associated with household activities:

Furnishings	Table, chair, lamp etc
Maintaining household cleanliness	Disinfectant bottle, scrubbing brush
Ornamentation	Figurine, picture

Eating and Drinking

Artefacts associated with preparing, serving and consuming food and beverages:

Storing food and drink	Bottle, jar
Serving and consuming food	Plate, bowl, cup, eggcup, platter, drinking glass, cutlery
Serving and consuming tea	Teacup, teapot, saucer, teaspoon
Serving and consuming	Unidentified hollow, unidentified flat
Preparing food	Baking dish, saucepan, milkpan

Personal

Artefacts associated with an individual's needs:

Accessory	Jewellery, bead, badge, eyeglasses
Clothing	Button, hook and eye, shoe, textile
Health care	Medicine bottle, syringe, pill box, bleeding bowl
Grooming and hygiene	Hair comb, hair brush, tooth brush, tooth paste jar, ointment jar, chamberpot

Recreational

Artefacts relating to children's play and adult's relaxation:

Children's play	Doll, marble, toy tea set
Competitive activities	Dominos, dice
Non-competitive activities	Paint jar, musical instrument, tobacco pipe

Social

Artefacts designed to facilitate social interaction between individuals and groups:

Currency	Coins
Educational	Writing slate
Religious	Rosary beads, crucifix

Tools and Equipment

Artefacts relating to agricultural or domestic work:

Sewing	Needle, pin, thimble
Weapons and ammunition	Cartridge, gun
Work tool	Shovel, pick, file
Writing and drawing	Pen, pencil, ink bottle
Aboriginal tool	Stone tool

Miscellaneous

Artefacts with an unidentifiable function and artefacts that may belong to more than one activity group:

Containers	Vessel or bottle that cannot be grouped into a specific activity e.g. Poison bottle, unidentified form
Unknown function	Unidentified function

Appendix 2
Date Ranges and Occupation Phases

Homestead	Artefact	Start Date	End Date	MNI
Pre-Martin occupation	coin	1697	1697	1
Total				**1**
Martin occupation	bottle	1600	1920	3
	pencil	1700	1920	1
	bottle	1750	1920	3
	teacup	1768	present	1
	ui flat	1768	present	1
	unidentified	1768	present	1
	ui hollow	1780	present	1
	unidentified	1794	present	1
	mug	1805	present	1
	plate	1805	present	1
	ui flat	1805	present	1
	ui hollow	1805	present	1
	unidentified	1805	present	1
	bottle	1820	1920	1
	bottle	1821	1920	1
	bottle	1821	present	1
	pin	1824	on	17
	button	1827	on	1
	ui flat	1828	present	1
	bottle	1830	1920	3
	ui flat	1835	present	2
	ui hollow	1835	present	1
	unidentified	1835	present	1
	button	1838	1900	1
	bottle	1838	1920	1
	bottle	1840	1920	1
	bottle	1844	1920	1
	bottle	1845	1920	1
	marble	1846	1920	1
	bottle	1852	1870	1
	bottle	1860	1900	1
	saucer	1860	present	1
	teacup	1860	present	1
	coin	1873	1873	1
Total				**57**
Post-Martin occupation	bottle	1888	1900	1
	bottle	1890	present	10
	jar	1890	present	1
	bottle	1895	on	1
	bottle	1900	1920	1
	bottle	1905	1919	1
	bottle	1920	on	3
	bottle	1920	present	9
	bowl	1921	on	1
	badge	1921	present	1
	bottle	1923	1930	1
	bottle	1930	present	6
	bottle/jar	1930	present	1
Total				**37**

Appendices

Tip	Artefact	Start Date	End Date	MNI
Pre-Martin phase	ui hollow	1794	1830	1
Total				**1**
Martin phase	bottle	1600	1850	1
	bottle	1600	1870	10
	bottle	1600	1920	11
	bottle/jar	1600	1920	1
	jar	1600	1920	1
	ui hollow	1600	1920	1
	bottle	1600	1930	1
	button	1700	1850	1
	pencil	1700	1920	2
	ui hollow	1743	on	1
	unidentified	1743	on	1
	bottle	1750	1920	1
	bowl	1768	present	1
	egg cup	1768	present	1
	jar	1768	present	1
	jug	1768	present	1
	plate	1768	present	6
	saucer	1768	present	3
	teacup	1768	present	6
	ui flat	1768	present	6
	ui hollow	1768	present	3
	unidentified	1768	present	1
	button	1770	on	3
	ui hollow	1780	1850	1
	covered bowl	1780	present	1
	dish	1780	present	1
	mug	1780	present	1
	serving dish	1780	present	1
	tureen	1780	present	1
	ui flat	1780	present	1
	ui hollow	1780	present	1
	jug	1782	1956	1
	bottle	1784	on	4
	lamp chimney	1784	on	7
	decanter	1790	on	2
	tumbler	1790	on	3
	saucer	1794	1850	1
	teacup	1794	1850	1
	ui flat	1794	1850	1
	bowl	1794	present	9
	covered bowl	1794	present	1
	mug	1794	present	1
	plate	1794	present	3
	platter	1794	present	1
	saucer	1794	present	6
	teacup	1794	present	29
	ui flat	1794	present	6
	ui hollow	1794	present	18
	ui teaware	1794	present	6
	unidentified	1794	present	3
	stopper	1799	present	1
	bottle	1800	1875	3
	bowl	1800	1875	1
	saucer	1800	1910	2
	toy teacup	1800	1910	1
	toy teapot	1800	1910	1
	ui hollow	1800	1910	1

(continued)

Appendices

(continued)

Tip	Artefact	Start Date	End Date	MNI
	stemware	1800	present	1
	corkscrew	1802	on	1
	unidentified	1805	1850	1
	bowl	1805	present	10
	covered bowl	1805	present	1
	drainer	1805	present	1
	jar	1805	present	12
	jug	1805	present	4
	knob	1805	present	1
	milkpan	1805	present	1
	mug	1805	present	3
	plate	1805	present	6
	platter	1805	present	1
	serving dish	1805	present	3
	spoon	1805	present	1
	teacup	1805	present	2
	tureen	1805	present	1
	ui flat	1805	present	21
	ui hollow	1805	present	19
	ui tableware	1805	present	1
	unidentified	1805	present	7
	plate	1820	1854	1
	bottle	1820	1870	29
	bottle	1820	1920	8
	saucer	1820	present	2
	teacup	1820	present	3
	ui hollow	1820	present	1
	bottle	1821	1920	3
	bottle/jar	1821	present	1
	jar	1821	present	1
	pin	1824	on	53
	button	1827	on	3
	bowl	1828	present	3
	jug	1828	present	1
	plate	1828	present	1
	platter	1828	present	1
	saucer	1828	present	1
	serving dish	1828	present	1
	teacup	1828	present	3
	ui flat	1828	present	1
	ui hollow	1828	present	1
	ui tableware	1828	present	1
	unidentified	1828	present	1
	bowl	1830	on	3
	plate	1830	1859	10
	platter	1830	1859	1
	tureen	1830	1859	2
	ui hollow	1830	1859	1
	bottle	1830	1875	1
	bowl	1830	1900	1
	bottle	1830	1920	3
	tumbler	1830	1920	1
	bottle	1834	1920	2
	basin	1835	present	1
	bowl	1835	present	1
	chamberpot	1835	present	1
	covered bowl	1835	present	1

(continued)

(continued)

Tip	Artefact	Start Date	End Date	MNI
	dish	1835	present	1
	egg cup	1835	present	1
	ewer	1835	present	3
	jug	1835	present	1
	ladle	1835	present	1
	plate	1835	present	3
	platter	1835	present	3
	saucer	1835	present	6
	serving dish	1835	present	1
	teacup	1835	present	3
	ui flat	1835	present	6
	ui hollow	1835	present	3
	ui tableware	1835	present	1
	unidentified	1835	present	3
	bottle	1836	1861	1
	stopper	1836	1913	1
	stopper	1838	on	1
	ui hollow	1838	on	1
	button	1838	1900	3
	bottle	1838	1920	1
	comb	1839	on	1
	bead	1840	on	1
	button	1840	on	2
	jar	1840	on	1
	doll	1840	1900	1
	bottle	1840	1920	1
	jar	1840	present	1
	bottle	1842	1868	5
	bottle	1842	1883	1
	unidentified	1842	1883	1
	bottle	1844	1870	3
	bottle	1844	1920	101
	bottle	1844	1925	1
	ui hollow	1845	1867	1
	bowl	1845	1890	1
	jug	1845	1890	1
	plate	1845	1890	3
	platter	1845	1890	1
	saucer	1845	1890	1
	serving dish	1845	1890	1
	teacup	1845	1890	9
	ui flat	1845	1890	7
	ui hollow	1845	1890	3
	unidentified	1845	1890	1
	vase	1845	1890	1
	bottle	1845	1920	1
	bead	1845	present	1
	bottle	1845	present	3
	jar	1845	present	1
	marble	1846	1920	2
	chamberpot	1847	1867	1
	doll	1850	1880	1
	button	1850	1900	11
	bottle	1850	1920	7
	stopper	1850	present	1
	plate	1851	1862	3
	ui flat	1851	1862	3

(continued)

Appendices

(continued)

Tip	Artefact	Start Date	End Date	MNI
	plate	1851	1882	1
	bottle	1855	on	5
	plate	1856	1858	5
	bottle	1859	1928	1
	unidentified	1859	present	1
	platter	1860	1860	2
	doll	1860	1900	1
	bottle	1860	1920	6
	saucer	1860	present	3
	teacup	1860	present	1
	ui hollow	1860	present	1
	unidentified	1860	present	1
	plate	1862	1871	2
	platter	1862	1871	2
	saucer	1862	1871	2
	ui hollow	1862	1871	1
	unidentified	1862	1871	1
	unidentified	1862	1882	1
	stopper	1863	on	1
	plate	1869	1882	1
	bottle	1869	1883	7
	stopper	1870	on	1
	bottle	1870	1920	1
Total				**709**
Post-Martin phase	jar	1880	1920	1
	bottle	1920	present	1
Total				**2**

Appendix 3
Summary of Activity and Function Groupings for Artefacts Recovered from the Tip

Domestic

Function	Qty	Weight	MNI	%
Furnishings	185	602.5	13	52.0
Maintaining the Household	6	58.4	2	8.0
Ornamentation	57	500.0	10	40.0
Total	**248**	**1,160.9**	**25**	**100.0**

Eating and Drinking

Function	Qty	Weight	MNI	%
Preparing Food	526	18590.4	14	1.9
Serving and Consuming Food	2,850	36,483.1	223	30.7
Serving and Consuming Tea	1,539	8,208.0	130	17.9
Serving and Consuming	2,279	8,796.7	123	16.9
Storing Food and Drink	8,231	69,548.4	237	32.6
Total	**15,425**	**141,626.6**	**727**	**100.0**

Personal

Function	Qty	Weight	MNI	%
Accessory	29	27.7	24	12.8
Clothing	272	210.5	103	54.8
Grooming and Hygiene	367	4,134.9	38	20.2
Health Care	72	476.2	23	12.2
Total	**740**	**4,849.3**	**188**	**100.0**

Recreational

Function	Qty	Weight	MNI	%
Children's Play	29	149.5	18	62.1
Competitive Activities	9	35.6	7	24.1
Non-competitive Activities	12	29.8	4	13.8
Total	**50**	**214.9**	**29**	**100.0**

Social

Function	Qty	Weight	MNI	%
Currency	1	11.7	1	100.0
Total	**1**	**11.7**	**1**	**100.0**

Tools and Equipment

Function	Qty	Weight	MNI	%
Sewing	93	17.6	61	81.3
Weapons and Ammunition	7	17.2	4	5.3
Work tool	24	135.9	3	4.0
Writing and Drawing	46	202.4	7	9.3
Total	**170**	**373.1**	**75**	**100.0**

Miscellaneous

Function	Qty	Weight	MNI	%
Containers	3,412	13,975.7	154	70.0
Unknown Function	220	913.1	66	30.0
Total	**3,632**	**14,888.8**	**220**	**100.0**

Bibliography

Archival Sources

The Argus

The Australian

Graham Papers – University of Melbourne Archives
James Graham's Letter Book

Heidelberg Historical Society
Viewbank File
Bartram Family File
Unidentified press clipping, 1862
Unidentified press clipping, 1866

Kerr's Melbourne Almanac and Port Phillip Directory
Compiled by William Kerr, 1841 and 1842 editions

The Melbourne Commercial Directory
1853 edition

The Melbourne Morning Herald and General Daily Advertiser

Port Phillip Directory
1847 edition

Port Phillip Gazette

Port Phillip Herald

Public Record Office of Victoria
VA 2624 Master in Equity, Supreme Court VPRS 7591/P2 Wills 1853–1960
Unit 17, File 12-586:
Will of Dr Robert Martin, 27 January 1873
Codicil, 15 July 1874
Affidavit, 22 October 1874
Affidavit, 11 February 1875
Unit 87, File 26-805:
Will of Mrs Lucy Martin, 7 August 1882
Affidavit, 9 January 1884
Affidavit, 11 January 1884
Affidavit, 19 January 1884
VA 2889 Registrar General's Department, VPRS 460/P Application's for Certificates of Title
Unit 1102:
Land Purchase, 31 January 1839
Land Title, 150140/16440
Lease of Viewbank to Cecilia H. Cockburn Campbell, 1 June 1875

Melbourne City Council, VPRS 5708 Rate Books

Sands and McDougall Melbourne and Suburban Directories
Published by Sands and McDougall, Melbourne, 1862 to 1874 editions.

References

Adams, W. H. 1991, Trade Networks and Interaction Spheres – a View from Silcott. In *Approaches to Material Culture Research for Historical Archaeologists*, edited by G. L. Miller, O. R. Jones, L. A. Ross and T. Majewski, Society for Historical Archaeology, Pennsylvania: 385–398.

Adams, W. H. 2003, Dating Historical Sites: The Importance of Understanding Time Lag in the Acquisition, Curation, Use and Disposal of Artifacts. *Historical Archaeology*, 37(2): 38–64.

Albert, L. S. and K. Kent 1971, *The Complete Button Book*. John Edwards, Stratford.

Allison, P. M. and A. Cremin 2006, Ceramics from the Old Kinchega Homestead. *Australasian Historical Archaeology*, 24: 55–64.

Ames, K. L. 1978, Meaning in Artifacts: Hall Furnishings in Victorian America. *Journal of Interdisciplinary History*, 9(1): 19–46.

Anderson, M. 1985, Marriage and Children in Western Australia, 1842–49. In *Families in Colonial Australia*, edited by P. Grimshaw, C. McConville and E. McEwen, George Allen & Unwin, Sydney: 49–56.

Anderson, M. 1992, Good Strong Girls: Colonial Women and Work. In *Gender Relations in Australia: Domination and Negotiation*, edited by K. Saunders and R. Evans, Harcourt Brace Jovanovich, Sydney: 225–245.

Appadurai, A. (ed.) 1986, *The Social Life of Things: Commodities in Cultural Perspective*. Cambridge University Press, Cambridge.

Attwood, B. 2009, *Possession: Batman's Treaty and the Matter of History*. Miegunyah Press, Melbourne.

Aussie Bottle Digger 2007, Dating Australian Bottles. Retrieved 3 January 2007 from www.users.bigpond.com/oz-riley/bottledating.html.

Australian Medical Pioneers Index 2006, Australian Medical Pioneers Index. Retrieved 11 July 2007 from www.medicalpioneers.com/cgi-bin/index.cgi?detail=1&id=2100.

Barwick, D. E. 1984, Mapping the Past: An Atlas of Victorian Clans 1835–1904. *Aboriginal History*, 8: 100–132.

Beaudry, M. 2006, *Findings: The Material Culture of Needlework and Sewing*. Yale University Press, New Haven.

Beaudry, M. C., L. J. Cook and S. A. Mrozowski 1991, Artifacts and Active Voices: Material Culture as Social Discourse. In *The Archaeology of Inequality*, edited by R. H. McGuire and R. Paynter, Blackwell, Oxford: 150–191.

Beaudry, M. C., J. Long, H. M. Miller, F. D. Neiman and G. W. Stone 2000, A Vessel Typology for Early Chesapeake Ceramics: The Potomac Typological System. In *Approaches to Material Culture Research for Historical Archaeologists*, edited by D. R. Brauner, Society for Historical Archaeology, Pennsylvania: 11–36.

Beaujot, A. 2012, *Victorian Fashion Accessories*. Berg, London.

Beer, J. 1989, Highland Scots in Victoria's Western District. In *Colonial Frontiers and Family Fortunes: Two Studies of Rural and Urban Victoria*, edited by J. Beer, C. Fahey, P. Grimshaw and M. Raymond, Melbourne University history monograph series No. 6, History Department, University of Melbourne, Melbourne: 12–78.

Beeston, J. 1994, *A Concise History of Australian Wine*. Allen & Unwin, Sydney.

Beeton, I. M. 1861, *Beeton's Book of Household Management*. S. O. Beeton, London.

Bell, R. C. 2000, *Board and Table Game Antiques*. Shire Albums, Shire Publications, Buckinghamshire.

Billis, R. and A. Kenyon 1932, *Pastoral Pioneers of Port Phillip*. MacMillan & Company, Melbourne.

Birmingham, J. 1992, *Wybalenna: The Archaeology of Cultural Accommodation in Nineteenth Century Tasmania*. Australian Society for Historical Archaeology, Sydney.

Birmingham, J. and K. Fahy 1987, Old Australian Pottery. In *Papers in Australian Historical Archaeology*, edited by J. Birmingham and D. Bairstow, Australian Society for Historical Archaeology: 7–11.

Boow, J. c.1991, *Early Australian Commercial Glass: Manufacturing Processes*. Heritage Council of New South Wales, Sydney.

Borrett, P. 2007, Corkscrew Guide. Retrieved 3 December 2007 from www.corkscrewsonline.com.

Bourdieu, P. 1977, *Outline of a Theory of Practice*. Translated by R. Nice, Cambridge University Press, Cambridge.

Bourdieu, P. 1984, *Distinction: A Social Critique of the Judgment of Taste*. Harvard University Press, Cambridge, Massachusetts.

Bowen, A. 2012, *Archaeology of the Chinese Fishing Industry in Colonial Victoria*. Studies in Australasian Historical Archaeology 3, Sydney University Press, Sydney.

Boyce, J. 2011, *1835: The Founding of Melbourne & the Conquest of Australia*. Black Inc., Melbourne.

Bride, T. F. 1969, *Letters from Victorian Pioneers*. William Heinemann, Melbourne.

Brighton, S. A. 2011, Middle-Class Ideologies and American Respectability: Archaeology and the Irish Immigrant Experience. *International Journal of Historical Archaeology*, 15(1): 30–50.

Broadbent, J. 1995, *Elizabeth Farm Parramatta: A History and a Guide*. Historic Houses Trust of New South Wales, Sydney.

Brooks, A. 1999, Building Jerusalem: Transfer-Printed Finewares and the Creation of British Identity. In *The Familiar Past? Archaeologies of Later Historical Britain*, edited by S. Tarlow and S. West, Routledge, London: 51–65.

Brooks, A. 2002, The Cloud of Unknowing: Towards and International Comparative Analysis of Eighteenth- and Nineteenth-Century Ceramics. *Australasian Historical Archaeology*, 20: 48–57.

Brooks, A. 2005a, *An Archaeological Guide to British Ceramics in Australia 1788–1901*. Australasian Society for Historical Archaeology and the La Trobe University Archaeology Program, Sydney.

Brooks, A. 2005b, Observing Formalities – the Use of Functional Artefact Categories in Australian Historical Archaeology. *Australasian Historical Archaeology*, 23: 7–14.

Brooks, A. 2007, Ceramics. In *The Same under a Different Sky?: A Country Estate in Nineteenth-Century New South Wales*, edited by G. Connah, BAR International Series, John and Erica Hedges, Oxford: 183–195.

Broome, R. 1984, *The Victorians: Arriving*. Fairfax Series, Fairfax, Syme & Weldon Associates, Sydney.

Broome, R. 2005, *Aboriginal Victorians: A History since 1800*. Allen & Unwin, Sydney.

Brown-May, A. 1998, *Melbourne Street Life*. Australian Scholarly Publishing, Melbourne.

Burke, H. 1999, *Meaning and Ideology in Historical Archaeology: Style, Social Identity, and Capitalism in an Australian Town*. Kluwer Academic/Plenum Press, New York.

Burley, D. 2000, Function, Meaning and Context: Ambiguities in Ceramic Use by the Hivernant Metis of the Northwestern Plains. In *Approaches to Material Culture Research for Historical Archaeologists*, edited by D. R. Brauner, Society for Historical Archaeology, Pennsylvania: 399–408.

Busch, J. 1991, Second Time Around: A Look at Bottle Reuse. In *Approaches to Material Culture Research for Historical Archaeologists*, edited by G. L. Miller, O. R. Jones, L. A. Ross and T. Majewski, Society for Historical Archaeology, Pennsylvania: 113–126.

Bushman, R. 1993, The *Refinement of America: Persons, Houses, Cities*. Vintage Books, New York.

Bibliography

Cameron, F. 1985, Analysis of Buttons, Clothing Hardware and Textiles of the Nineteenth Century Chinese Goldminers of Central Otago. Honours thesis, Anthropology Department, University of Otago, Dunedin.

Campbell, J. 2002, *Invisible Invaders: Smallpox and Other Diseases in Aboriginal Australia 1780–1880*. Melbourne University Press, Melbourne.

Cannon, M. 1971, *Australia in the Victorian Age: Who's Master? Who's Man?* John Currey O'Neil, Melbourne.

Cannon, M. 1975, *Australia in the Victorian Age 3: Life in the Cities*. Thomas Nelson Australia, Melbourne.

Carlin, S. 2000, *Elizabeth Bay House: A History & Guide*. Historic Houses Trust of New South Wales, Sydney.

Carney, M. 1998, A Cordial Factory at Parramatta, New South Wales. *Australasian Historical Archaeology*, 16: 80–93.

Casella, E. C. 2005, "Games, Sports and What-Not": Regulation of Leisure and the Production of Social Identities in Nineteenth Century America. In *The Archaeology of Plural and Changing Identities: Beyond Identification*, edited by E. C. Casella, Springer, New York: 163–189.

Casella, E. C. and S. K. Croucher 2010, *The Alderley Sandhills Project: An Archaeology of Community Life in (Post-) Industrial England*. Manchester University Press, Manchester.

Casey, M. 1999, Local Pottery and Dairying at the DMR Site, Brickfields, Sydney, New South Wales. *Australasian Historical Archaeology*, 17: 3–37.

Casey, M. 2005, Material Culture and the Construction of Hierarchy at the Conservatorium Site, Sydney. *Australasian Historical Archaeology*, 23: 97–113.

Chadwick, R. 1958, The Working of Metals. In *A History of Technology. Volume V: The Late Nineteenth Century C.1850–1900*, edited by C. Singer, E. J. Holmyard, A. R. Hall and T. I. Williams, Oxford University Press, New York: 605–635.

Cheltenham Museum 2006, Keeping Cool: Fans from the Art Gallery & Museum's Collection. Retrieved 15 November 2006 from www.cheltenhammuseum.org.uk/search/fans_info_sheet.pdf.

Clark, C. 1986, *The American Family Home 1800–1960*. University of North Carolina Press, Chapel Hill.

Cochran, M. D. and M. C. Beaudry 2006, Material Culture Studies and Historical Archaeology. In *The Cambridge Companion to Historical Archaeology*, edited by D. Hicks and M. C. Beaudry, Cambridge University Press, Cambridge: 191–204.

Connah, G. 1977, Wool, Water and Settlement: The Archaeological Landscape of Saumarez Station. *Armidale and District Historical Society Journal*, 20: 117–127.

Connah, G. 1986, Historical Reality, Archaeological Reality: Excavations at Regentville, Penrith, New South Wales, 1985. *The Australian Journal of Historical Archaeology*, 4: 29–42.

Connah, G. 1993, *The Archaeology of Australia's History*. Press Syndicate of the University of Cambridge, Melbourne.

Connah, G. 2001, The Lake Innes Estate: Privilege and Servitude in Nineteenth-Century Australia. *World Archaeology*, 33(1): 137–154.

Connah, G. 2007, *The Same under a Different Sky?: A Country Estate in Nineteenth-Century New South Wales*. BAR International Series, John and Erica Hedges, Oxford.

Connah, G., M. Rowland and J. Oppenheimer 1978, *Captain Richards' House at Winterbourne: A Study in Historical Archaeology*. Department of Prehistory and Archaeology, University of New England, Armidale.

Connell, R. W. and T. H. Irving 1980, *Class Structure in Australian History: Documents, Narrative and Argument*. Longman Cheshire, Melbourne.

Consultants, G. M. H. 1999, The Cumberland/Gloucester Streets Site, the Rocks: Archaeological Investigation Report. Report submitted to the Sydney Cove Authority, Sydney.

Copeland, R. 1998, The Marketing of Blue and White Wares. In *True Blue: Transfer Printed Earthenware*, edited by G. B. Roberts, Friends of Blue, Oxfordshire: 15–18.

Courtney, K. 1998, Piece Pipes: Clay Tobacco Pipes from the Site of "Little Lon", Melbourne, Australia. Masters thesis, School of Fine Arts, Classical Studies and Archaeology and Department of History, University of Melbourne, Melbourne.

Coysh, A. W. and R. K. Henrywood 1989, *The Dictionary of Blue and White Printed Pottery 1780–1880*, Vol. 2. Antique Collectors' Club, Woodbridge.

Crook, P. 2000, Shopping and Historical Archaeology: Exploring the Contexts of Urban Consumption. *Australasian Historical Archaeology*, 18: 17–28.

Crook, P. 2011, Rethinking Assemblage Analysis: New Approaches to the Archaeology of Working-Class Neighborhoods. *International Journal of Historical Archaeology*, 15(4): 582–593.

Crook, P., L. Ellmoos and T. Murray 2003, *Assessment of Historical and Archaeological Resources of the Cumberland and Gloucester Streets Site, the*

Rocks, Sydney. Archaeology of the Modern City 1788–1900 Series, Volume 3, Historic Houses Trust of New South Wales, Sydney.

Crook, P., L. Ellmoos and T. Murray 2005, *Keeping up with the McNamaras: A Historical Archaeological Study of the Cumberland and Gloucester Streets Site, the Rocks, Sydney*. Archaeology of the Modern City 1788–1900 Series, Volume 8, Historic Houses Trust of New South Wales, Sydney.

Crook, P., S. Lawrence and M. Gibbs 2002, The Role of Artefact Catalogues in Australian Historical Archaeology: A Framework for Discussion. *Australasian Historical Archaeology*, 20: 26–38.

Crook, P. and T. Murray 2004, The Analysis of Cesspit Deposits from the Rocks, Sydney. *Australasian Historical Archaeology*, 22: 44–56.

Cummins, C. (ed.) 1971, *Heidelberg since 1836: A Pictorial History*. Heidelberg Historical Society, Heidelberg.

Cunnington, C. W. and P. Cunnington 1951, *The History of Underclothes*. M. Joseph, London.

Davey, P. (ed.) 1987, *The Archaeology of the Clay Tobacco Pipe: X. Scotland*. BAR British Series 178, Oxford.

Davidoff, L. and C. Hall 2002, *Family Fortunes: Men and Women of the English Middle Class, 1780–1850*. Routledge, London.

Davidson, D. C. and R. J. S. MacGregor 2002, *Spectacles, Lorgnettes and Monocles*. Shire Album, Shire Publications, Buckinghamshire.

Davies, M. and K. Buckley 1987, *Archaeological Procedures Manual: Port Arthur Conservation and Development Project*. Occasional Paper No. 13, Department of Lands, Parks and Wildlife, Hobart.

Davies, P. 2001a, A Cure for All Seasons: Health and Medicine in a Bush Community. *Journal of Australian Studies*, 70: 63–72.

Davies, P. 2001b, Isolation and Integration: The Archaeology and History of an Otways Forest Community. PhD thesis, Archaeology Program, School of Historical and European Studies, La Trobe University, Melbourne.

Davies, P. 2005, Writing Slates and Schooling. *Australasian Historical Archaeology*, 23: 63–69.

Davies, P. 2006a, *Henry's Mill: The Historical Archaeology of a Forest Community*. Bar International Series: Studies in Contemporary and Historical Archaeology 2, Archaeopress, Oxford.

Davies, P. 2006b, Mapping Commodities at Casselden Place. *International Journal of Historical Archaeology*, 10(4): 343–355.

Davies, P. in press, Archaeology and Religion at the Hyde Park Barracks Destitute Asylum, Sydney. *Historical Archaeology*, 47(4).

Davison, G. 1978, *The Rise and Fall of Marvellous Melbourne*. Melbourne University Press, Melbourne.

De Castella, H. 1861, *Australian Squatters*. Translated by C. B. Thornton-Smith in 1987. Melbourne University Press, Melbourne.

De Cunzo, L. A. and B. Herman 1996, *Historical Archaeology and the Study of American Culture*. Henry Francis duPont Winterthur Museum, Winterthur, Delaware.

De Serville, P. 1980, *Port Phillip Gentlemen and Good Society in Melbourne before the Gold Rushes*. Oxford University Press, Melbourne.

De Serville, P. 1991, *Pounds and Pedigrees: The Upper Class in Victoria 1850–1880*. Oxford University Press, Melbourne.

Deetz, J. 1977, *In Small Things Forgotten*. Doubleday, New York.

des Fontaines, J. 1990, Wedgwood Whiteware. *Proceedings of the Wedgwood Society*, 13: 1–8.

Deutsher, K. M. 1999, *The Breweries of Australia: A History*. Lothian Books, Melbourne.

Dingle, T. 1984, *The Victorians: Settling*. Fairfax, Syme & Weldon Associates, Sydney.

Douglas, M. and B. Isherwood 1978, *The World of Goods: Towards an Anthropology of Consumption*. Penguin Books, Ringwood.

Dunstan, D. 1994, *Better Than Pommard! A History of Wine in Victoria*. Australian Scholarly Publishing and Museum Victoria, Melbourne.

Dyster, B. 1989, *Servant & Master: Building and Running the Grand Houses of Sydney 1788–1850*. New South Wales University Press, Sydney.

Eckstein, E. and G. Firkins 2000, *Gentlemen's Dress Accessories*. Shire Albums, Shire Publications, Buckinghamshire.

Ellis, A. 2001, Toy Stories: Interpreting Childhood from the Victorian Archaeological Record. Honours thesis, Archaeology Program, School of Historical and European Studies, La Trobe University, Melbourne.

Ellis, M. H. and M. B. Yeh 1997, Categories of Wax-Based Drawing Media. *WAAC Newsletter*, 19(3).

Evans, R. and K. Saunders 1992, No Place Like Home: The Evolution of the Australian Housewife. In *Gender Relations in Australia: Domination and Negotiation*, edited by K. Saunders and R. Evans, Harcourt Brace Jovanovich, Sydney: 175–196.

Ewins, N. 1997, *'Supplying the Present Wants of Our Yankee Cousins ...': Staffordshire Ceramics and the American Market 1775–1880*. City Museum and Art Gallery, Stoke-on-Trent.

Fisher, S. 1966, *English Ceramics*. Ward Lock & Co., London.

Fitts, R. 1999, The Archaeology of Middle-Class Domesticity and Gentility in Victorian Brooklyn.

Bibliography

Historical Archaeology, 33(1): 39–62.

Fitzgerald, S. 1987, *Rising Damp: Sydney 1870–90*. Oxford University Press, Melbourne.

Flanders, J. 2003, *The Victorian House: Domestic Life from Childbirth to Deathbed*. Harper Collins, London.

Fletcher, M. 1984, *Costume in Australia 1788–1901*. Oxford University Press, Melbourne.

Fletcher, M. 1989, *Needlework in Australia: A History of the Development of Embroidery*. Oxford University Press, Melbourne.

Ford, G. 1995, *Australian Pottery: The First 100 Years*. Salt Glaze Press, Wodonga.

Foucault, M. 1973, *The Order of Things: An Archaeology of the Human Sciences*. Vintage Books, New York.

Frankel, D. 1979, Excavations at Elizabeth Farm House 1972. *The Artefact*, 4: 39–56.

Friedman, J. 1994, *Consumption and Identity*. Studies in Anthropology and History, Harwood Academic, Switzerland.

Furlong, K. 2002, Investigating Bottles from the "Viewbank" Excavation Site. Assignment for the 'History in the Field' subject at Melbourne University, Melbourne.

Fussell, G. 1966, *The English Dairy Farmer 1500–1900*. Frank Cass & Co., London.

Garden, D. 1972, *Heidelberg: The Land and Its People 1838–1900*. Melbourne University Press, Melbourne.

Genealogical Society of Victoria 1970, Port Phillip Pioneer Pedigrees: No. 2 – the Martin Family of Banyule and Viewbank, Heidelberg. *Ancestor*, 8(5): 105–108.

Gibb, J. 1996, *The Archaeology of Wealth: Consumer Behaviour in English America*. Springer, New York.

Giddens, A. 1973, *The Class Structure of Advanced Societies*. Hutchinson University Library, London.

Glassie, H. 1975, *Folk Housing in Middle Virginia: A Structural Analysis of Historic Artefacts*. University of Tennessee Press, Knoxville.

Glassie, H. 1977, Archaeology and Folklore: Common Anxieties, Common Hopes. In *Historical Archaeology and the Importance of Material Things*, edited by L. Ferguson, Special Publication Series No. 2, Society for Historical Archaeology, Lansing: 23–35.

Glassie, H. 1982, *Passing the Time: Folklore and History of an Ulster Community*. O'Brien Press, Dublin.

Godbold, N. 1989, *Victoria: Cream of the Country*. Griffin Press, Adelaide.

Godden, G. 1964, *Encyclopaedia of British Pottery and Porcelain Marks*. Barrie & Jenkins, London.

Godden Mackay Logan, Austral Archaeology and La Trobe University 2004a, Casselden Place, 50 Lonsdale Street, Melbourne, Archaeological Excavations Research Archive Report, Volume 3(I): Artefact Reports. Report for ISPT and Heritage Victoria, Melbourne.

Godden Mackay Logan, Austral Archaeology and La Trobe University 2004b, Casselden Place, 50 Lonsdale Street, Melbourne, Archaeological Excavations Research Archive Report, Volume 3(Ii): Artefact Reports. Report for ISPT and Heritage Victoria, Melbourne.

Gojak, D. and I. Stuart 1999, The Potential for the Archaeological Study of Clay Tobacco Pipes from Australian Sites. *Australasian Historical Archaeology*, 17: 38–49.

Goodwin, L. B. R. 1999, *An Archaeology of Manners: The Polite World of the Merchant Elite of Colonial Massachusetts*. Kluwer Academic/Plenum Press, New York.

Gosnell, J. 2006, John Price/ Price & Gosnell/ John Gosnell & Co. (1677 to Present). Retrieved 19 December 2006 from www.gosnell.org.uk.

Gothard, J. 2001, *Blue China: Single Female Migration to Colonial Australia*. Melbourne University Press, Carlton South, Vic.

Graham, K. 2005, The Archaeological Potential of Medicinal Advertisements. *Australasian Historical Archaeology*, 23: 47–53.

Graham, M. 1981, *Australian Glass of the 19th and Early 20th Century*. David Ell Press, Sydney.

Graham, M. c.1979, *Printed Ceramics in Australia*. Occassional Paper No. 2, Australian Society for Historical Archaeology, Sydney.

Graham, S. (ed.) 1998, *A Man About Town: The Letters of James Graham, Victorian Entrepreneur, 1854–1864*. Melbourne University Press, Melbourne.

Green, H. 1983, *The Light of the Home: An Intimate View of the Lives of Women in Victorian America*. Pantheon Books, New York.

Griffin, D. and E. C. Casella 2010, 'We Lived Well at the Hagg': Foodways and Social Belonging in Working-Class Rural Cheshire. In *Table Settings: The Material Culture and Social Context of Dining Ad 1700–1900*, edited by J. Symonds, Oxbow, Oxford: 101–111.

Griffin, R. 2004, Fireplaces. In *The Art of Keeping House: A Practical and Inspirational Guide*, edited by Historic Houses Trust of New South Wales, Hardie Grant Books, Melbourne: 48–55.

Griggs, H. J. 2001, By Virtue of Reason and Nature: Competition and Economic Strategy in the Needle Trades at New York's Five Points 1855–1880. *Historical Archaeology*, 35: 76–88.

Hagger, J. 1979, *Australian Colonial Medicine*. Rigby, Adelaide.

Hammerton, A. J. 1979, *Emigrant Gentlewomen: Genteel Poverty and Female Emigration, 1830–1914*. Croom Helm, London.

Hardesty, D. L. 1994, Class, Gender Strategies, and Material Culture in the Mining West. In *Those of Little Note*, edited by E. M. Scott, University of Arizona Press, Tucson: 129–145.

Hayes, S. 2007, Consumer Practice at Viewbank Homestead. *Australasian Historical Archaeology*, 25: 87–103.

Hayes, S. 2008, Being Middle Class: An Archaeology of Gentility in Nineteenth-Century Australia. PhD thesis, Archaeology Program, School of Historical and European Studies, La Trobe University, Melbourne.

Hayes, S. 2011a, Amalgamation of Archaeological Assemblages: Experiences from the Commonwealth Block Project, Melbourne. *Australian Archaeology*, 73: 13–24.

Hayes, S. 2011b, Gentility in the Dining and Tea Service Practices of Early Colonial Melbourne's 'Established Middle Class'. *Australasian Historical Archaeology*, 29: 33–44.

Heidelberg Relief Organisation 1933, *Souvenir: Heidelberg Old and New 1860–1933: Back to Heidelberg Municipality*. Heidelberg Relief Organisation, Melbourne.

Heinson, G., S. Lawrence, G. Jackman, N. Fathianpour, L. McKenzie and J. Harrington 1996, A Geophysical Investigation of the Viewbank Archaeological Site: A Preliminary Report. Report for Flinders University of South Australia and Heritage Victoria, Melbourne.

Hellman, V. R. and J. K. Yang 1997, Previously Undocumented Chinese Artifacts. In *Historical Archaeology of an Overseas Chinese Community in Sacramento, California*, edited by M. Praetzellis and A. Praetzellis, Anthropological Studies Center, Sonoma State University Academic Foundation, California, Volume 1: 155–202.

Heritage Victoria 2004, Archaeological Artefacts Management Guidelines. Heritage Victoria, Melbourne.

Heritage Victoria 2005, Viewbank Excavation 1999. Retrieved 3 April 2005 from www.heritage.vic.gov.au/page.asp?pf=1&submit_action=&ID+113&level1=Information&level2=Archaeology&level3=Viewbank%20Excavation.

Hester, T. R., H. J. Shafer and K. L. Feder 1997, *Field Methods in Archaeology*. Mayfield, Mountain View, California.

Higman, B. W. 2002, *Domestic Service in Australia*. Melbourne University Press, Melbourne.

Hirst, J. 1988, Egalitarianism. In *Australian Cultural History*, edited by S. L. Goldberg and F. B. Smith, Cambridge University Press, Cambridge: 58–77.

Hodder, I. 1982, *Symbols in Action: Ethnoarchaeological Studies of Material Culture*. Cambridge University Press, Cambridge.

Hopton, A. J. 1950, Rural Port Phillip, 1834 to 1851. *Journal and Proceedings of the Royal Australian Historical Society*, XXXVI: 297–392.

Hourani, P. 1990, Spatial Organisation and the Status of Women in Nineteenth Century Australia. *Australian Historical Archaeology*, 8: 70–77.

Howell-Meurs, S. 2000, Nineteenth-Century Diet in Victoria: The Faunal Remains from Viewbank. *Australasian Historical Archaeology*, 18: 39–46.

Iacono, N. 1999, Miscellaneous Artefacts Reports. *The Cumberland/Gloucester Streets Site, The Rocks: Archaeological Investigation Report*, Volume 4, Part 2. Godden Mackay Heritage Consultants, Report submitted to the Sydney Cove Authority, Sydney: 11–118.

Israel, F. L. (ed.) 1968, *1897 Sears Roebuck Catalogue*. Chelsea House, New York.

Johnson, E. 1999, *Needlework and Embroidery Tools*. A Shire Book, Shire Publications, Buckinghamshire.

Johnson, M. 1996, *An Archaeology of Capitalism*. Blackwell, Oxford.

Jones, O. 2000, A Guide to Dating Glass Tableware: 1800 to 1940. In *Studies in Material Culture Research*, edited by K. Karklins, Society for Historical Archaeology, Pennsylvania: 141–232.

Jones, O. and C. Sullivan 1989, *The Parks Canada Glass Glossary: For the Description of Containers, Tableware, Flat Glass, and Closures*. Canadian Parks Service, Environment Canada, Ottawa.

Karklins, K. 1985, *Glass Beads: The 19th Century Levin Catalogue and Venetian Bead Book and Guide to Description of Glass Beads*. Canadian Parks Service, Environment Canada, Ottawa.

Karskens, G. 1999, *Inside the Rocks: The Archaeology of a Neighbourhood*. Hale and Iremonger, Sydney.

Karskens, G. 2001, Small Things, Big Pictures: New Perspectives from the Archaeology of Sydney's Rocks Neighbourhood. In *The Archaeology of Urban Landscapes: Explorations in Slumland*, edited by A. Mayne and T. Murray, University of Cambridge, Cambridge: 69–85.

Karskens, G. and S. Lawrence 2003, The Archaeology of Cities: What Is It We Want to Know? In *Exploring the Modern City: Recent Approaches to Urban History and Archaeology*, edited by T. Murray, Historic Houses Trust of New South Wales in association with La Trobe University, Sydney: 89–111.

Kingston, B. 1994, *Basket, Bag and Trolley: A History of Shopping in Australia*. Oxford University Press, Melbourne.

Kiplinger, J. 2004, Those Wonderful Gizmos Which Hold Us Together. Retrieved 10 May 2004 from www.fabrics.net/joan101.asp.

Kirkman, W. T. 2007, R. E. Dietz Compendium. Retrieved 29 November 2007 from www.lanternnet.com/compendium.htm.

Klein, T. 1991, Nineteenth-Century Ceramics and Models of Consumer Behaviour. *Historical Archaeology*, 37(1): 77–91.

Knehans, M. M. 2005, The Archaeology and History of Pharmacy in Victoria. *Australasian Historical Archaeology* (23): 41–46.

Kociumbas, J. 1992, *Possessions 1770–1860*. The Oxford History of Australia, Volume 2, Oxford University Press Australia, Melbourne.

Kociumbas, J. 1997, *Australian Childhood: A History*. Allen & Unwin, Sydney.

Lampard, S. 2004, Urban Living: The Respectable of Jane Street, Port Adelaide. In *National Archaeology Students Conference: Explorations, Investigations and New Directions*, edited by D. Arthur and A. Paterson, National Archaeology Students Conference, Adelaide: 26–32.

Lampard, S. 2009, The Ideology of Domesticity and the Working-Class Women and Children of Port Adelaide, 1840–1880. *Historical Archaeology*, 43(3): 50–64.

Lampard, S. and M. Staniforth 2011, The Demon Drink: Working-Class Attitudes to Alcohol in Nineteenth-Century Port Adelaide. *Australasian Historical Archaeology*, 29: 5–12.

Lane, T. and J. Serle 1990, *Australians at Home: A Documentary History of Australian Domestic Interiors from 1788 to 1914*. Oxford University Press, Melbourne.

Lawrence, S. 1998, The Role of Material Culture in Australasian Archaeology. *Australasian Historical Archaeology*, 16: 8–15.

Lawrence, S. 2000, *Dolly's Creek: An Archaeology of a Victorian Goldfields Community*. Melbourne University Press, Melbourne.

Lawrence, S. 2003, Exporting Culture: Archaeology and the Nineteenth-Century British Empire. *Historical Archaeology*, 37(1): 20–33.

Lawrence, S. 2006, *Whalers and Free Men: Life on Tasmania's Colonial Whaling Stations*. Australian Scholarly, Melbourne.

Lawrence, S., A. Brooks and J. Lennon 2009, Ceramics and Status in Regional Australia. *Australasian Historical Archaeology*, 27: 67–78.

Lawrence, S. and P. Davies 2011, *An Archaeology of Australia since 1788*. Springer, New York.

Lawson, E. 2004, Flowers & Plants. In *The Art of Keeping House: A Practical and Inspirational Guide*, edited by Historic Houses Trust of New South Wales, Hardie Grant Books, Melbourne: 82–93.

Lawson, E. and S. Carlin 2004, The Dining Table. In *The Art of Keeping House: A Practical and Inspirational Guide*, edited by Historic Houses Trust of New South Wales, Hardie Grant Books, Melbourne: 94–101.

Legge, M. 1986, *The Apothecary's Shelf: Drug Jars and Mortars 15th to 18th Century*. National Gallery of Victoria, Melbourne.

Leone, M. P. 1999, Setting Some Terms for Historical Archaeologies of Capitalism. In *Historical Archaeologies of Capitalism*, edited by M. P. Leone and P. B. Potter, Jr., Kluwer Academic/Plenum Press, New York: 3–22.

Leone, M. P. 2005, *The Archaeology of Liberty in an American Capital: Excavations in Annapolis*. University of California Press, Berkeley.

Leone, M. P. and P. B. Potter, Jr. (eds.) 1999, *Historical Archaeologies of Capitalism*. Kluwer Academic/Plenum Press, New York.

Lewis, M. 1988, Pioneering: Early Lime and Cement. In *Two Hundred Years of Concrete in Australia*, edited by Concrete Institute of Australia, North Sydney.

Lindbergh, J. 1999, Buttoning Down Archaeology. *Australasian Historical Archaeology*, 17: 50–57.

Logan, H. C. 1959, *Cartridges: A Pictorial Digest of Small Arms Ammunition*. Bonanza Books, New York.

Loudon, J. C. 2000, *Encyclopaedia of Cottage, Farm and Villa Architecture and Furniture*. Donhead, Shaftesbury.

Lucas, G. 2006, *An Archaeology of Colonial Identity: Power and Material Culture in the Dwars Valley, South Africa*. Springer, New York.

Lydon, J. 1993a, Archaeology in the Rocks, Sydney, 1979–1993: From Old Sydney Gaol to Mrs Lewis' Boarding-House. *Australasian Historical Archaeology*, 11: 33–42.

Lydon, J. 1993b, Task Differentiation in Historical Archaeology: Sewing as Material Culture. In *Women in Archaeology: A Feminist Critique*, edited by H. du Cros and L. Smith, Department of Prehistory, Research School of Pacific Studies, Australian National University, Canberra: 129–133.

Lydon, J. 1998, Boarding-Houses in the Rocks: Mrs Ann Lewis' Privy 1865. In *Redefining Archaeology: Feminist Perspectives*, edited by M. Casey, D. Donlon, J. Hope and S. Wellfare, ANH Publications, Canberra: 138–144.

Lydon, J. 1999, *Many Inventions: The Chinese in the Rocks 1890–1930*. Monash Publications in History, Melbourne.

Mackay, E. A. 1934, Medical Men as Pastoral Pioneers. *The Medical Journal of Australia*, II(14): 476–483.

Majewski, T. and M. O'Brien 1987, The Use and Misuse of Nineteenth-Century English and

American Ceramics in Archaeological Analysis. In *Advances in Archaeological Method and Theory*, edited by M. Schiffer, Academic Press, New York: 97–209.

Majewski, T. and M. B. Schiffer 2001, Beyond Consumption: Toward an Archaeology of Consumption. In *Archaeologies of the Contemporary Past*, edited by V. Buchli and G. Lucas, Routledge, London: 26–50.

Marsden, G. 1998, Introduction. In *Victorian Values: Personalities and Perspectives in Nineteenth-Century Society*, edited by G. Marsden, Longman, London.

Marsh, M. 1990, *Suburban Lives*. Rutgers University Press, New Brunswick.

Mattick, B. E. 2010, *A Guide to Bone Toothbrushes of the 19th and Early 20th Centuries*. Xlibris, Bloomington.

Maynard, M. 1994, *Fashioned from Penury: Dress as Cultural Practice in Colonial Australia*. Cambridge University Press, Cambridge.

Mayne, A. and S. Lawrence 1998, An Ethnography of Place: Imagining "Little Lon". *Journal of Australian Studies*, 57: 93–107.

Mayne, A. and T. Murray (eds.) 2001, *The Archaeology of Urban Landscapes: Explorations in Slumland*. New Directions in Archaeology Series, Cambridge University Press, Cambridge.

McCarthy, J. 1988, The New Gold Mountain: Chinese Non-Settlement in Northern Australia. In *Archaeology and Colonisation: Australia in the World Context*, edited by J. Birmingham, D. Bairstow and A. Wilson, Australian Society for Historical Archaeology, Sydney: 139–148.

McCarthy, J. 1989, Archaeological Investigation: Commonwealth Offices and Telecom Corporate Building Sites, the Commonwealth Block, Melbourne, Victoria, Volume 1: Historical and Archaeological Report. Report for Department of Administrative Services and Telecom Australia by Austral Archaeology, Melbourne.

McCarthy, J. P. and J. A. Ward 2000, Sanitation Practices, Depositional Processes, and Interpretive Contexts of Minneapolis Privies. *Historical Archaeology*, 31(1): 111–129.

McCarthy, P. 2001, Values and Identity in the "Working-Class" Worlds of Late Nineteenth-Century Minneapolis. In *The Archaeology of Urban Landscapes: Explorations in Slumland*, edited by A. Mayne and T. Murray, University of Cambridge, Cambridge: 145–153.

McCracken, G. 1988, *Culture and Consumption: New Approaches to the Symbolic Character of Consumer Goods and Activities*. Indiana University Press, Indianapolis.

McKendrick, N., J. Brewer and O. H. Plumb 1982, *The Birth of Consumer Society: The Commercialization of Eighteenth-Century England*. Indiana University Press, Indianapolis.

McKenzie, L. 1996, Viewbank Homestead Project 1996. Paper given at the Australasian Society for Historical Archaeology Annual Conference.

McKenzie, L. 1997, Forgotten but Not Lost: Viewbank Homestead Excavation Report 1996–1997. Report for Heritage Victoria, Melbourne.

Merriam-Webster 2007, Word for the Wise: Antimacassar. Retrieved 29 November 2007 from www.merriam-webster.com/cgi-bin/wftwarch.pl?041907.

Mezey, B. 2005, Reflections on Casselden Place through Its Jewellery. Honours thesis, Archaeology Program, School of Historical and European Studies, La Trobe University, Melbourne.

Miller, D. 1985, *Artefacts as Categories*. Cambridge University Press, Cambridge.

Miller, D. 1987, *Material Culture and Mass Consumption*. Basil Blackwell, Oxford.

Miller, D. 1995, *Acknowledging Consumption: A Review of New Studies*. Routledge, London.

Miller, D. 2008, *The Comfort of Things*. Polity, Malden, MA.

Miller, D. 2010, *Stuff*. Polity Press, Cambridge.

Miller, D., M. Rowlands and C. Tilley 1995, *Domination and Resistance*. Routledge, London.

Miller, G. 1980, Classification and Economic Scaling of Nineteenth-Century Ceramics. *Historical Archaeology*, 14: 1–40.

Miller, G. 1986, Of Fish or Sherds: A Model for Estimating Vessel Populations from Minimum Vessel Counts. *Historical Archaeology*, 20: 59–85.

Miller, G. 1991, A Revised Set of Cc Index Values for Classification and Economic Scaling of English Ceramics from 1787 to 1880. *Historical Archaeology*, 25: 1–25.

Miller, G. 2000, A Revised Set of Cc Index Values for Classification and Economic Scaling of English Ceramics from 1787 to 1880. In *Approaches to Material Culture Research for Historical Archaeologists: A Reader from Historical Archaeology*, edited by D. R. Brauner, Society for Historical Archaeology, Tucson: 86–109.

Miller, G. L., O. R. Jones, L. A. Ross and T. Majewski 1991, Approaches to Material Culture Research for Historical Archaeologists: Introduction. In *Approaches to Material Culture Research for Historical Archaeologists*, edited by G. L. Miller, O. R. Jones, L. A. Ross and T. Majewski, Society for Historical Archaeology, Pennsylvania: 1–10.

Mitchell, S. 2009, *Daily Life in Victorian England*, Second Edition. Greenwood Press, London.

Moi, T. 1991, Appropriating Bourdieu: Feminist

Theory and Pierre Bourdieu's Sociology of Culture. *New Literary History*, 22: 1017–1049.

Moore, S. 1995, *Table Knives and Forks*. Shire Albums, Shire Publications, Buckinghamshire.

Mrozowski, S. A. 2006, *The Archaeology of Class in Urban America*. Cambridge University Press, Cambridge.

Mrozowski, S. A., G. H. Ziesing and M. C. Beaudry 1996, *Living on the Boott: Historical Archaeology at the Boott Mills Boardinghouses, Lowell, Massachusetts*. University of Massachusetts Press, Amherst.

Muir, A.-L. 2003, Ceramics in the Collection of the Museum of Chinese Australian History, Melbourne. *Australasian Historical Archaeology*, 21: 42–49.

Murray, T. 2006, Integrating Archaeology and History at the "Commonwealth Block": "Little Lon" and Casselden Place. *International Journal of Historical Archaeology*, 10(4): 395–413.

Murray, T. 2011, Poverty in the Modern City: Retrospects and Prospects. *International Journal of Historical Archaeology*, 15: 572–581.

Murray, T. and A. Mayne 2001, Imaginary Landscapes: Reading Melbourne's "Little Lon". In *The Archaeology of Urban Landscapes: Explorations in Slumland*, edited by A. Mayne and T. Murray, University of Cambridge, Cambridge: 89–105.

Myatt, F. 1981, *An Illustrated Guide to Pistols and Revolvers*. Landsdowne Press, London.

Neale, R. S. 1972, *Class and Ideology in the Nineteenth Century*. Routledge & Kegan Paul, London.

Niall, B. 2002, *The Boyds: A Family Biography*. Melbourne University Press, Melbourne.

Niall, B. 2004, *Martin Boyd: A Life*. Melbourne University Press, Melbourne.

Nix, M. 2005, Silk Gloves and Cast Iron Boilers: A Study of Cargoes for Scotland to Australia, 1820–1824. *Australasian Historical Archaeology*, 23: 25–39.

Noel Hume, I. 1969, *A Guide to Artifacts of Colonial America*. Alfred A. Knopf, New York.

Orser Jr., C. E. 1994, Consumption, Consumerism, and Things from the Earth. *Historical Methods*, Spring 1994, 27(2): 61–70.

Parker, R. 1984, *The Subversive Stitch: Embroidery and the Making of the Feminine*. Women's Press, London.

Parks Canada 1992, *Classification System for Historical Collections*. Canadian Parks Service, Environment Canada, Ottawa.

Paynter, R. 1988, Steps to an Archaeology of Capitalism. In *The Recovery of Meaning: Historical Archaeology in the Eastern United States*, edited by M. P. Leone and P. B. Potter, Jr., Smithsonian Institution Press, Washington DC: 407–433.

Paynter, R. 1999, Epilogue: Class Analysis and Historical Archaeology. *Historical Archaeology*, 33(1): 184–195.

Pensabene, T. S. 1980, *The Rise of the Medical Practitioner in Victoria*. Health Research Project Research Monograph, Australian National University, Canberra.

Peters, S. J. 1996, Viewbank Homestead Heidelberg: An Historical Survey. Report for Heritage Victoria, Department of Planning and Development, Melbourne.

Petrow, B. 2007, Pen Facts. Retrieved 9 January 2008 from www.woodpensonline.com/history.htm.

Pollon, F. 1989, *Shopkeepers and Shoppers: A Social History of Retailing in New South Wales from 1788*. The Retail Traders' Association of New South Wales, Sydney.

Porter, J. and Å. Ferrier 2006, Miscellaneous Artifacts from Casselden Place, Melbourne. *International Journal of Historical Archaeology*, 10(4): 375–393.

Praetzellis, A. and M. Praetzellis 1992, Faces and Facades: Victorian Ideology in Early Sacramento. In *The Art and Mystery of Historical Archaeology: Essays in Honor of James Deetz*, edited by A. E. Yentsch and M. C. Beaudry, CRC Press, Florida: 75–99.

Praetzellis, A. and M. Praetzellis 2001, Mangling Symbols of Gentility in the Wild West: Case Studies in Interpretive Archaeology. *American Anthropologist*, 103(3): 645–654.

Praetzellis, A., M. Praetzellis and M. R. Brown III 1988, What Happened to the Silent Majority? Research Strategies for Studying Dominant Group Material Culture in Late Nineteenth-Century California. In *Documentary Archaeology in the New World*, edited by M. Beaudry, Cambridge University Press, Cambridge: 192–202.

Presland, G. 1994, *Aboriginal Melbourne: The Lost Land of the Kulin People*. McPhee Gribble, Melbourne.

Priestley, S. 1984, *The Victorians: Making Their Mark*. Fairfax, Syme & Weldon Associates, Sydney.

Pritchett, J. and A. Pastron 1983, Ceramic Dolls as Chronological Indicators: Implications from a San Francisco Dump Site. In *Forgotten Places and Things: Archaeological Perspectives on American History*, edited by A. E. Ward, Centre for Anthropological Studies, Albuquerque: 321–334.

Prossor, L., S. Lawrence, A. Brooks and J. Lennon 2012, Household Archaeology, Lifecycles and Status in a Nineteenth-Century Australian

Coastal Community. *International Journal of Historical Archaeology*, 16(4).

Proudfoot, H., A. Bickford, B. Egloff and R. Stocks 1989, *Australia's First Government House*. Allen & Unwin, Sydney.

Pynn, B. R. 2007, Antique Toothpaste Pot Lids: Something to Smile About. Retrieved 9 January 2007 from www.deanantiques.com/PLG/articles.htm.

Quirk, K. 2008, The Victorians in 'Paradise': Gentility as Social Strategy in the Archaeology of Colonial Australia. PhD thesis, Anthropology Department, University of Queensland, Brisbane.

Reckner, P. E. and S. A. Brighton 1999, "Free from All Vicious Habits": Archaeological Perspectives on Class Conflict and the Rhetoric of Temperance. *Historical Archaeology*, 33(1): 63–86.

Richards, T. 1990, *The Commodity Culture of Victorian England: Advertising and Spectacle 1851–1914*. Stanford University Press, Stanford.

Rodriguez, A. C. and A. Brooks 2012, Speaking in Spanish, Eating in English; Ideology and Meaning in Nineteenth-Century British Transfer Prints in Barcelona, Anzoategui State, Venezuela. *Historical Archaeology*, 46(3): 47–62.

Rotman, D. 2009, *Historical Archaeology of Gendered Lives*. Contributions to Global Historical Archaeology, Springer, New York.

Roycroft, R. and C. Roycroft 1979, *Australian Bottle Price Guide*. No. 3, Australian Bottle Review, Deniliquin.

Russell, P. 1993, In Search of Woman's Place: An Historical Survey of Gender and Space in Nineteenth-Century Australia. *Australasian Historical Archaeology*, 11: 28–32.

Russell, P. 1994, *'A Wish of Distinction': Colonial Gentility and Femininity*. Melbourne University Press, Melbourne.

Russell, P. 2003, Cultures of Distinction. In *Cultural History in Australia*, edited by H.-M. Teo and R. White, University of New South Wales Press, Sydney: 158–260.

Russell, P. 2010, *Savage or Civilised? Manners in Colonial Australia*. New South, Sydney.

Samford, P. M. 2000, Response to a Market: Dating English Underglaze Transfer-Printed Wares. In *Approaches to Material Culture Research for Historical Archaeologists*, edited by D. R. Brauner, Society for Historical Archaeology, Pennsylvania: 56–85.

Saunders, K. and R. Evans (eds.) 1992, *Gender Relations in Australia: Domination and Negotiation*. Harcourt Brace Jovanovich, Sydney.

Schiffer, M. B. 1987, *Formation Processes of the Archaeological Record*. University of New Mexico Press, Albuquerque.

Schlereth, T. 1979, Material Culture Studies in America: Notes toward a Historical Perspective. *Material History Bulletin*, 8: 89–98.

Serle, G. 1971, *The Rush to Be Rich: A History of the Colony of Victoria, 1883–1889*. Melbourne University Press, Melbourne.

Shackel, P. A. 1993, *Personal Discipline and Material Culture: An Archaeology of Annapolis, Maryland 1796–1870*. The University of Tennessee Press, Knoxville.

Shackel, P. A. 2000, Craft to Wage Labor: Agency and Resistance in American Historical Archaeology. In *Agency in Archaeology*, edited by M.-A. Dobres and J. E. Robb, Routledge, New York: 232–246.

Shaw, A. G. L. 1996, *A History of the Port Phillip District: Victoria before Separation*. Melbourne University Press, Melbourne.

Skeggs, B. 1997, *Formations of Class and Gender: Becoming Respectable*. Sage, London.

Sklar, K. 1973, *Catharine Beecher*. Yale University Press, New Haven.

Skooldays 2008, Cap Guns. Retrieved 9 January 2008 from www.skooldays.com/categories/toys/ty1304.htm.

Snyder, J. 1997, *Romantic Staffordshire Ceramics*. Schiffer Publishing, Atglen.

South, S. 1977, *Method and Theory in Historical Archaeology*. Academic Press, New York.

Spencer-Wood, S. 1987, *Consumer Choice in Historical Archaeology*. Plenum Press, New York.

Sprague, R. 1981, A Functional Classification for Artifacts from 19th and 20th Century Historical Sites. *North American Archaeologist*, 2(3): 251–261.

Sprague, R. 2002, China or Prosser Button Identification and Dating. *Historical Archaeology*, 36(2): 111–127.

Spreadborough, R. and H. Anderson 1983, *Victorian Squatters*. Red Rooster Press, Ascot Vale.

Staniforth, M. 2003, *Material Culture and Consumer Society: Dependent Colonies in Colonial Australia*. New York, Kluwer Academic/Plenum.

Staniforth, M. and M. Nash 1998, *Chinese Export Porcelain from the Wreck of the Sydney Cove (1797)*. The Australian Institute for Maritime Archaeology, Special Publication No. 12, Brolga Press for the Australian Institute for Maritime Archaeology, Adelaide.

Sussman, L. 1997, *Mocha, Banded, Cat's Eye and Other Factory-Made Slipware*. Studies in Northeast Historical Archaeology No. 1, Council for Northeast Historical Archaeology, Boston.

Sussman, L. 2000, Objects Vs. Sherds: A Statistical Evaluation. In *Studies in Material Culture Research*, edited by K. Karklins, Society for

Historical Archaeology, California, Pennsylvania: 96–103.

Sykes, M. 1988, Lace Makers' Bobbins. In *The Antique Collector*, edited by National Magazine Co., London.

Symonds, J. 2003, An Imperial People? Highland Scots, Emigration and the British Colonial World. In *Archaeologies of the British: Explorations of Identity in Great Britain and Its Colonies 1600–1945*, edited by S. Lawrence, Routledge, London: 138–155.

Tarlow, S. 2007, *The Archaeology of Improvement in Britain, 1750–1850*. Cambridge University Press, Cambridge.

Thompson, E. 1994, *Fair Enough: Egalitarianism in Australia*. University of New South Wales Press, Sydney.

Toy, A. and R. Griffin c.1990, *The Language of the Fireplace*. Historic Houses Trust of New South Wales, Sydney.

Vader, J. 1975, *Antique Bottle Collecting in Australia*. Summit Books, Sydney.

Veres, M. 2005, Introduction to the Analysis of Archaeological Footwear. *Australasian Historical Archaeology*, 23: 89–96.

Vines, G. 1993, *Farm and Dairy: The Agricultural and Dairy Farms of Melbourne's West*. Melbourne's Living Museum of the West, Melbourne.

Walker, R. 1984, *Under Fire: A History of Tobacco Smoking in Australia*. Melbourne University Press, Melbourne.

Wall, D. D. 1992, Sacred Dinners and Secular Teas: Constructing Domesticity in Mid-19th-Century New York. *Historical Archaeology*, 25: 69–81.

Wall, D. D. 1994, *The Archaeology of Gender: Separating the Spheres in Urban America*. Plenum Press, New York.

Waterhouse, R. 1995, *Private Pleasures, Public Leisure: A History of Australian Popular Culture since 1788*. Longman Australia, Melbourne.

Watson, D. 1984, *Caledonia Australis: Scottish Highlanders on the Frontier of Australia*. Collins, Sydney.

Watts, P. 1985, Historic Gardens – the Vaucluse House Experience. In *Bringing a House to Life*, edited by Australian Council of National Trusts/Historic Houses Trust of New South Wales, The Australian Council of National Trusts, Canberra: 54–61.

Weaver, F. 1991, An Archaeological Survey of the Lower Plenty River. Report for Melbourne Metropolitan Board of Works, Melbourne.

Webb, J., T. Schirato and G. Danaher 2002, *Understanding Bourdieu*. Allen & Unwin, Sydney.

Webster, S. 2004, Floors & Floorcoverings. In *The Art of Keeping House: A Practical and Inspirational Guide*, edited by Historic Houses Trust of New South Wales, Hardie Grant Books, Melbourne: 36–47.

Wegars, P. 2007, Asian American Comparative Collection: Artifact Illustrations. Retrieved 22 May 2007 from www.uidaho.edu/LS/AACC/illus.htm.

White, G. 1966, *European and American Dolls and Their Marks and Patents*. Chancellor Press, London.

Wilkie, L. 2000, Not Merely Child's Play: Creating a Historical Archaeology of Children and Childhood. In *Children and Material Culture*, edited by J. S. Derevenski, Routledge, London: 100–113.

Willacy, E. 1981, Report on Viewbank Tip Trench Excavation Conducted by Archaeological and Anthropological Society of Victoria, April 1980. Report for the Archaeological and Anthropological Society of Victoria, Melbourne.

Woodhead, E. 1991, *Trademarks on Base-Metal Tableware*. Parks Service, Environment Canada, Ottawa.

Woodhead, E. I., C. Sullivan and G. Gusset 1984, *Lighting Devices in the National Reference Collection, Parks Canada*. National Historic Parks and Sites Branch, Parks Canada, Ottawa.

Woolfall, R. J. 2006, Woolfall Glass Bottle. Retrieved 29 November 2007 from www.antique-bottles.net/forum/m-44310/mpage-1/tm.htm#78419.

Wurst, L. 2006, A Class All Its Own: Explorations of Class Formation and Conflict. In *Historical Archaeology*, edited by M. Hall and S. W. Silliman, Blackwell, Malden: 190–206.

Wurst, L. and R. K. Fitts 1999, Introduction: Why Confront Class? *Historical Archaeology*, 33(1): 1–6.

Wurst, L. and R. H. McGuire 1999, Immaculate Consumption: A Critique of the "Shop Till You Drop" School of Human Behaviour. *International Journal of Historical Archaeology*, 3(3): 191–199.

Yamin, R. 1998, Lurid Tales and Homely Stories of New York's Notorious Five Points. *Historical Archaeology*, 32(1): 74–85.

Yamin, R. 2001, Alternative Narratives: Respectability at New York's Five Points. In *The Archaeology of Urban Landscapes: Explorations in Slumland*, edited by A. Mayne and T. Murray, Cambridge University Press, Cambridge: 154–170.

Yamin, R. 2002, Children's Strikes, Parents' Rights: Paterson and Five Points. *International Journal of Historical Archaeology*, 6(2): 113–126.

Yentsch, A. 1991, The Symbolic Divisions of Pottery: Sex-Related Attributes of English and Anglo-American Household Pots. In *The Archaeology of Inequality*, edited by R. H. McGuire and R. Paynter, Blackwell, Oxford: 192–230.

Young, L. 1998, The Material Construction of Gentility: A Context for Understanding the Role of Women in Early Nineteenth Century Sites. In *Redefining Archaeology: Feminist Perspectives*, edited by M. Casey, D. Donlon, J. Hope and S. Wellfare, Research School of Pacific and Asian Studies, Australian National University, Canberra, 29: 134–137.

Young, L. 2003, *Middle-Class Culture in the Nineteenth Century: America, Australia and Britain*. Palgrave Macmillan, Hampshire.

Young, L. 2004, 'Extensive, Economical and Elegant': The Habitus of Gentility in Early Nineteenth Century Sydney. *Australian Historical Studies*, 36(124): 201–220.

Young, L. 2010, Gentility: A Historical Context for the Material Culture of the Table in the 'Long 19th Century'. In *Table Settings: The Material Culture and Social Context of Dining Ad 1700–1900*, edited by J. Symonds, Oxbow, Oxford: 133–143.

Index

Aboriginal experiences 7, 9–10
alcohol 36, 67–68
archaeology
    archaeological site 4–5, 18
    excavation 17–20
    interpretation 3, 75
architecture 59, 70
artefacts
    see ceramics, clothing, bottles, glass, jewellery
    cataloguing 21–22
    processing 20–21

Batman, John 7
Batman's treaty 7
beads 38–39, 45, 71, 72
bedrooms 60, 75
    children's 70
    servants' 61
beverages 34, 36, 46, 52
beverage storage 36–38
bobbins 45, 65
bottles 36–38, 46, 48, 51–53, 75
    aerated water 36, 52, 53
    alcohol 36, 68
    blacking 42
    condiment 36, 48, 51
    ink 45, 51, 62
    medicine 42, 51, 62, 73
    perfume 41, 51, 72
Bourdieu, Pierre 2–3, 76
Boyd, Lucy (neé Martin) 13–14, 15, 16, 69–70, 72
Boyd, Captain John Theodore 13–14, 16
breakfast 65–67, 74, 75
British society 1, 66, 76–77
buttons 39–40, 47, 65, 71

Casselden Place, Melbourne 1, 42, 51, 64, 75
ceramic 26–29, 32–34, 34–36, 48
    bone china 26, 28, 32
    chamber pots 41, 49, 53, 57, 73
    Chinese 26, 27, 28, 38, 52
    coarse earthenware 25, 38
    conjoining 23
    moralising china 34, 70, 77
    matching sets 23, 29, 33–34, 50, 57, 62–63, 65–66, 68, 69, 73, 75, 76
    porcelain 46, 50
    redware 26, 33, 37–38, 53
    stoneware 37–38, 42, 45, 46, 53
    tableware 23, 26–29, 33, 49, 53, 57, 65–67, 68, 70, 75, 76, 77
    teaware 26, 32–34, 49, 53, 57, 65–66, 69, 75

    tin-glazed earthenware 46
    toiletware 41, 76
        sets 57, 70, 73, 75, 76, 77
    white granite 25, 26, 28, 29, 32, 34, 46, 50–51, 53, 65, 67, 70
    whiteware 26, 34, 46, 51
    yellowware 25
childhood 13–14, 34–35, 42–43, 70–71, 77
    education 13, 14, 45, 64, 71
    play 43–44, 64, 70
class 1–4, 77–78
class negotiation 1–4, 49, 76–77
clay pipes 44, 63
clothing 39–41, 71–72
    fasteners 40–41
    shoes and boots 41
coins 44, 47, 48
Collins Street, Melbourne 12, 53, 55, 58, 74, 77
conjoins 21, 23
consumerism 2, 4
consumer practice 49, 53, 57–58
cutlery 31, 67
    matching sets 67

dairying 8, 53, 57, 63–64
department stores 55, 57
depositional patterns 22, 23
dining 27, 65–68
dining room 60, 66, 68
dinner 66
dinner parties 68
dinner service 26–29, 66, 77
dolls 43, 51, 70, 71
domestic artefacts 24–38
domesticity 13, 64, 76
drawing room 60, 64, 68
dress
    see clothing

education 7, 12, 13, 14, 45, 64, 71
embroidery 64, 65, 69
'established middle class' 4, 5, 11, 75, 76

family roles 14–15
farming 7, 8, 63–64
fashion 67, 70, 71, 72, 75
fireplaces 47, 60, 75
folding fan 39, 72
food preparation 25–26
food storage 36–38
furnishings 24, 60, 69

gaming pieces 43–44, 64

garden 8, 15, 18, 57, 59, 63, 77
gender 14, 59–60
gentility 1–4, 49, 59, 65, 75–78
glass
    see also bottles
    dessert glasses 30, 67
    drinking glasses 29, 57, 67–68
    tableware 29–30
gold rush 4, 8
gothic style 51, 70
Graham, James 12, 13, 14, 15, 68, 69
grooming 41–42, 73

habitus 3
hall 60, 61, 69
health 42, 72–74
Heidelberg, Victoria 5, 8, 26, 55–56, 61, 63–64
Heritage Victoria 1, 5, 17, 18, 20, 21
horses 15, 63
husband
    death of 15–16
    role of 14
hygiene 41–42, 72–74, 77

immigrants 1, 4, 7, 76
    Chinese 52
    female 4
imported goods 53, 57

jewellery 24, 38–39, 53, 70, 72

kitchen 48, 61, 66

lace making 39, 45, 65
leisure 3, 60, 64–65, 69, 77
library 60
lighting 24
Little Lon, Melbourne 1, 75
lunch 66

maintaining the household 24
makers' marks 22, 33, 36–37, 42, 46, 49, 51, 53, 75
markets 49–53, 57
marriage 4, 13–14, 15, 69, 77
Martin, Charlotte 12, 13, 15, 68, 69, 72
Martin, Dr Robert 5, 7, 11–12, 13–14, 15–16, 60, 62, 69, 71
Martin, Edith 13, 14, 15
Martin, Emma 13, 15
Martin, Lucy (neé Gear) 9, 10, 12–13, 15–16, 61, 62, 69, 71, 72
Martin, Lucy
    see Boyd, Lucy
Martin, Robert William Kirby (Willy) 13, 14, 15, 16, 35, 63, 69, 70, 71
Martin, Sarah Anne Jane (Annie) 13, 14, 15, 69
matching sets
    see ceramic
material culture 1, 2, 3–4, 23, 59, 75–77
meals 63, 65–66, 75
medical profession 7, 12
medicine 42, 62, 73–74
Melbourne, Victoria 1, 7–8

middle class 1–4, 7, 11, 14, 61, 62, 64, 69, 70, 76–77
minimum number of individuals (MNI) 21
mourning 39–40, 72

needlework 60, 64–65, 76
netting 45, 65
New Zealand 11, 15, 49

ointment jars 41–42, 46, 73, 77
orchard 57–58, 63
ornamentation 24–25

pastoralism 4, 7, 10, 11, 63–64
personal accessories 38–39
personal appearance 3, 41–42, 71–72, 77
personal artefacts 38–42
place of manufacture 21, 49
Port Phillip Association 7
Port Phillip District 7–8
preparing food 25–26
public versus private 14, 59, 75

recreation
    see leisure
recreational artefacts 42–44
recycling 57
religion 69–70, 76
respectability 1, 2, 8
The Rocks, Sydney 1, 42

school 8, 71
Scottish 4, 7, 11, 69
scullery 60–61
servant bells 48, 61–62
servants 5, 15, 57, 59–62, 65, 66, 70, 75, 77
    ceramics 62–63, 66, 73
    domestic 15, 61–62
    housekeeper 15, 16, 61, 62
    smoking 63
    work 62–63
service area 61
serving and consuming food 26–34
sewing 40, 44–45, 47, 60, 62, 64–65, 71, 77
shopping 13, 49, 53–57, 76, 77
shopping arcades 55, 57, 75
site formation 22, 23–24, 47
slate pencils 45, 47, 71
social artefacts 44
social events 13, 68–69
social mobility 1, 2, 3, 4, 76, 77, 78
spending 55, 77
squatters 7
storing food and drink 36–38
study 60
'Summer Flowers' pattern 27, 29, 53, 66, 67

taste 3, 49, 60, 67, 68, 71, 75, 76
tea 60, 65, 66–67, 69
tea service 32–34, 65, 66, 67, 69, 75
time lag 22, 23
tools and equipment 44–45
toothbrush 41, 57

Index

toothpaste 41–42, 51, 73
toys 42–43, 48, 71
    dolls 43, 51, 53, 57, 70, 71, 75
    marbles 43, 51, 70
    tea sets 42–43, 70, 71
trade catalogues 57
type series 21–22

urban archaeology 1–2

Victoria 8, 10, 11, 22, 26, 52–53, 63, 71, 76
Viewbank homestead 4–5
    excavation 17–20
    layout 18–19, 59–62, 68
    history 8–10
    location 4–5
    tip 5, 17, 18–20, 23–24

wallpaper 18, 60, 61, 75

weapons and ammunition 45
white granite
    see ceramics
wife
    role of 14, 65
women
    housework 61, 64
    husband determining position of 3, 13
    motherhood 13, 69
    work 62
    role in determining class position 3, 55, 69, 76, 77
    role of 13, 60, 70, 76
work 13, 44–45, 62–64
working class 2, 8, 57, 61, 62, 64, 75, 76
    archaeological sites 1
writing and drawing 45